How He
Mastered the Universe

How He-Man Mastered the Universe

Toy to Television to the Big Screen

BRIAN C. BAER

McFarland & Company, Inc., Publishers
Jefferson, North Carolina

LIBRARY OF CONGRESS CATALOGUING-IN-PUBLICATION DATA

Names: Baer, Brian C., 1985– author.
Title: How He-man mastered the universe : toy to television to the
    big screen / Brian C. Baer.
Description: Jefferson, North Carolina : McFarland & Company, Inc.,
    Publishers, 2017 | Includes bibliographical references and index.
Identifiers: LCCN 2016045106 | ISBN 9781476665900 (softcover :
    acid free paper) ∞
Subjects: LCSH: He-Man figures—History. | He-Man and the masters
    of the universe (Television program : 1983–1985) | He-Man and
    the masters of the universe (Television program : 2002–2004) |
    He-Man and the masters of the universe (Motion picture) | Action
    and adventure television programs. | Action and adventure films. |
    Superhero television programs. | Superhero films. | Comic books,
    strips, etc. | Mattel, Inc.
Classification: LCC NK4894.3.H46 B34 2017 | DDC 688.7/2—dc23
LC record available at https://lccn.loc.gov/2016045106

BRITISH LIBRARY CATALOGUING DATA ARE AVAILABLE

ISBN (print) 978-1-4766-6590-0
ISBN (ebook) 978-1-4766-2706-9

Front cover illustration by Eamon O'Donoghue

Printed in the United States of America

McFarland & Company, Inc., Publishers
    Box 611, Jefferson, North Carolina 28640
    www.mcfarlandpub.com

For Von

Table of Contents

Preface
Man-E-Prefaces

He-Man has been a part of my life since the day of my birth. In a waiting room outside of the maternity ward in a small hospital in Albert Lea, Minnesota, my three-year-old-brother Von was playing with some action figures. When the nurse came to invite him into the room to meet his new baby brother, he refused. The woman said he would need to wear the sanitary smock to enter the sterile room, and that would cover up his *Masters of the Universe* t-shirt.

"But this is He-Man," Von told her. "He's the best! I want my brother to know who He-Man is." And so, my very first day, I learned.

Later, when the time came for me to come home, my parents told my brother that I'd brought him a present. They handed him a brand new Stratos action figure, from the first wave of the Masters of the Universe line. He looked up at them, bewildered. "How did he know this was the one I wanted?" he asked.

Though the cartoon was off the air by the time I was old enough to appreciate it, I grew up with dozens of VHS tapes full of recorded episodes and several of the bright, blocky action figures that felt massive in my small hands. The theme song was a constant anthem in our house. It was years later when I saw the *Masters of the Universe* film for the first time, and seeing the familiar characters appear slightly different, and in live-action, sparked the fascination in me all over again. I spent the next several years tracking down the film's reviews, actors' interviews, and overall trivia, just as so many young people grew up collecting the rare action figures and home video releases of the Filmation cartoons. The favorite things from our childhoods always have a special place in our hearts, but for many of us of a certain age, there's something extra special about He-Man.

The well-worn He-Man t-shirt my brother wore to the hospital on the day of my birth. It was likely one of the first things I ever saw.

The characters mean a lot to a lot of different people. For many children of the '80s, Masters of the Universe is a way to remember our formative years. It's a way to introduce our children to the things we marveled at when we were their age. It is also a remarkably agile franchise, with a new edition popping up every few years (*He-Man and the Masters of the*

Universe, 1983; the live-action *Masters of the Universe* film, 1987; *The New Adventures of He-Man*, 1990; and another animated reboot in 2002) to hook a new generation.

As this is written in 2016, there have been new movie adaptation rumors swirling for the past several years. Some 30 years ago, *Masters* was panned for being the first film based on an action figure. And now, we live in a world with four *Transformers* films and two based on *GI Joe*, along with many more sequels and spin-offs announced for each. It's no longer uncommon even for board games like Battleship to be adapted into a big-budget adventure film.

Pop culture has finally caught up with He-Man.

Mattel debuted the Masters of the Universe toy line in 1982, and it was a runaway success. Characters like Man-At-Arms and Evil-Lyn, along with the heroic He-Man and dastardly Skeletor, struck some special chord in the hearts and minds of children across the planet.

Certainly some of this can be attributed to the size of the figures; He-Man was not a small, fragile toy, like the 3¾-inch Star Wars toys Hasbro had been releasing since the late '70s. He was a big, powerful toy to match the big, powerful character. More so, he was wish fulfillment in its most basic form: a man of solid muscle who would take any beating a young child's imagination could come up with. And with the swivel-waist "power punch" feature, he was a toy that could return that beating in kind.

There was an elegance in the simplicity of the characters and their world. He-Man and Skeletor were engaged in the ultimate battle of good versus evil. As "the most powerful man in the universe," He-Man was as virtuous as he was physically strong, an aspirational figure. His nemesis, Skeletor, did not simply wear a black hat, he was a walking personification of fear and death. His face was the stark yellow skull of Memento Mori, and his skin was blue, otherworldly and unsettling when compared to the tan muscles and handsome face of his adversary. There were dozens of other figures, along with their vehicles and play sets, but it was always just as easy to separate the good guys from the bad.

The world they inhabited, Eternia, was designed to maximize playability. The land was a bizarre combination of sword and sorcery and science fiction. He-Man was a brawny barbarian with a John Carter–like chest harness who carried a battle axe, yet he could ride on the back of a giant green tiger as easily as he could fit in a flying car shaped like a falcon. There were castles and ray-guns and mermen and magic. In Eternia, anything could go. There were enough outlandish accessories and bizarre characters to keep up with a young child's imagination.

There was nothing else like it on the market, and it opened the doors to a new level of imagination and physicality in action figures. The action figures were packaged with a minicomic to explain more about the characters and their world. Eager to capitalize, Mattel pushed into storybooks and full-length comic books from DC Comics, video games, trading cards, and all other sorts of merchandise. Everything the hero attacked fell easily, and Masters of the Universe was a hit in all its many forms. Soon, it seemed only natural the He-Man brand would expand onto the airwaves.

In 1983, the Filmation company created the animated series *He-Man and the Masters of the Universe*. Lou Scheimer and the Filmation animators pushed the toy's concept further than the simplistic mythology shown in the minicomics. The animators were much more interested in telling stories than merely selling products; they created characters like Orko, the floating magical comic relief, and stressed the concept of He-Man's secret identity, Prince Adam. These additional wrinkles became some of the best known and well-loved elements of the He-Man franchise.

Like its action figure inspiration, the TV show also broke new ground. Cross-media marketing, like a children's show based on a toy line, was unheard of in the early '80s. There was even some question of its legality. Filmation took the risk to create the *Masters* cartoon, and then had to find someone to air it.

Even with the success of the toy line, the major television networks were unwilling to take the risk. And so Scheimer made the very uncommon move to sell the show directly to syndication; forgoing the traditional first run on the major networks, he sold the series to individual, local stations. These stations could smell a hit, and *He-Man and the Masters of the Universe* did not disappoint.

The show was not without controversy. There was plenty of fuss from concerned parents about the cartoon's perceived violence, along with the ethics of broadcasting what many considered a "program-length commercial."[1] Still, it ran for two 60-episode seasons, produced a spin-off in *She-Ra: Princess of Power*, and sold plenty more toys. With He-Man at his peak, Mattel began looking for another way to capitalize.

However groundbreaking the animated series had been, in the mid–'80s, a live-action film based on an action figure was absolutely unheard of. *Masters of the Universe* would be the first. Still, the company put the call out to Hollywood, courting several studios before deciding on Cannon Films, the scrappy B-movie studio whose shady bookkeeping practices had left them, unbeknownst to Mattel, teetering on the verge of bankruptcy.

Cannon hired first-time feature director Gary Goddard to helm the project. Goddard battled Mattel to treat the source material with a serious eye instead of as a marketing tool, and fought Cannon to ensure the crew got paid when the project slipped over budget and behind schedule. In the end, Cannon closed production before filming had completed. Goddard was forced to pay out of pocket to get the last few shots needed to complete the climactic showdown between He-Man and Skeletor.

The film, against all odds and despite box office failure, emerged as highly watchable. Goddard brought a keen attention to lighting, as well as set and costume design, giving *Masters* a unique look. The script also kept the pace brisk enough to keep the plot from collapsing in on itself. It brought a surprising edge to many of the characters, to stop them from coming off as too "kiddie" to be enjoyable for adult audiences. Though Dolph Lundgren's performance as He-Man is fodder for the cult classic and "so bad, it's good" audiences, the film also featured a mesmerizing turn from future Academy Award nominee Frank Langella as Skeletor.

But it was all for naught. After He-Man blazed a trail with innovative action figures and the first cartoon based on a toy, critics considered a live-action movie a bridge too far. Compounding issues, *Masters* was released as the He-Man fad had begun to fade. Cannon, in its money troubles, was not able to market the film properly. The box office receipts both companies anticipated didn't come through. When it was removed from theaters, the figures sat unsold on toy store shelves, and Cannon quietly slumped its way out of business.

There have been a few more attempted resurgences of the brand since the 1987 film, each with varying degrees of success. But nothing has been able to match the levels of excitement He-Man and his friends had initially inspired. While Mattel's attempts to connect with new audiences have floundered, its core fan base has stayed faithful. The children who grew up on the toys, cartoons, and film have grown into adults with fond memories and the disposable income to feed their nostalgia. Mattel began releasing new action figures in the old style through their direct order service online. This new line, called Masters of the Universe Classics, evolved to include the Filmation-centric Club Grayskull.

When the *Masters of the Universe* film was released in 1987, critics and audiences were confused by the idea of a live-action film based on an action figure. Nearly 30 years later, though, that idea has come into vogue. After multiple movies based on media franchises who followed He-Man's path from toy to cartoon and beyond, there are rumblings once again of another Masters movie.

At every phase of his evolution, He-Man has left a mark on the landscape of popular culture. After the overwhelming success of the action figure, he was the first one to break through to animated adventures. It didn't take long for the imitators to follow, though. When the popularity of the Masters of the Universe characters began to fade in the latter half of the '80s, it was eclipsed by the likes of GI Joe and Transformers, other franchises who began on the toy shelves and followed the path blazed by He-Man.

Decades later, those same franchises would follow him onto the big screen, with much larger budgets and, occasionally, better receptions at the box office. As recognized as the *He-Man and the Masters of the Universe* cartoon is for shaping a generation and the boundaries of cross-media franchises, the ground broken by the *Masters* film is often overlooked. As the forgotten cornerstone of pop culture turns 30, its place in history and its impact on our modern world of entertainment is due for reconsideration.

How He-Man Mastered the Universe will look at He-Man throughout the ages, from his contentious creation and initial success, and the controversies he caused. Time will also be spent on the Filmation company and its pivotal contributions to the Masters of the Universe brand, the rocky history of the Cannon film group, which was responsible for the failures the *Masters* film, and the director, stars, and designers who were responsible for its successes. I will also be checking in on the current state of the Masters of the Universe brand and the dedicated He-Man fans who have been with the character through his many changes.

Masters of the Universe not only provided fun and familiar characters to a generation, it also marked a turning point in the way we consume our popular culture. Nearly every popular franchise since 1982 has succeeded due to the ground broken by He-Man. Though many beloved characters have graced our toy boxes and television sets and movie theater screens, there's always been something special about He-Man.

This book would not be possible without the help of some wonderful people.

I'd like to thank Gary Goddard, William Stout, Corey Landis, Stephen Tolkin and Tim Seeley for their time and for agreeing to speak with me for this project. Those interviews could not have happened without the help of Tom King and Blake J. Harris, among others. I received assistance from He-Man fans around the world and across the internet, including Peter Eckhart, Jérémie Damoiseau, James Eatock, the Power and Honor Foundation, the members of the he-man.org forums, and the resources of

Wiki Grayskull (he-man.wikia.com), the Battle Ram blog (battleram.word-press.com), and the Grayskull Museum (www.grayskullmuseum.com).

I am eternally grateful to John T. Atkin and James Sawyer. The research and interviews they did for Sawyer's Masters of the Universe Movie site (www.motomovie.com) was a huge source of inspiration and very helpful in the formation of this book. The interviews collected by Blake J. Harris for his article "How Did This Get Made: Masters of the Universe (An Oral History)" for slashfilm.com was also key. Photos of the figures were taken by Rachael Layne, courtesy of the Jedi Alliance of Spokane, Washington. Many illustrations from the film's production were provided by William Stout. The fantastic cover is courtesy of Eamon O'Donoghue.

Gigantisaur-sized thanks to Chris Carlson and Scott Eubanks for the encouragement and early, critical eye, and to Harmony Mason for her patience and support. I would have been lost in the Sands of Time without Vance Kotrla and Joseph Haeger's incredible notes and edits. All overly-meticulous questions about minute pop culture details were directed toward Colby Park, Glenn Case, and James O'Coyne. Special accommodations were provided by B-Hatch and Glenn/Ron.

An extra special Preternia thank you goes to my parents, who have always been supportive of my career choice, and to my brother Von for introducing me to He-Man all those years ago.

Good journey, everyone!

Introduction
The Power of ... Introduction!

A lot has changed since 1982.

A toy isn't enough anymore. In fact, a toy isn't considered successful without its matching lunchbox, comic book series and prose novel tie-ins, Saturday morning cartoon with syndication and home video releases, a video game released across multiple platforms, and a live-action Michael Bay film franchise with platinum-selling soundtracks.

The modern definition of a successful brand depends entirely on its presence across the vast spectrum of contemporary media. The concept of cross-media franchises is not new, exactly, but it has been gaining momentum like a snowball rolling downhill. Speed picks up, and new layers are collected as the franchise becomes broader and more powerful. As technology expands the possibilities for our entertainment, a franchise develops new venues for exploitation.

A toy cannot simply be a toy. A toy must be an idea, vast and mutable, to be interpreted into any shape or size for any age group or demographic. A toy must be a way of life, as toymakers are inviting their consumers to define themselves by it. The things we enjoy become the things we love, and what we love is who we are. There are plenty of ways to spend money to express ourselves and show our love.

For example, we can look to one of the most successful franchises of the 2000s: Harry Potter. As Jay Lemke wrote in *Critical Analysis Across Media: Games, Franchises, and the New Cultural Order*: "The Harry Potter franchise is a new kind of cross-media or meta-media object. The complete experience of its 'discourse' involves participation with all these media: not just reading the books, but also viewing the films (which differ significantly from the books) and the DVDs (which include material not

8

in the theatrical-release films), playing the videogames, wearing the clothing, buying the toys, visiting the websites which are linked to the books, films, and videogames, and even perhaps eating the candy."[1] Harry Potter is far from alone. Every successful commercial property for the past several decades have been a multi-pronged attack, from the fast food tie-ins to *Star Wars Episode I: The Phantom Menace* to the music videos from the soundtrack to the movie adaptation of *Fifty Shades of Grey*.[2]

Many of these multi-faceted strategies are purely mercenary: if your fan base loves your toy/film/book/et cetera, they are more likely to pay money for its tie-ins and adaptations. If a fan likes a movie, they might play its video game. If a movie is received well enough, it may warrant a sequel, or its own cartoon. Fans will want to wear a t-shirt announcing their fandom. If they like the comic book, they might read the novel it was based on. The wider the net is spread, the more viable options there are for the fans to spend their money on. Every dollar they spend on your franchise is a dollar not going to a competitor.

The omnipresence of merchandise elevates the brand from mere entertainment to a lifestyle. Fans are encouraged to label themselves as such, so there can be no question of who is a "Trekkie" (*Star Trek* fan) or a "Whovian" (*Doctor Who* fan) or a "Twihard" (*Twilight* fan) based on nothing more than their hats, scarves, and haircuts. Symbols and logos become perfect fodder for tattoos; we are literally branded by our favorite brands.

In 2005, film historian Edward Jay Epstein wrote about Hollywood's "Midas formula" for *Slate* magazine. After listing the most profitable media franchises of the time, such as *Star Wars* (1977), *Spider-Man* (2002), and *Pirates of the Caribbean* (2003), he noted that they all tend to follow the same outline in terms of story and storytelling approach.

One key factor involves aiming for the correct audience: children. Many of the most successful and profitable media franchises are based on children's books or comic books, which are typically seen as a kid-friend medium, along with action figures and theme park rides. Original concepts, such as a *Star Wars*, still skew toward children's sensibilities. In order to keep that ideal demographic, most cross-media brands steer away from overly violent or sexual themes. According to Epstein, "This ensures the movie gets the PG-13 or better rating necessary for merchandizing tie-ins and for placing ads on children's TV programming."[3]

The plot lines of these successful franchises may feel familiar to audiences as well. The stories tend to follow the structure of Joseph Campbell's "Monomyth," also called "The Hero's Journey" or the "Hero with a

Thousand Faces." As Campbell described the archetypical tale, "A hero ventures forth from the world of common day into a region of supernatural wonder: fabulous forces are there encountered and a decisive victory is won: the hero comes back from this mysterious adventure with the power to bestow boons on his fellow man."[4]

An awkward or weak young person receives a call to adventure and discovers something special in themselves, something that allows them to overcome darkness and return home a hero. The story was common before the likes of Luke Skywalker and Peter Parker, but continues to resonate with audiences for a reason. Viewers love to see themselves in the protagonists, to imagine their own adventures and escapes from the mundane. This fantasy actualization of power and success brings them back again and again, be it for a sequel or for another franchise altogether.

The Monomyth structure also suits itself well to children's stories. Many successful media franchises feature a young person as the hero, allowing for another way for their ideal market to identify with the story and characters. In the example of Harry Potter, the characters may also grow older as the stories progress, allowing them to age with the audience. Thus stories may darken or mature to keep pace with the developing tastes. Those initial fans can go onto introduce younger siblings or even their children to the same stories, letting them grow up with the characters, like they did.

Name recognition goes a long way. Readers or viewers may not be as willing to invest the time and money in what is deemed an untested product. But when a property conquers one medium and jumps to another, even if an individual is not a fan of the original product the new version is based on, it is seen with a level of cross-media pedigree. Merely recognizing that product and seeing it has been successful enough to warrant a jump into another medium can speak to its value, and encourage consumption.

If the property is an original concept, it will revolve around characters ideal for translation into toys and other merchandise. For example, if a successful franchise character wasn't originally based on an action figure, they can still get an action figure made in their honor soon thereafter.

Another key element to Epstein's "Midas formula" is cutting edge technology. No matter what the level of special effect sophistication is when the film or television branch of the franchise comes about, everything must be top of the line to make the maximum impact. If audiences, especially children, aren't gripped by the wonder of what they're watching, they won't be as likely to buy, or ask their parents to buy, the subsequent merchandise. Audiences continually grow jaded at a younger age, so new frontiers must be broken in order to win a war for dwindling attention spans.

In these "special effects movies," the special effects truly are the star of the show. While there may be a "big name" actor or two in the cast, the lead is often played by someone previously undiscovered. And though actors like Christopher Reeve (Superman) or Daniel Radcliffe (Harry Potter) go on to successful careers with soaring paychecks, they are often stuck in contracts to play that same character in sequels for surprisingly low pay.

There are exceptions to every rule, of course. Despite plenty of borrowing, *The Matrix* was an original film, instead of being based on a well-known property. *Twilight*'s target audience is made up of teens instead of their younger siblings. Johnny Depp was already an expensive, household-name actor when he signed on for the first *Pirates of the Caribbean* movie, and other franchises, such as the novel *Fifty Shades of Grey*, likely hadn't anticipated the level of success that would require them to branch out into the cinematic domain. Still, there are more than enough successful brands that follow the formula to lend credence to Epstein's article.

However, strict adherence to what has worked before is no guarantee of a hit franchise. The footnotes of popular culture are littered with brand names that attempted to expand but fell apart for a variety of reasons.

Rights issues, such as actors' likenesses, held back the expansions like *The Real Ghostbusters* (1993), an animated tie-in to the '80s film *Ghostbusters*. Overestimating a concept's appeal (the pulpiness of *The Adventures of Buckaroo Banzai Across the 8th Dimension* in 1984) or an actor's drawing power (Ryan Reynolds in 2011's *Green Lantern*) can bring franchise dreams crashing down. Audience's appetites and expectations can be difficult to predict. Even potential franchise "slam dunks," such as the Will Smith vehicle and TV adaptation *Wild Wild West*, can fall apart.[5]

One key example is the 1998 remake of the famous Toho Studios monster, Godzilla. The project came together as Hollywood had truly ironed out their media franchise formula: a brand that was already a household name was paired with producer Dean Devlin and director Roland Emmerich, the masterminds behind hits like *Stargate* (1994) and *Independence Day* (1996). *Godzilla* had top-tier actors and action figures, a soundtrack filled with popular artists, an animated series debuting the same year, fast food tie-ins, and a family-friendly PG-13 rating. Still, *Godzilla* is now an infamous example of a Hollywood franchise flop.

The official budget for the film was $130 million, a number which typically doesn't account for marketing, which was extensive. When the worldwide box office gross came in at $379 million, it wasn't enough for the studio moneymen to consider it a success. Tri-Star already had two sequels in the works when *Godzilla* premiered. These were both scrapped quietly.[6]

So where did *Godzilla* go wrong? By most accounts, the failure came down to an issue of quality. The film was lambasted by critics, "winning" the Golden Raspberry award for Worst Remake or Sequel, and was widely disliked by a majority of audiences as well.[7] Though negative reviews don't necessarily kill a franchise, audience support is very important. A movie can get decent box office receipts from crowds that leave unsatisfied, but franchises are built of repeat viewings. Audiences need to love a film, or a toy, or any other brand seedling so much they'll be excited to see it or play with it again and again, until they can experience it in another format.

Many also saw the franchise as expanding too broadly, too quickly. The entire endeavor appeared calculated, like a cynical plot to raise as much money as possible. It's possible the audiences were turned off by an apparent desperation.

There is no easy way to make a successful cross-media franchise. Even now, when the "Midas formula" has been so perfected, there is no guarantee a wide-branching concept will not wither and die with no sequel in sight.

The cross-media franchise was born of adaptation, a method of borrowed storytelling that's been common for well over a century.

Sherlock Holmes Baffled was released in 1900. There is some debate about whether it is an adaptation in the true sense of the word, as it is not abundantly clear whether the man in the silent film is intended to be Holmes. More likely, some argue, the character's name was included in the title to capitalize on his fame.

As Sir Arthur Conan Doyle was still writing stories about Holmes at the turn of the century, this could be seen as an early attempt of one media to exploit the success of another. Unlike other early adaptations of Lewis Carroll or the Brothers Grimm, *Baffled* had a symbiotic relationship with the then-current stories. Fans of the books could see the character in live action, and vice versa.

Another early example of a film adaptation working as cross-media brand was the *Tarzan of the Apes* silent feature of 1918. Edgar Rice Burroughs was still writing his Tarzan novels at the time, and the film and its sequel, *The Romance of Tarzan*, are considered very faithful adaptations of his first book.

Still, many consider the true founder of multimedia branding to be Walt Disney, as his studio created *Snow White and the Seven Dwarfs* in 1937. The film is rightly considered a classic cornerstone of cinema, informing the contemporary Disney princess "formula" and our modern interpretation of fairy tales.

Disney also used *Snow White* to introduce the concept of a movie soundtrack. As a musical, the film had a host of original songs written for it, which Disney released in conjunction with the theatrical run. It was nominated for Best Original Score at that year's Academy Awards, and set the standard for multimedia releases. It is especially notable for being an official tie-in made by the same studio as the film, not a tie-in from selling the rights to company specializing in a different form of media. In that aspect especially, *Snow White* was ahead of its time.

The net of cross-media properties was spread wider by Superman. He first appeared in *Action Comics* #1, in June of 1938 and took America by storm. National Comics, soon to become DC Comics, wasted no time in expanding the visibility of the world's first superhero. As author Jake Rossen explains in *Superman Vs. Hollywood*, Superman's creators, Jerry Siegel and Joe Shuster, did not own the rights to their own creation, and had no say in the way he was used. They were "entitled to no recompense when their character appeared in another medium," Rossen wrote. "If National felt the urge to prostitute him in wildly unfaithful incarnations, the duo could do little but sigh."[8]

But adaptations, especially those first ones, were good to Big Blue. Today, everyone knows the famous line "Look, up in the sky! It's a bird! It's a plane!" and know that the character is described as "faster than a speeding bullet! More powerful than a locomotive! Able to leap tall buildings in a single bound!" Many know Superman's pal, Jimmy Olsen, and the bald head of the villainous Lex Luthor, not to mention the deadly effects of Kryptonite, the radioactive pieces of his home world. However, these famous elements of the mythology did not appear in the original comic book pages. Adaptations expanded the mythos and shifted the focus of the character, taking him from smaller feats, like stopping an abusive husband in Action Comics #1, to flying around the globe fast enough to reverse time in 1978's *Superman: The Movie*. In fact, the character only became the character we now know him as once he began appearing in multiple formats.

Superman was less than one year old when he became a "strange visitor" to another kind of storytelling: newspaper comic strips. The *Superman* strip first appeared in January of 1939, and went on to debut the magical prankster character Mr. Mxyzptlk and Luthor's now standard appearance, complete with a bald head. These changes would go on to be incorporated into the monthly Superman comics and the public consciousness.

In February of the next year, Superman made the leap to radio. *The Adventures of Superman* brought the character to life through Bud Collyer, who alternated his voice from meek to booming to differentiate between Clark Kent and Superman, a technique that has been used in practically every incarnation since. The series also bolstered the supporting cast, introducing Kent's boss, Perry White, and photographer Jimmy Olsen, who have become mainstays of the comics and future adaptations. Perhaps most importantly, radio gave us Kryptonite. When Collyer needed a break from the recording schedule, the showrunners created Superman's signature weakness as a way to write out the show's star for several episodes at a time. Per Rossen, "listeners sat in rapt attention as Superman did little more than moan in the background, felled by the noxious mineral."[9]

The year 1941 brought about the *Superman* series of animated shorts by Fleischer Studios. The pilot episode was nominated for an Academy Award, and the series is still highly regarded to this day. The cartoon carried over many innovations from the radio series, including Collyer and the voice cast, while adding elements like the "Up, up, and away" catchphrase. It even introduced the idea of Clark Kent dashing into a telephone booth of all places to his costumed identity.[10] As these cartoons were initially played before feature films in cinemas, *Superman* also marks the character's first appearance on the big screen.

The next year, a novel also titled *The Adventures of Superman* was released, retelling the character's origins in greater detail. And so within five years of his creation, Superman had spread across several branches of media, not including the merchandising, or the eventual live-action serials, films, and TV shows. In addition to the impressive success of these adaptations, it is also of particular importance to see how the innovations in one medium influenced the other. More than mere tie-ins, the disparate works built upon one another and made the brand stronger in terms of content as well as visibility.

The effects of National/DC's expansionary ideas are still being felt in popular culture today, and a great many franchises have followed in Superman's footsteps.

As time progressed, new and varied forms of media became available. With the dawn of television, home video, and video games, film studios and other tastemakers have hurried to keep up with the times. Along with these leaps in technology, more conglomerated companies own the means to release their own tie-in media. This allows for a uniformity of creative vision: no longer allowing the maker of a cartoon spin-off to, for example, drastically alter the source material.

Studios, publishers, toy companies and the like have also learned from the successful multimedia expansions of the past. Original music released as film soundtracks, as opposed to just orchestral scores, are now common for non-musicals. Films such as 1989's *Batman* were released with both tie-in scores and soundtrack albums. Cross-media endeavors, such as a tie-in cartoon, are prepared in conjunction with a film or video game just like the t-shirts and other merchandise. It has become expected to release your product like a tidal wave across these varied forms.

This was taken a step further in 2008 with the success of Marvel Comics' *Iron Man* film. In a post-credit sequence, top-tier actor Samuel L. Jackson appeared, surprisingly unannounced, in a role as superhero handler Nick Fury. One quick mention of forming a team of superheroes over the course of the next few Marvel movies sent fans' excitement over the top.

Audiences were energized by the dangling carrot of sequels and spin-offs and a whole "cinematic universe," where one character could pop up in another's film and the events of *Film A* could have ramifications in *TV Show B*. Quickly, building the franchise into interlocking films became the key motivating factor instead of simply an efficient way to maximize profitability. With each successive Marvel film, their Cinematic Universe grew wider and profits soared.

This became the norm. DC Comics, Marvel's four-color rival, announced their own cinematic universe in 2013. In 2015, toy company Hasbro announced a "multi-property universe" of their own, to consist of existing movie franchises GI Joe and Transformers along with new, live-action incarnations of '80s toys like M.A.S.K. and the Micronauts.[11] That year, Universal Studios began talk of uniting its remakes of classic monster movies the same way.[12]

Every successful movie wasn't merely required to have a matching toy line or videogame, it also needed to fit into a broader universe of collective stories. Dangling plot threads became common place, and the arcs of cinematic universes trumped the individual stories of single films. Release dates for sequels or spin-offs began to be announced before the original film was even released. Well-received cartoon series were cancelled if they don't sell enough tie-in merchandise.[13] Every branch of a cross-media empire must be successful or the entire endeavor is considered a failure.

And so media franchises are capable of expanding too broadly, collapsing under their own weight, and the entire Universe can be felled quickly if one aspect underperforms. Studios must be cautious even as they invest billions of dollars, and filmmakers must approach transmedia like a wary safe-cracker. Even as wide-reaching media franchises have become the standard operating procedure for our entertainment, there are seldom safe bets. How does Hollywood know what properties are ideal for the big screen, small screen, book and t-shirt and everything in between?

Media franchises have come a long way since *Sherlock Holmes Baffled* to reach the levels of the modern transmedia matrixes and cinematic universes. But as quickly as technology developed to allow for these new branches of media and ease of their exploitation, the road was not always simple or easy. There were battles to be fought over the correct place of franchises, especially those following the "Midas formula" closely enough to focus on an audience of children.

Two important breakthroughs in the emergence of the modern media franchise belong to the same franchise: Masters of the Universe.

Masters followed the "Midas formula" almost perfectly. It began life as an action figure, with He-Man and his friends and enemies targeting perfectly the young male demographic interested in strength and wish fulfillment in the ultimate battles between good and evil. It built a solid brand with a very recognizable name before attempting to break into the other forms of entertainment available in the early 1980s.

However, it was the first toy to attempt such a leap. Before the animated series *He-Man and the Masters of the Universe* debuted in 1983, no other action figure brand had attempted to cross into the world of children's cartoons, and with good reason: such adaptations were heavily regulated by the Federal Communications Commission.

There had been rules set in place for decades to govern the amount of advertising allowed on the airwaves, and special attention was given to those that were targeting children. The latter was guarded even more zealously by grassroots watchdog groups. ACT, or Action for Children's Television, was the loudest voice speaking against advertisements during children's programming. That group of concerned parents would monitor the shows for a correct amount of advertising time, and making sure the presenters or programs themselves weren't advertising a product. If a certain show or broadcaster were not following the FCC's regulations to the letter, they would threaten to report them to the government. Their threats tended to work.

The ACT's track record was more mixed in their dealings with the National Association of Broadcasters. They began pressuring the NAB in the 1970s to do away with advertising during children's broadcasting altogether, but succeeded only in limiting commercial time from 16 minutes per hour to 12. Still, the group was a well-known crusader looking to protect impressionable children by enforcing regulations. But in the 1980s, "regulations" became a dirty word.

Newly elected president Ronald Reagan appointed Mark Fowler as the chairman of the FCC in 1981. Following Reagan's free market approach, Fowler began rolling back the regulations that had been determining television content to give corporations a shot at winning over Saturday morning audiences. "Television is just another appliance," he said in 1981, "it's a toaster with pictures. We've got to look beyond the conventional wisdom that we must somehow regulate this box, we must single it out."[14]

Just like that, television became another element of American life and entertainment left to be determined by the open market. Objections from groups like the ACT about advertisements directed at children, or what they'd determined was marketing disguised as content, would no longer hold back enterprising toy manufacturers. This also opened the doors for cross-media franchises to expand into new territory.

This threshold was approached gingerly at first in 1982, with an animated series based on the video game Pac-Man. The home video game market then was not the powerhouse it would later become, so the show was a minimal success and didn't cause too many waves with concerned parents. The impact of *The Pac-Man Show* was largely symbolic.

No punches were pulled when Mattel and Filmation unleashed *He-Man and the Masters of the Universe* a year later. Though it was already a very profitable toy line, the entire concept of turning a toy into a cartoon was too untested for the major networks. Even some smaller, regional broadcasters were uncertain. There was no guarantee success in the toy store shelves could translate to high ratings and happy sponsors. And then there was the wrath of the ACT.

Though they were defanged by the FCC's recent reversals, the groups of upset parents were not giving up their fight for advertisement-free children's programming. Broadcasters were still wary of facing their wrath, or inspiring more to join their cause by airing something that really was "a thirty-minute toy commercial."

There was also some concern over the stories Filmation would be telling. Would it be too violent? Would it send the wrong messages about power and weapons? Would the villains, like the skull-faced Skeletor, be too scary? Mattel and Filmation worked to address each concern in the program, but minds were not necessarily set at ease.

In the end, *He-Man and the Masters of the Universe* premiered and Reagan's free market spoke. The show was a hit.

The networks noticed this, and so did the toy manufacturers. Within the next few years, GI Joe, Transformers, Teenage Mutant Ninja Turtles, and other toy properties followed He-Man and Skeletor onto the airwaves. The market was glutted, and the decade became infamous for the not-so-subtle advertising of cartoons based on toys.

Soon, the symbiosis between toy lines and their accompanying cartoons grew stronger. Instead of using a cartoon to bolster the success of an already-existing toy brand, it was made in conjunction with the same product it was capitalizing on. The action figures would hit the shelves at the same time as their series debuted, blurring the line between the two products far more than ever. Thanks to an enterprising Mattel and the raw appeal of the He-Man character, media franchises turned a pivotal corner.

The heroes of Eternia were also responsible for the next leap forward a few years later. Though popular franchise characters had been adapted into celluloid from mediums like books (*Sherlock Holmes Baffled*), comics (1978's *Superman: The Movie*) and TV (1970's *House of Dark Shadows*), an action figure brand had yet to be brought to life in a live-action movie. With the blockbuster success of the He-Man cartoon, Mattel saw no reason not to push the boundaries once again. The company began the process of finding a movie studio to sell the rights to.

They quickly received the same treatment from studios they'd received from television broadcasters. Some were interested in trying to spin a household name for toys and children's programming into a verifiable action film, but the toy company also received a great deal of cold shoulders. Whether due to filmmakers' creative concerns or a more general cinematic snobbery, He-Man had to prove himself all over again.

Mattel accepted one of several bids, this one from the Cannon Film Group. Cannon had a reputation in Hollywood as a scrappy underdog studio, often skewing toward exploitation, and typically more focused on producing a remarkable number of films than the quality each one contained. Still, they'd produced some bona fide hits in the '80s, such as the dance picture *Breakin'* (1984) and Chuck Norris vehicles like *Missing in Action* (1984). A Cannon film was a guarantee of a finished movie made for a reasonable, if not minuscule, budget. Without investing too much into the film, Mattel reasoned it could get a sizeable return from the box office based on their franchise's name recognition alone.

The production of *Masters of the Universe* was fraught with problems, though. The impending bankruptcy of Cannon Films and waning popularity of the He-Man toy line backed the idealistic first-time director Gary Goddard into a corner. With building pressure and slashed budgets, the director was forced to pay out of pocket just to see the project through to completion. The movie was released on August 7, 1987. The resulting box office wasn't what Mattel or Cannon had hoped for.

However, *Masters of the Universe* as a film displayed just how strong the franchise was as a mutable concept. Though jettisoning many of the fan-favorite Filmation characters and ideas, the end product stayed true to the Masters of the Universe brand. It was still unmistakably He-Man: the villains were cruel and monstrous, the heroes were brawny but pure, and elements of both sword-and-sorcery and science-fiction were uniquely juggled. Even moving a majority of the film's events to Earth from the outlandish Eternia couldn't distance it from the source material.

Though *Masters* emerged as a shockingly competent film, given its behind-the-scenes problems, it wasn't the carbon copy of the cartoon many fans wanted to see. General audiences stayed away. For most, a motion picture based on a children's toy was far too unusual and an utterly untested idea.

Approaching the 30th anniversary of *Masters of the Universe*, it's obvious how much that mindset has changed. Between 1987 and 2017, the idea of a live-action film based on a toy franchise became rather common-place.

The ivory tower of cinema was chipped away at slowly throughout the late '80s and '90s. Tim Burton's *Batman* and *Batman Returns* made impressive strides for comic book adaptations in 1989 and 1992, and they were quickly followed up and imitated. The Garbage Pail Kids made the leap from gross-out trading cards to the big screen in 1987, and the Super Mario Bros. video game became a movie in 1993, but neither went over very well. *Garbage Pail Kids* is roundly considered one of the worst films of all time, and the surprisingly cheerless *Super Mario Bros.* isn't remembered much more fondly.

Then in 2007, Michael Bay and Hasbro rode a wave of '80s nostalgia to box office glory with the first installment of their Transformers film franchise. While ostensibly respectful to the established mythology of the heroic Autobots and evil Decepticons, Bay inserted time-tested elements to make the adaptation a success: goofy, non-sequitur humor, the inferred patriotism of American soldiers as supporting cast members, a dorky boy meets cool girl storyline, and plenty of gratuitous shots of Megan Fox bending over. Though many fans weren't pleased by the backseat their old action figures took to Shia LaBeouf's shenanigans, there were enough references to the original to win them over.

Transformers was a palpable hit, and more than that, it was a cross-media juggernaut. After its big opening weekend came the new action figures, the new animated series, the trailers for the next film, and so on. Twenty years after *Masters of the Universe* made its attempt, audiences were finally ready for a blockbuster movie based on a toy franchise.

Hasbro followed this success with their other big toy property from the 1980s: GI Joe. Though 2009's *GI Joe: The Rise of Cobra* did fairly well at the box office, it wasn't as well received as its predecessor was.

Audiences found it cartoonish and overly broad, while critics poked at its plot holes and disappointing special effects. Worse, hardcore Joe fans complained about the liberties taken by director Stephen Sommers. Still, one disappointment did not end the new cross-media expectations. The Joes got their sequel. *Transformers* got four, and counting.

These blockbuster adaptations added fuel to the fire of franchise expansion. *Transformers* led to films like *Iron Man* and *The Avengers* (2012), big-budget and crowd-pleasing, but still shockingly faithful to the source material for their devoted followers.

Despite reworking the franchise to fit the new medium and reach broader demographics, the existing fan base is recognized to be one of the most powerful tools in a brand name's arsenal. Even more dormant franchises, like that of Masters of the Universe, can count on a devoted group of followers to clamor for more material featuring their favorite characters. But those characters still need to be handled correctly. If situations like the first *GI Joe* film are an indication, Hollywood has learned that the importance of appeasing this ready-made demographic cannot be overstated.

With the success of these massively expansive media franchises comes scholarly interest and study. What makes certain franchises, like *Star Wars*, take off while others, like the 1998 remake of *Godzilla*, crash and burn? How does one concept expand properly into other field? How do the creators know when they've over-expanded? By studying the current pop culture landscape, we can attempt to anticipate the next big trend for studios or, as cynics have been mentioning for years, when the "bubble" of seeming-niche franchises like superhero films will burst. Looking backward allows us to see ahead.

But those two massive strides in the evolution of pop culture, the formerly plastic He-Man's jaunt into animation and live-action, are not highlighted in the annals of pop culture history like Burton's *Batman* or Joss Whedon bringing the failed film property of *Buffy the Vampire Slayer* to success on TV. By studying the rise of the Masters of the Universe franchise, we can get a grasp on the early trailblazer to the modern interpretation of cross-media phenomena. When we look at where the brand began, and the way it grew, we can watch the adolescence of our own experiences in pop culture.

1

The Secret History
of He-Man

A line can be drawn down the center of the history of all media franchises, and that line can be labeled *Star Wars*. When the film, retroactively titled *Episode IV: A New Hope*, debuted in 1977, the rules of moviemaking changed, but so did the world of tie-ins. The film was a shocking success, so much so that the action figures line being produced by Kenner were not even ready for sale yet. Toy-hungry film fans had to settle for a coupon promising them the plastic replicas one year later.

As caught off guard as Kenner was, they were still the smart ones. George Lucas had approached toy companies before the premiere and got a fair number of doors slammed in his face. The price tag for the rights to the characters, reportedly upward of $750,000, scared away some prospects. More so, at the time, *Star Wars* was more than an untested product; it was downright risky. Many insiders were skeptical about the film's chances.

The film's success left several toy companies smarting. Some never recovered. In addition to the terrific name recognition factor, the better-late-than-never Kenner figures also revolutionized the industry for their smaller scale, each one measuring only 3¾" tall. The Mego Corporation, best known for their 8" World's Greatest Super Heroes line, passed on the license and were later unable to compete with the newer, smaller, cheaper action figures. They were bankrupt by 1982.

Mattel was another established toy company kicking themselves. The company, best known for the profitable and beloved Barbie line, had been unable to make a successful action figure toy line for boys. Not only did they not buy the rights to make Star Wars figures, they also had nothing in place to compete with the evil Darth Vader or the blonde, sword-wielding Luke Skywalker.

In the market for a strong brand name to create toys for, Mattel was approached by CPI, or Conan Properties, Inc. This was in early 1980, while production was still underway for the live-action *Conan the Barbarian* film, based on the character by Robert E. Howard. The movie's producers were interested in an action figure tie-in.

With the film set for release in 1982, there was not much time to put a new toy line together. Mattel was considering redressing a male action figure called Big Jim, a 9½" toy that had failed to catch on before this, in barbarian attire to make the deadline. Jim's slim build was not going to match the big screen Conan, played by the former bodybuilder Arnold Schwarzenegger, but it was the best they could do on such short notice.

These plans changed when executives were given a sneak peek at the Conan film. Mattel's marketing department was reportedly "appalled at its violence and dropped the license" quickly.[1] Action figures were, after all, a market for children, who were clearly not the key demographic for *Conan the Barbarian*. If they were going to have a successful male action figure line, it would need to be approached from a more family-friendly angle.

By December of 1981, Mattel had had enough. They issued a memo to their development teams, lamenting that once the company is hired to make the tie-in toys for a soon-to-be hit film, "its [sic] too late for us to tool up an entirely new line. If we had a generic male action figure license tooled up the lead times and expenses involved in getting into licenses would be a lot less."[2] By creating a "generic" action figure line, something to keep on hand for alteration once the right film's producers came along, they wouldn't be caught behind the eight ball like Kenner had been with *Star Wars*.

This mindset changed quickly, though. The toy company decided not to wait for the Hollywood producers to come to them. Why pay for the rights to a hit brand name when they could build one themselves?

The company began focus testing, a process of interviewing kids and their parents about their reactions to the vaguest concepts for proposed new toy lines. "What would you want to play with," they asked, or "What would you consider buying for your children?" Two of the ideas bandied about were "Space Military à la *Star Wars*" and "Barbarian Monster Fantasy." In the end, though, the toy Mattel would decide on would be a unique combination of the two.

As with many successful and profitable ideas, there is not an easy answer to the question of who created it. Despite the occasional CEO who would take credit, there are two people believed to be responsible for the first He-Man action figure: Roger Sweet, one of Mattel's toy designers, and graphic artist Mark Taylor. The two of them, however, are not interested in sharing the honor.

Sweet was working as a lead designer for Mattel's preliminary design department in 1980, when the call for a "generic" male action figure went out. Calling on his interest in bodybuilding and the overly muscular fantasy artwork of Frank Frazetta, he wanted to make a toy of outlandish proportions, grimacing and crouched for action, instead of the Mego and Star Wars toys who stood straight and looked out blandly from the toy aisle shelves. He took Big Jim figures and accentuated the musculature beyond human limitations. In his book *Mastering the Universe: He-Man and the Rise and Fall of a Billion-Dollar Idea*, Sweet explains the focus on making a toy that made the competition look "wimpy" in his singularly eccentric voice: "My thought was that an unbelievably ripped hombre like that would be compelling for boys, since every boy—or man, for that matter—would love to have the kind of anacondas hanging from his shoulders that make people draw back in awe."[3]

Although Mattel was now looking for an original concept, there was still a focus on keeping it "generic." Anything too specific would pigeonhole a concept and potentially limit marketing. To combat this, Sweet picked a perfectly open-ended name for his creation.

He would be called He-Man.

As the top ranking concepts from the company's focus testing were "Space Military à la *Star Wars*," "Current Military à la G.I. Joe," and "Barbarian Monster Fantasy," Sweet costumed his new muscle-bound figure in a costume representative of each. He-Man, he wanted to prove, was a unique character who was generic enough to be dropped into any genre. The space figure he created came with a jetpack and a helmet which resembled, more than a little, that of the *Star Wars* bounty hunter Boba Fett. The military figure came with an assault rifle and wore the turret of a Panzer tank over his head. For the barbarian figure, Sweet turned to Mark Taylor.

Taylor was working as an artist and designer for the company's Visual Design department. In addition to his artwork on the boxes of various Barbie toys, he provided illustrations for other Mattel employee's product pitches. He agreed to make a template for Sweet to use. When he got it, Sweet stated it wasn't what he had in mind. The character's physique was too "average," for starters.

"I discarded Mark's designs for a helmet, shin guards, wrist bracelets, and weapon," he later wrote. "I used only his designs for a chest halter, cape, and fur loincloth." In the next line Sweet stresses, "these elements were Mark's only contributions to the origination of He-Man and the general concept for Masters of the Universe."[4]

Though it's not clear which exact Taylor sketch Sweet used to create his prototype, his claims to have created the majority of the character is not easy to accept. Wrist bracelets from a Taylor sketch labeled "Torak: Hero of Pre-History," dated 1979, match the barbarian figure's almost precisely. In addition, much changed from that original prototype to the finished product. The character's darker skin was lightened to a more "all-American" shade of tan, and his long, black hair turned into a blond Prince Valiant bob. The colors of the costume, as well, were brightened to appeal to children. Beyond the muscles, crouch and grimace, the only elements that remained from the prototype was the chest harness with the iron cross symbol, which Sweet had stated came from Taylor's illustration.

Because of the numerous, and often undated, sketches Taylor had created over the years, the credit for who originated the character of He-Man is complicated. According to Taylor, he was also a fan of Frank Frazetta artwork and had been tinkering with a barbarian character since he was young. Fueled by the conviction of both Sweet and Taylor's arguments, the debate over who created the characters and concepts have become a bit of a controversy.

In the early 2010s, filmmakers Corey Landis and Roger Lay, Jr., began interviewing the former Mattel employees who were present in the early days of the Masters of the Universe franchise. When they asked who originated the ideas, they heard many different stories. Even after years of interviews and editing their footage into a documentary titled *Toy Masters*, Landis still felt uncertain who had the legitimate claim. "I will say that memory is tricky," he said, "and people do tend to pick things from the ether at the same time. Conan, Frazetta, etc., was all bubbling at the same time and it's not surprising that two people both claim they originated [Masters of the Universe] with all of those references in the air."[5]

Any concrete evidence to back Sweet's claim was literally tossed out years ago. In his book, the toymaker recalled that after his time with Mattel, he threw away a manila envelope of documents and work orders that would have proved his sole ownership of the idea. Also supposedly chucked out were the three original He-Man prototypes.[6]

The story of who did what, and when, were relegated to hazy memories.

The first line of Masters of the Universe figures was released on 1982 with the full backing of Mattel. Despite the multiple reasons to play it safe with an untested, original brand, the company invested $19 million in advertising, a figure far above the norm.

The initial line contained He-Man and arch-nemesis Skeletor, along with the heroic Man-At-Arms, Teela, and Stratos, and the villainous Beast Man and Mer-Man. Mattel had considered including a character named The Goddess, but executives were unsure a boys' toy line could support a second female figure. At the last minute, she was replaced with the more ambiguous "cosmic enforcer" Zodac.[7]

He-Man's companion, pet, and transportation, the mighty Battle Cat, was released separately. The other vehicles included the Wind Raider, Battle Ram, and the iconic Castle Grayskull was the line's big playset.

These first action figures had barely scratched the surface of the Masters of the Universe concept's potential, as Roger Sweet saw it. "I do feel like 1982 line was a bare-bones collection with little in the way of product variety, creativity, and styling," he complained.[8] He described the figures as "low-tech" and blamed Taylor for skewing the characters designs more toward the sword and sorcery aspect of Eternia. For a world that

The heroic He-Man rides his handy transportation/sidekick, Battle Cat. Each sold separately. (Photograph by Rachael Layne.)

encompassed both magic and sci-fi elements, he worried the Masters were underutilizing what made them so special.

While the initial figures didn't dig too deep into space fantasy, their vehicles certainly did. The Wind Raider was a sleek and colorful hover-craft, and the blocky Battle Ram introduced the MOTU visual of animal motifs, something that would appear more and more often in future vehicles and playsets. Unlike the ominous Castle Grayskull, they were both clearly made from science and not magic.

The character of Man-At-Arms was also utterly sci-fi. While his fellow figures were monsters and barbarians, Taylor designed him with a high-tech version of a Spanish conquistador's breastplate and helmet. At this nascent stage of the MOTU mythology, Taylor was inspired by Piers Anthony's novel *Sos the Rope* and envisioned Eternia as a once advanced planet who had sunk into a post-apocalyptic, medieval society. Powerful technology still existed in the ruins of the previous culture. Man-At-Arms would not use magic like Skeletor, but instead, Taylor said, "he digs down and brings out their technology, which gives him a huge advantage over everyone else!"[9]

As the toys continued to expand into the realm of science-fiction with the successive waves of Masters of the Universe, they were still limited by the realities of production. In order to keep costs down, Mattel relied on a small number of reusable parts. All male characters were limited to either a muscular human torso or a furry one, which also doubled as scales. Arms and legs were either human, furry, or more reptilian. Only the heads were personalized. As such, the bird-like Stratos was virtually identical to the mammalian Beast Man from the neck down. Everyone but Teela, the token female character, came with the same uniform set of furry barbarian shorts. It didn't matter if they were highly advanced like Man-At-Arms, or lived underwater like Mer-Man; furry shorts for all.

Other corners were cut as well. Designers returned to the premade molds for the failed Big Jim line once more, turning an ordinary jungle cat into the ferocious Battle Cat. While the new paint job and accessories went a long way, this was largely possible due to the difference in scale. A cat designed for a 9½" figure could be fitted with a saddle for the 5½" He-Man. This was repeated in 1984's wave, with a repaint to create Battle Cat's evil foil, Panthor. Big Jim's falcon also made the transformation into the heroic Zoar and the villainous Screeech.

It wasn't just the animals. Teela was repainted to create Skeletor's companion Evil-Lyn. Even He-Man would be repainted to be sold as an evil robotic doppelgänger called Faker. Twice.

The evil Skeletor atop Panthor, who was released in the third wave of Masters of the Universe figures, in 1984. (Photograph by Rachael Layne.)

Still, the limitations of the figures did not impede the toys' ability to inspire imaginations and fuel Good vs. Evil playtime for a generation. They were a hit. That initial line of Masters of the Universe figures did an impressive $38 million worth of business in 1982. The next year, business more than doubled to $80 million. The year after, sales were over $110 million.

Masters of the Universe rode into 1983 under pressure to keep the line as successful as before. The figures for this second wave pushed further into the sci-fi territory championed by Roger Sweet, with clever action features like Ram-Man's spring-loaded charge. It contained no He-Man, and was heavier on the side of the villainous "Evil Warriors." In additional to Teela's counterpart, Evil-Lyn, and the evil He-Man duplicate Faker, the line introduced Skeletor's new henchmen, the three-eyed Tri-Klops, and the Frankensteinian cyborg Trap Jaw.

The second year's playset, Point Dread, was modest compared to Castle Grayskull. It was a small, windowed structure which appeared to be made of the same roughhewn green rock as the castle, so it could be set on top of a turret to expand the original set. Inside were sci-fi computer consoles, and the top was fitted with a massive perch for the Talon Fighter,

Left to right: Man-At-Arms, Beast Man, Teela, Stratos, Zodac, and Mer-Man made up the rest of the first wave from 1982. (Photograph by Rachael Layne.)

a bird-shaped jet it came packaged with. The Talon Fighter was large enough to fit two figures, and came with a handle for its owner to hold while maneuvering it through a make-believe battle against evil.

Early on, Mattel realized the storytelling potential of the franchise. Eternia was a world made richer by its contradictions. He-Man was a barbarian superhero in a world of monsters and castles and animal-shaped sci-fi vehicles. There could be a story behind every ray gun, a myth behind every magic sword. Why did Skeletor have blue skin? What, exactly, was a "cosmic protector"? What made He-Man the most powerful man in the universe?

These ideas were explored through a series of minicomics packaged with each action figure or vehicle. Each comic worked to introduce the characters and their world to the toy's new owner. They could read about the heroic He-Man and the importance of defending Castle Grayskull from Skeletor to better inform their playtime. It also worked as an incentive to buy the other figures, to read more about their favorite characters and their adventures.

Likely not anticipating the dizzying heights of success, continuity was not a major focus in the earliest minicomics stories. It is likely that Mattel had not even decided to take the Masters of the Universe property to television at the point the comics were created. When that leap was taken, quite a bit was changed.

He-Man is introduced as a great warrior from a primitive jungle tribe who ventures out into the greater realms of Eternia. He has no secret identity, but he does still have a great destiny ahead of him as the protector of Grayskull. After rescuing a green-skinned Goddess, who was later changed into the character of the Sorceress, he is gifted with a set of weapons and other enchanted tools. He has two chest harnesses, which are confusingly identical in appearance. One grants superhuman strength and another which gives him an impenetrable force field.

Man-At-Arms appears as Taylor envisioned him, a scavenger after the "Great Wars" from a tribe identified as the "Masters of All Weapons." Teela is a blond-haired "Warrior Goddess," seen as formidable in combat but also subject to periodic kidnappings by the villains.

The Skeletor of these early minicomics is a being from another dimension, one where the inhabitants seemingly all look like he does. During the Great Wars, a supernatural breach was opened and he became trapped on Eternia. All of his attempts to steal the power held within Castle Grayskull is to reopen that interdimensional passageway to bring his people through to conquer.

Another element brought about early on was the Power Sword, though it would evolve over the next two years, as well. It was introduced as a "key" to Castle Grayskull, needed to open the great drawbridge of the skull's mouth and access the great powers inside. To protect the castle, the Goddess split the Power Sword in two and scattered those pieces across Eternia. Only when they were united could someone gain entrance and become a master of the universal power kept within.

By the time the first minicomic begins, Skeletor has already obtained one of those halves. Though He-Man comes into possession of the other, he is not the one commonly depicted with it in those early stories. Instead, Skeletor is often seen waving it around and using it to cast spells or shoot energy bolts. Before the Power Sword is given more prominence in the Filmation cartoons, He-Man was nearly always drawn with his large, two-bladed battle axe.

The multiple versions of the Power Sword are easily explainable by the realities of these first action figures: the swords that most characters were packaged with all looked like that. The tiny swords were made to fit together like in the stories. The thinness of each one's plastic led them to curve from heat and regular play.

The early stories were appropriately thin to let the focus rest of the characters' visuals and the action features of their vehicles. Those first few comics leaned more on the Robert E. Howard style of fantasy, with more emphasis on damsels in distress and the muscular men defeating magical villain to save them. Those were the issues released with the first wave of Masters of the Universe figures in 1982. The sci-fi concepts were introduced in the comics for the next wave.

With the next group of figures released in 1983, Mattel brought in noted comics artist Mark Texeira. The visuals changed from storybook format, with one image per page, to a more traditional comic book format. The scripting was transferred to Gary Cohn, who began incorporating more sci-fi elements and hammering out more precise mythos for Eternia. Despite saddling He-Man and the other characters with overly-formal and stilted sword-and-sorcery dialogue, the writing began to nudge into some more substantive territory. Cohn also introduced some wonderful, if unexplored, sci-fi and fantasy concepts to Eternia, such as Teela being a clone of the Goddess given life by one of Skeletor's schemes, and Procrustus, a giant stone god who holds the core of the planet together with his four arms.

Creating compelling storylines and believable characters from a line of action figures is not, strictly speaking, the easiest job in the world. The minicomics' creators had a certain amount of flexibility in the first two years of the MOTU franchise, as they were not beholden to any previous incarnations of those characters. To some extent, their imaginations could run free, as long as the good guys were good and everyone looked enough like their toy.

The creators were still bound by the page count and the target age range, but the biggest difficulty would lie in creating a story that showcased a new character or vehicle without the entire story feeling like mere advertising. In addition, the early creators weren't exactly fans of the source material.

Artist Mark Texeira has since confessed it was a mere paycheck gig for him. Gary Cohn, who wrote the scripts for Texeira, felt more strongly. After agreeing to write the comics for a friend working as the editor, he was shown the MOTU action figures he'd be writing about. "I looked at them and pronounced them among the ugliest and most ridiculous toys I'd ever seen," Cohn recalled years later. "I thought 'He-Man' was the silliest name for a character I'd ever heard."[10]

Still, the two of them worked together to create the seven minicomics that were packaged with the second wave of Masters of the Universe figures and vehicles. They found a common ground, their interests in mythology and pulpy Conan the Barbarian stories, and funneled that into the world of Eternia. "He-Man's universe was similar to Robert E. Howard's world," Texeira said, citing the novella *Red Nails* as a particular influence.[11] Texeira, who later became well-known for his work on characters like the Incredible Hulk for Marvel Comics, said he is still presented those same minicomics to be signed at conventions.

Despite having no attachment to the characters of their stories, Cohn recalled having fun writing the stories as "throwaway fluff." He was pleasantly surprised, years later, to hear from the fans who remembered their minicomics fondly.[12]

Cohn's stories are recognized for the free-wheeling imagination, and for the charmingly awkward way he handled the necessary product placement. In the story "The Magic Stealer," for example, a weakened Goddess collapses into He-Man's arms when he asks for her to teleport him to battle Skeletor. "I cannot," she says, "I no longer have enough power. You must take ... The Attak-Trak!" Cut to He-Man climbing into one of the brand new vehicle, each sold separately.

Mattel stepped up production for 1984's third wave, as the *He-Man and the Masters of the Universe* animated series was at the peak of its popularity. There were nearly double the number of figures released, along with all the trimmings of vehicles, accessories, animal sidekicks, and playsets.

Both He-Man and Skeletor received new figures, these ones with "Battle Armor" chest plates which could show damage from their epic conflicts. The new recruits to He-Man's Heroic Warriors were Fisto, the bee-man Buzz-Off, and a colorful cyborg named Mekaneck, whose neck extended to giraffe-like proportions. Also released were two characters introduced by the cartoon show: the magician Orko, unable to levitate in his plastic form, and He-Man's pink-clad alter ego, Prince Adam. For transportation, our heroes had the battery powered Dragon Walker and a robotic horse called Stridor.

Battle Armor Skeletor was joined by some new Evil Warriors: Fisto's counterpart, Jitsu, the crab-man Clawful, alligator-man Whiplash, spider-man Webstor, and Kobra Khan, a lizard-man who also functioned as a squirt gun.

The playset for this wave was Skeletor's base of operations, Snake Mountain, which acted as an evil counterpoint to the first wave's Castle Grayskull. It was shaped like a big, purple mountain, complete with giant snake heads and a built-in voice changing microphone feature, to make a kid's voice sound deep, dark, and evil. By moving one of the snake faces' mouths, it could look like mountain itself was speaking.

Although Snake Mountain first appeared in the animated series, there was some miscommunication between Filmation and Mattel. The cartoon version, possibly based on an early design for the playset, was stark and nearly pitch black. It had one snake wrapped up the mountain's jagged peak, with a waterfall of lava pouring over one side. The toy itself had something similar in a bright green snake's head stretching above the mountaintop, but it was also decorated with other ghoulish faces for the voice-changing feature. Its colors were more vibrant, and it came with platforms and bridges built in for a more changes for the heroes and villains to battle across the mountainside.

That one discrepancy aside, the toy line began to mirror He-Man's animated adventures very closely beginning with wave three. Recognizing the power of synchronizing the narrative of the Masters of the Universe brand, Mattel swept aside previous approaches and backstories to the characters. The descriptions given in advertisements and on the back of their toy's packaging were updated to reflect the new, better known continuity of *He-Man and the Masters of the Universe*. The amount of changes required varied from character to character, but the core conceits remained the same. In this sort of mutability of storytelling possibilities, He-Man showed his true strength.

The toy series continued on, with the next two years introducing new villains like Hordak and his evil Horde, and King Hiss and the villainous Snake Men. While these later characters would occasionally appear in the cartoons, they were primarily introduced to the toy-buying public through the minicomics. While these pack-in stories were initially created with little thought to continuity for the brand's burgeoning mythos, they became one of the most important ways of telling the stories of He-Man.

After Texeira and Cohn's comics for the second wave of figures, they were replaced by a rotating band of creators including Alfredo Alcala, the artist for the first four comics, and Michael Halperin, who had written the story bible for the Filmation cartoon *He-Man and the Masters of the Universe*, which had debuted at this point. The characters and tone began to match that of the popular animated incarnation, and several TV episodes were adapted into the comics altogether.

Many of the later creators tasked with Mattel's minicomics took the material more seriously. The main goal, as writer Michael Halperin described it, was keeping things consistent. He worked as a liaison between the animators and the toy creators, ironing out the looks and behaviors of the characters, while also establishing their motivations and backstories. Uniting these different branches of the fledgling media empire under one head writer, he said, produced "three solutions at once: consistency, the basis for a series, and a sales tool."[13]

The minicomics and animated series began to fall into step under Halperin's watch. Several minicomics were based on episodes of *He-Man and the Masters of the Universe*, as adapted by Halperin, though they were not exact duplicates. As tied together as the different writers were, there were different lags in production time for the animators, comic artists, and toy makers. When the character of Prince Adam was folded into the Filmation cartoon, his color scheme had not been finalized before the first minicomic featuring him was released. Similar discolorings happened with Teela and King Randor. When there was confusion over the look of Skeletor's Snake Mountain, the comic artists sided with toy, so their version also looks nothing like what the toy buyers saw in the syndicated show.

All told, there were 49 minicomics released between 1981 and 1987. Beyond that were the full-sized issues released by DC Comics, a read-along record, children's storybooks from Golden Books in the U.S. and Ladybird Books in the UK, the official *He-Man and the Masters of the Universe* magazine, a newspaper comic strip beginning on 1986, and many others.

There are several standouts throughout the various stages of the minicomics. They are remarkable for either the art or story quality, the lasting impacts on characters or their story universe, or general memorability for a generation of fans who grew up reading them.

Contained below are explorations and explanations of three of these stories. It is not intended to be comprehensive.

"The Vengeance of Skeletor" (1982)

The last of the initial Don Glut and Alfredo Alcala minicomics from the first wave of MOTU figures, this story sees Skeletor organize his minions Beast Man and Mer-Man into a direct assault on He-Man and his allies for control of Castle Grayskull. The previous three minicomics had displayed the skull-faced villain's trickery and scheming, with only one of his henchmen at a time.

Skeletor sends the two out to ambush He-Man, saying: "before he can use one his super-weapons against you, you will destroy him." The two take him by surprise, and from beyond a ridge, Teela sees Mer-Man dragging the hero away.

Chucked into the ocean, He-Man awakens to struggle against a large creature which resembles a fanged octopus. He reaches the surface, but the unnamed monster is still squeezing the life out of him. Spotting the battle from above, Stratos swoops in for the rescue.

Realizing Skeletor must be counting on his death, He-Man tells his friend they must hurry to press their advantage. They find Teela, who thanks "the Universal Powers" for his safety, and says she saw Beast Man loping off toward Castle Grayskull.

The castle is described as an "ancient place of wonders that was built by unknown hands sometime before the Great Wars." It is inhabited by the wispy, ephemeral spirit of Grayskull, who has charged He-Man and his friends with its protection. Skeletor had already gained entrance to it in the minicomics by this point; he briefly usurped the great power inside, though only using it to animate suits of armor and levitate weapons. So far, there had been nothing on the scale of the intergalactic domination he promised.

He-Man, Stratos, and Teela attack the villains outside of Castle Grayskull, tricking Skeletor's henchmen into firing their weapons at one another. Incensed, Skeletor turns on his own failing minions, shocking Mer-Man with a magic bolt from his half of the Power Sword. He-Man interrupts to stop this torture, running Skeletor over with the Battle Ram. The narration explains that as much as he hates Skeletor, "he hated more to see a master do harm to a slave."

The early stories, especially before the moral-loaded Filmation cartoons, had more of an edge to them. Though He-Man is always portrayed as a good guy, this is one of the earliest instances of his true nobility shining through.

"The Ordeal of Man-E-Faces" (1983)

As the second of the minicomics from Cohn and Texeira, this story was laid out in traditional comic book style and allowed the reader into the mind of Skeletor via thought balloons. It is especially noteworthy for being the first to shine a light on the broader Eternia society outside of the wastelands surrounding Castle Grayskull. The first page's caption tells us as much, by announcing the action is taking place within "the Royal Palace of Eternia."

He-Man and Teela are standing in a small crowd, watching a performance on a small Commedia dell'arte-style stage. The sole performer is Man-E-Faces, a character in a blue space suit and helmet covered in sci-fi wires and cable. In true Eternian fashion, of course, he is also shirtless.

Man-E-Faces was a figure introduced in the second wave of Masters of the Universe. His action feature was all in his head: by turning a knob, the face inside his helmet would change from a normal human to a vicious monster. This minicomic is used as an origin story for the character, as Skeletor forces him to drink a magic potion which creates the monster persona and places the multi-faced character under his evil control. Man-E-Faces memory of this is wiped, giving Skeletor a sleeper agent within the Palace.

The actor is giving a performance for the King and Queen of Eternia, in their first appearances as well, when Skeletor magically appears. As He-Man attacks, Man-E-Faces is activated. His monster identity takes control, and he easily swats away Man-At-Arms and abducts Teela. As he teleports them away, Skeletor gloats he will sacrifice her to a demon to gain entrance to Castle Grayskull.

The Goddess, now called the Sorceress, arrives to transport He-Man to Teela's rescue. As he battles the demon, the Sorceress reverts Man-E-Faces to his normal state so he can free Skeletor's captive. The unlucky actor is caught between the two magic-users, switching back and forth between man and monster, until a third face appears. No longer good or evil, simply a blank-faced robot. Skeletor flees, and the Sorceress worries that he may once again take control of Man-E-Faces.

"The Ordeal of Man-E-Faces" is a prime example of the strengths of the Cohn and Texeira stage of the minicomics. Along with expanding the narrative scope and providing important insight into the day-to-day life, and the system of government, of Eternians, they also introduce an element of moral complexity into the good vs. evil dynamic. Following his introduction in this story, owners of a Man-E-Faces action figure could portray him as a hero, a villain, or an innocent stuck in the middle, just as the comics and cartoons would do.

"Grizzlor: The Legend Comes Alive!" (1985)

This minicomic from the fourth wave of Masters of the Universe worked to introduce the character of Grizzlor, a villainous figure from the evil Horde, a new group of bad guys intended to mix up the power struggle of Eternia. By not focusing on He-Man only fighting Skeletor and his minions, the story options widened. In addition, an influx of new characters meant even more toys to sell: there were 13 figures in wave four, and five of them were from the Horde.

By this point the minicomics, and the Masters of the Universe brand as a whole, had really hit its stride. The character designs were all but flawlessly matched between animation, action figure, and comic pages.

The tone and characterizations had become ironed out, as well. Even the minicomics' artwork had jumped up a notch.

"Grizzlor: The Legend Comes Alive!" is most notable for that artwork, as provided by animator Bruce Timm. This is some of Timm's earliest comics work, and the Grizzlor story is his first solo penciling gig. His signature style is already apparent in these pages, a bold and expressive take on characters that would later be deemed as iconic in his work on DC Comics cartoons. Along with writer Paul Dini, he would be responsible for *Batman: The Animated Series* (1992–1995), *Superman: The Animated Series* (1996–2000), and the one-two punch of *Justice League* (2001–2004) and *Justice League Unlimited* (2004–2006).

This minicomic, not attributed to any writer, concerns a group of Eternian heroes: Teela, Man-At-Arms, Fisto, and Buzz-Off. The four are on a trek across the desert for unexplained reasons, and as they camp for the night, Buzz-Off tells the legend of Grizzlor. Teela is spooked by the tall tale, but Man-At-Arms tells her not to worry: Buzz-Off tells scary stories around the camp fire on every trip.

The next day, however, Buzz-Off comes across some footprints which can only belong to the fabled Grizzlor. No one believes him, but someone watching through a magic portal from the evil dimension, the Fright Zone. It is Hordak, the leader of the evil Horde, and he just happens to control the Grizzlor.

He sends the monster through the portal to abduct Teela, wanting to use her connection to the Sorceress to, what else, steal the power of Castle Grayskull. Try as the heroes may, they can't stop Grizzlor without sending Buzz-Off back to the castle to bring He-Man. Once he shows up, Hordak and his minion are sent packing.

By 1984, He-Man was already cemented as a success in toy stores, book shops, and television. That's when the lawyers showed up.

Conan Properties, Inc., the people who held the copyright for the character of Conan the Barbarian, saw the impressive trajectory of Mattel's own muscular barbarian character and cried foul. Spotting some visual similarities between the two characters, and they noted that before He-Man's debut, Mattel had been supplied with a lot of pre-production material about the look of the cinematic Conan, before he was played by Arnold Schwarzenegger in 1982. He-Man, CPI claimed, was nothing more than "Conan disguised with a blond wig."[14]

CPI brought suit against Mattel for all number of infringements, including copyright and trademark, along with fraud, breach of contract, and unfair competition. Mattel countered with a claim of fraud against CPI, insisting He-Man and the Masters of the Universe characters were all original, and nothing had been borrowed or repurposed from their brief flirtation with a Conan toy line. The two companies went to court in lieu of their fictional warriors drawing their swords.

Due to the long, winding road of Conan's life as an intellectual property, CPI could only claim control of the character from 1977 on. In the court documents, it is not clarified where they obtained these rights from, and they could only claim that He-Man was infringing on the eight copyrights they had, consisting of the Marvel Comics Conan stories from the late 1970s. Anything more conceptual than that fairly recent incarnation was not able to be used in the case. CPI could make no claim to the original Howard stories.

The court mulled the case over for five years, not delivering a verdict until 1989. They determined that Conan the Barbarian, as a character, existed in the public domain. CPI owned the rights to the Marvel comic books, but there was no way to prove that if He-Man did borrow from the appearance of Conan, they were taking from a public domain version instead of the one CPI had the copyright for. But the official judgment went further than that.

"One of the first rudiments of intellectual property," the court's statement read, "is that no one may copyright an idea."[15] A character like Conan, they posit, is not original enough in the legal sense to accuse another of infringing. Any creator naturally brings his or her own inspirations to the table, meaning nothing is wholly original. Howard, many believe, was inspired by Viking tales and characters like Tarzan by Edgar Rice Burroughs, but that does not mean Conan was infringing on these concepts.

The court agreed that He-Man was likely influenced by Conan, visually if nothing else, but not to any extent that would constitute an infringement. Sweet agrees just as much in *Mastering the Universe*, claiming, "Conan was a minor source of inspiration for He-Man, but the physically powerful paintings of Frank Frazetta's barbarians played a much greater role in my mind."[16] The fantasy artwork of Frazetta had depicted Conan on many occasions, but also other warrior, barbarian, and sci-fi characters in the same trademark style.

In the end, all of CPI's claims relating to trademarks were thrown out. Though some contractual issues were likely settled behind the scenes, He-Man emerged unscathed.

Whatever elements of the Conan look or mythos were appropriated were likely not responsible for the surging popularity of the Masters of the Universe franchise in those early years. Instead, Mattel's focus on keeping the property "generic" saved it from being pigeon-holed as just a "Barbarian Monster Fantasy" toy or just a "Space Military" toy.

The inherent flexibility of the characters and the scope of the world of Eternia kept possibilities excitingly broad. While this was expressed in the varieties of character types and genre stories to be explored, it also opened Masters of the Universe up to be molded into different shapes to make it perfect for different types of media. While He-Man started out as a toy, that is not where he would remain.

Mattel's executives had grand plans of exploiting the recent relaxation of FCC regulations. They were going to bring their action figure to animation, no matter how strange such an idea may seem to both audiences and television networks in 1983. The next step would be to find an animation company willing to take such a risk.

2

Enter Filmation!

When Filmation Associates made a splash on Saturday mornings with *The New Adventures of Superman*, no one was more surprised than its founders.

Animators Lou Scheimer and Hal Sutherland formed the company in 1963 after stints at Larry Harmon Pictures working on a Popeye cartoon. After some minor projects, the two teamed with producer Norm Prescott to begin work on an animated sequel to iconic musical *The Wizard of Oz*. The project skidded to a halt over budgetary issues, so the fledgling Filmation crew turned back to television. Their original ideas failed to get traction, and their freelance work for commercials could only pay the bills for so long. By 1965, the future was looking bleak.

That's when they received the call. DC Comics editor Mort Weisinger was looking to bring Superman back to television after the sudden, and suspicious, suicide of Superman actor George Reeves in 1959. While it was determined replacing Reeves on *The Adventures of Superman* would be in bad taste, DC felt the property had laid dormant in the realm of TV for too long. This time, they wanted to take a different approach. By returning the character to animation, the storytelling options would move beyond what they producers could manage on a TV budget. Once again, the sky could be the limit. But first things first: DC wanted a tour of the Filmation studio.

When the call came in, however, Filmation had two employees: Scheimer and Sutherland. Their studio, if it could be called that, consisted of them and over 20 empty desks. What followed was one of the strangest scams in the history of cartooning.

Scheimer called DC back and said they were far too busy and could not let their staff be distracted for a tour. He did invite them during the studio's one weekly visiting time, between noon and one o'clock on a

Wednesday. The Filmation crew then called in every favor they had to get friends and family to man the desks during their lunch hours. Their makeshift "employees," made up of seasoned animators and complete novices, pretended to be working on the finished cels of the *Journey Back to Oz* project. Ted Knight, the man later known for announcing the *Super Friends* cartoon, was brought in to voice unseen employees outside of the office door during the meeting. The reception area was occupied by a store mannequin.

As Scheimer told the story years later, they were in the office discussing the details with DC's Whitney Ellsworth as time was running out for their "employees'" lunch hour. One of them, George Reilly, knocked on the door. He needed to return to work at Hanna-Barbera, but he announced that he had a toothache.

"I said, 'Okay, George, you can go to the dentist,'" Scheimer recalled. "He shut the door, and I turned around to Hal and said, 'Make sure we dock that son of a bitch!'"[1]

Filmation's ruse worked. They were signed to make *The New Adventures of Superman* series, and the modest price per episode paid by DC kept the company afloat. Scheimer and Sutherland were even able to hire some of their pretend-employees for real. The show was not only well received by the audience, it also helped Superman take another great leap forward for pop culture.

Before 1966, most television programs were created and controlled by the very companies that would advertise during the show. They would make everything to their own specifications and then find a network, like NBC or CBS, to broadcast it. Instead of finding a sponsor for the cartoon, the way the Kellogg cereal company had sponsored *The Adventures of Superman* live-action series in the 1950s, DC wasn't letting another company get between them and their lucrative property. Making the show themselves, DC could keep their same Superman comics writers and bear down on Filmation, a young, hungry company, to make sure Superman looked exactly the same as artist Curt Swan made him look on the newsstand every month. The finished cartoon was sold to CBS directly.

The other big change in cartoons at this time was the scheduling. Most animated series were considered family entertainment and played in the evenings. *The New Adventures of Superman* and these other new cartoons would be the first to move to a new time slot: Saturday mornings.

Just like that, Filmation had a hit show and were on the cutting edge of the new animation paradigm. All they had to do was keep it up. The company attempted to capitalize by developing pilots for a few other concepts, mainly original ideas, but they didn't take off. Scheimer blamed the failure of these sophomore efforts, such as *The Adventures of Dirk Digit*, for being too strange for audiences' tastes. And so they turned back to what they knew would work.

DC teamed with the company again to adapt another comic book hero: Aquaman. This time, the animators had a chance to flex their creative muscles. The entirely undersea setting for *Aquaman* gave the series a unique look and color palate, and a wavy underwater effect was created by moving one oiled acetate in front of the characters, at a different speed than how everything else on the screen was moving. This series, paired with the last to form *The Superman/Aquaman Hour of Adventure*, was another success.

By this point, Filmation had developed their signature style. Namely, in order to keep costs down, their scripts were built around the use of stock footage. Episodes would show the same clips of characters moving, like Superman flying or Aquaman swimming, connected by the original animation for the elements unique to that particular story. These familiar shots could be reversed, inverted, or anything else to keep the episode from appearing too repetitive.

The company utilized a method of limited animation, or animating one moving part of one character, such as Jimmy Olson's arm, while the rest of his body would remain stationary. The frame rate was also lower than other animation companies, making their cartoons appear to move jerkily instead of more smoothly, like a big budget Disney movie.

Costs were cut wherever possible. Backgrounds, and nearly everything else, were up for recycling. Monsters could be recolored to appear again as different monsters. Scheimer admitted, "We would also occasionally have the characters put their hands up by their mouths as they talked—as if they were scratching their chin or thinking—which meant we didn't have to animate their lips."[2]

This style allowed for more care to be taken on the design of the characters, which tended to be human instead of a cartoony or anthropomorphized animal, and also on the scripts, which were recognized for being a cut above their competitors.

Throughout the rest of the '60s, Filmation stuck to established properties. Aquaman was replaced to create *The Batman/Superman Hour*, and that show continued to dominate Saturday mornings. They adapted the Hardy Boys, the popular series of boy's adventure and mystery novels, and started making animated series based off of successful live-action films. In 1967, they premiered *Journey to the Center of the Earth*. It was followed the next year with *Fantastic Voyage*.

By the end of the decade, many were criticizing children's television for violence. Even Sutherland and Scheimer's adventure programs like *Batman/Superman*, which were considered rather tame, had a wary eye cast upon them. The company decided to move away from comic book superheroes, but not from comic books altogether.

Filmation's next great adaptation came in the form of America's favorite teenager: Archie Andrews. The fan base was already in place, and the more light-hearted tone would fit the direction Saturday morning cartoons were heading. As much as the concept seemed to be a slam dunk, it still needed some alterations before it hit the airwaves.

Hot Dog, the goofy pet of Archie's pal Jughead, was introduced. Archie's publishers did not provide writers for the show, the way DC had for Superman and Batman, but the company found the characters well enough established that there were no problems. Due to the character's conflicts and motivations, like Archie falling in love with both Betty and Veronica, Filmation tried to skew their audience for what came to be called "the Tween group." Still, nothing was too racy or dark to throw off the kiddies. To help sell the show's image as more of a "mature" children's program, a "canned" laugh track was incorporated so it could better resemble the sorts of live shows that were marketed at older kids, like *Rowan & Martin's Laugh-In*.

The biggest change to the source material was the way *The Archie Show* incorporated music. In the comics, the Riverdale gang had formed a band, "The Archies." The cartoon pushed that concept further, separating two independent stories with what could be considered a "music video" of the friends playing an original song.

For the music, Filmation turned to "the man with the golden ear," Don Kirshner.[3] Best known as a producer and a musical kingmaker, Kirshner had just had a falling out with another television band: The Monkees. Freed from the demands of live actors, he was eager to show he could form another hit musical act.

Utilizing a crew of seasoned session musicians and songwriters, Kirshner delivered the music, which turned out to be even more successful than the high-rated show. The infectious brand of bubblegum pop connected with audiences on both TV and radio. The first album from "The Archies" cracked the Billboard Top 100, and animated segments of the band playing the single "Bang-Shang-A-Lang" was broadcast during the Ed Sullivan Show on November 17, 1968, in lieu of a live act.

The second album released, *Everything's Archie*, contained the pop mega-hit "Sugar, Sugar." Written by pop virtuosos Jeff Barry and Andy Kim, Kirshner distributed the single to DJs without mentioning who sang it to avoid the stigma of "a cartoon band." Once radio's gatekeepers learned the truth, it was too late; the song rocketed to the number one spot and stayed there for four weeks.

"Sugar, Sugar" was certified as a gold record, signifying over one million copies sold,[4] and became Billboard's number one song for the year of 1969. In the list of biggest hit singles from that decade, Filmation's fictional The Archies is sandwiched between the Beatles, with "Hey, Jude" in 1968, and Simon and Garfunkel's "Bridge Over Troubled Water" in 1970.

As *The Archie Show* itself would be a Saturday morning mainstay. It went through many iterations, such as *Archie's TV Funnies* and *The U.S. of Archie*, for the next decade or so.

Filmation continued into the 1970s, powered by successes like their Archie spin-off, *The Sabrina the Teenage Witch Show*, and the beloved *Fat Albert and the Cosby Kids*, based on characters from Bill Cosby's standup routines. The show ran for eight seasons, and were hosted by Cosby in live-action introduction and conclusion segments. The company also continued their tradition of creating spin-offs or animated sequels to well-known series like *My Favorite Martian* and their *The Brady Bunch* cartoon, *The Brady Kids*.

With continued pressure on the companies producing children's programming from organizations like Action for Children's Television, Filmation continued to steer clear of perceived violent content. The focus remained on incorporating music, along with introducing more educational content. Shows like *Fat Albert* began including morals, where characters wrap up each episode by stressing the importance of friends, family, and other wholesome values. Already a household name, Scheimer and company made sure nobody could accuse Filmation of trying to corrupt the minds of children.

Their next big success came in the form of 1973's *Star Trek: The Animated Series*. Filmation managed to reunite nearly the entire live-action cast, along with original showrunner Gene Roddenberry and script editor Dorothy "D.C." Fontana. Though the animation was limited and relied heavily on stock footage, Fontana and the returning writers from the original live-action *Star Trek* episodes were able to depict more strange new worlds and alien life forms. The character's limited mobility fit well with the series' talky, intellectual approach. Although it would be played on Saturday mornings, alongside children's cartoons, Roddenberry and Filmation worked to make the show as sophisticated as possible.

Before the debut, producer Norm Prescott announced, "This is the first attempt to do an adult show in animation."[5] Nobody involved seemed certain such a "bold experiment," wagering children would want more intelligent programs and that adults would tune in on Saturday mornings, would pan out.

It was not an entirely successful venture. Nielson ratings showed that young children, the bread and butter of Saturday mornings, were not tuning in in the big numbers network had hoped for.

The next year, the episode "How Sharper than a Serpent's Tooth" won the Daytime Emmy Award for Outstanding Children's Series. It was the first Emmy award won by Filmation, and by the Star Trek franchise as a whole. It is still considered the only "major" Emmy won by any Trek TV series.

The 1970s were rounded out by more tried-and-true properties, like more Archie shows and *The New Adventures of Batman,* featuring the voices of Adam West and Burt Ward, and other adaptations of once-popular live-action shows, such as *The New Adventures of Gilligan.* Filmation also began to branch out and make their own live-action shows, like the superhero series *Shazam!* and the sci-fi *Jason of Star Command.*

The company was remaining solid, despite the fact there were more misses than hits. In addition, the landscape of children's television was constantly evolving. Filmation was able to keep ahead of the curve by introducing their live-action series, but they did not have enough success to move away from animation altogether. The world of animation was becoming more expensive. Many other companies had begun outsourcing animation tasks to cheaper countries, but Filmation remained loyal to the local Los Angeles animator unions. "Made in the USA" was proudly stamped on their products, but that didn't make them any cheaper to produce. Jobs were beginning to dry up.

That's when they were approached by Mattel.

The Mattel company had learned the power of good television marketing decades earlier. When Walt Disney's *The Mickey Mouse Club* debuted in 1955, the toy company paid $500,000, a staggering amount for the time, to sponsor the show's first year. The show was a hit, Disney used the money to build the Disneyland park, and the advertising paid off for Mattel far better than expected.

By the early 1980s, recognizing the storytelling potential of the Masters of the Universe characters and looking to capitalize on the Reagan administration's deregulation of children's programming, Mattel wanted to push the boundaries. Thomas Kalinske, Senior Vice President of Marketing, brought the property to Filmation's founder Lou Scheimer, showing him the recently published DC Comics adaptations of the figures.

"Mattel came to me with this wild barbarian with blonde hair waving in the wind, hatchets, axes, and all kinds of weapons and mayhem going on," Scheimer later wrote. "I said, 'You can't do that for kids!' With Action for Children's Television running around, and parents all concerned about content, there was no way anyone would let this on the air."[6]

Recognizing some potential in the characters, and what could be a much needed hit, Filmation asked for some time and liberties to find their own approach to the material. Immediately, nearly everything from the minicomics were thrown out. The basics from Mattel's vision of Eternia remained in place, but nearly everything else was open to reinterpretation.

Anything deemed "too scary" was dropped, and wary of the prevalent watchdog groups, the inherent violence was toned way down. To balance out Skeletor's ghoulish appearance, he was given a less than frightening voice, and was portrayed as barely more competent than his goofy henchmen. The kids watching at home would know that Eternia's heroes were never in any real danger.

Filmation was known for producing educational, moral programming for young people through shows like *Fat Albert*, and this was a trend they wanted to continue. So not only would the fighting be minimized, the episodes were also based around a lesson for the audience. While Prescott and Scheimer maintained this was their standard approach for all of their shows, it would also be useful when groups like the ACT began to protest *He-Man*.

In order for children to better connect with The Most Powerful Man in the Universe, the company returned to what they'd learned producing *Shazam!* In that live-action series, and later a cartoon as well, a young boy named Billy Batson could say the magic word, "Shazam," and be transformed into the adult superhero Captain Marvel. An unstoppable, hypermasculine idol was great, they figured, but a vulnerable, realistic protagonist was even better. And so they added Prince Adam, He-Man's alter ego.

The character had been formulated in Mattel in the early days, and in a very different form, and had already been used in one of the DC Comics stories as He-Man's secret identity. Filmation altered the character's look, namely adding the infamous pink and white color scheme, and revised his personality as well.

Adam was designed to be a normal human boy, someone with flaws and self-doubt. He would be uncertain but good-hearted, wanting to do the right thing until things became too dangerous. At the last moment, he could draw the Power Sword, which was now no longer in two halves, and say the magic words, "By the power of Grayskull, I have the power!" In a handy sequence of stock footage, the Prince would transform into the superhuman He-Man. Whether due to Filmation's limitations, or Mattel's interest in using the same body parts for every character, Prince Adam appeared the same age as his counterpart, and even had the same muscular build. Neither character wore a mask. Still, his secret identity stayed remarkably secret.

Adam was further fleshed out with a supporting cast. In addition to the characters who began as action figures, Man-At-Arms and Teela, he was given parents, Randor and Marlena, the King and Queen of the kingdom of Eternos. He-Man's ferocious green pet, Battle Cat, was given a secret identity in the cowardly Cringer. Cringer could talk, but Battle Cat just growled in most episodes.

The animators also created Orko, the floating comic relief character. He was written as equal parts powerful and bumbling, and was also much less mature than He-Man and the other characters. That way, as there were seldom any younger characters, Orko could play the part of the child who needed to learn how to behave, or how to be brave, over the course of an episode. In true Filmation fashion, Orko's name was changed from "Gorpo," so his stock footage could be flipped as needed without the "G" on his chest appearing backward. Turning that into an "O" meant the same clips could be used as much as needed.

The company was also working with Mattel's Michael Halperin to draft the story bible, a comprehensive list of backstories and motivations. They began to solicit scripts as the character designs were finalized. Though many Eternians were based on existing action figures, some needed to be tweaked to better show the newly revised continuity. Man-At-Arms, for example, was given a moustache in the cartoon to better identify him as older than Adam and Teela, and make him more of a father figure. The Sorceress, formerly called The Goddess, was revamped completely.

In the meantime, the company began to shop the show, now titled *He-Man and the Masters of the Universe*, around to the networks for a Saturday morning timeslot. Although the foreign markets were an easy sell for a company with Filmation's reputation for quantity, if not quality, American networks like ABC and NBC resisted.

He-Man already had a stigma. The toys looked inherently violent, and their appearances in comic books didn't prove differently, even when they met cartoon-friendly Superman in *DC Comics Presents* issue 47 in 1982. It would not be a good fit the more educational direction Saturday morning cartoons were heading in.

In addition, a cartoon series designed to show off action figures was untested waters. Even Mattel designers like Sweet saw the show as "blurring the line between children's programming and flat-out advertising."[7] Though such programs were now technically legal under President Reagan's administration, there was no guarantee how audiences would react. They could just as easily be turned off by a so-called "30-minute toy advertisement."

Networks decided to play it safe, so Mattel and Filmation opted to sell the show to local channels through the country, a process called syndication. TV shows typically went to syndication this way only after they had been broadcast on a major network; the same network who selected the show from an animation company's proposal and made demands about its content. By skipping the network's middle man, Filmation was given more creative control than any project they'd had before. They were now free to stray from the government's restrictions on content.

They were given the full support of Mattel, and the name recognition of the toy line was enough to sell the regional TV stations. The toy company also bartered with commercial time with these stations. A local station could get a great deal on the new He-Man cartoon by giving up some of the advertising time during the program. If they allowed Mattel to air commercials for their products during the show, which was also a commercial for their products, they could get a soon-to-be hit show for next to nothing. This was too good for most stations to pass up. By Mattel's accounts, about 90 percent of local TV stations in the United States picked up *He-Man and the Masters of the Universe*.

He-Man would not, however, be going to Saturday mornings. Regional TV channels would typically have an afternoon block of syndicated shows played every weekday, between 3 p.m. and 5 p.m. This made for so-called "appointment viewings," where children would either hurry home from school or hurry through their homework in order to watch their favorite programs. This also meant additional exposure for the show, at least five times as much as a normal Saturday morning series. Most TV series only went to syndication once they'd been on the air for enough years to have a catalogue of finished episodes. *He-Man and the Masters of the Universe* was pre-selling 65 episodes, enough new episodes for one quarter of a year's weekdays. For the remainder of the year, they could be played as repeats and still have enough variety to keep from appearing too repetitive.

It would be a monumental task for Filmation. The company hired on more animators and accepted scripts from outside writers just to keep up.

One such writer was Paul Dini, who went on to become a well-known writer for DC Comics. Working with former MOTU minicomics artist Bruce Timm, he was a writer for and co-creator of the DC Animated Universe, consisting of the multiple Emmy Award winner *Batman: The Animated Series* and many others. Though the *He-Man* cartoon was some of Dini's earliest work, his episodes are still considered fan favorites. He has given interviews about his experiences working on the series for the DVD box set releases, and in 2015's *The Art of He-Man and the Masters of the Universe*.

In the latter, Dini expressed appreciation for Filmation's route through syndication, as it opened up more possibilities for the writers. "We all wanted to raise the bar as much as we could," he said, "and try to tell stories that hadn't been done before in traditional Saturday-morning action-adventure. We didn't have network executives giving us creative notes and we had a lot of episodes with which to experiment."

The long seasons allowed for more narrative flexibility, he continued: "Anyway, when you've maxed out the epic Skeletor-attacks stories, the Orko-feels-unappreciated stories, and the giant-beasts-run-wild stories you start looking around for something new to write."[8] This led to more characters and monsters created out of whole cloth instead of the Mattel figures, including Sh'Gora, Dini's take on a Lovecraftian "Elder God" in his episode "To Save Skeletor."

Though the writers sent the characters off in different directions as often as they could, the resulting episodes were largely held to formula by the stock footage sequences, guaranteeing villains like Skeletor and Evil-Lyn were never far away. The structure was ensured by the adherence to the moral of each episode, which characters like He-Man, Teela, or Orko would re-emphasize to the audience after the story's climax.

As *He-Man and the Masters of the Universe* was debuting on television, Filmation brought it to the big screen. Three episodes were edited together and played at locations across the country, including a red carpet event at Mann's Chinese Theatre in Los Angeles. That event hosted a He-Man themed hot air balloon and actors dressed as the heroes and villains of Eternia. Invitations were sent out to children's groups, specifically, to spread the brand name to the target market and do a little last minute focus testing. But watching the excitement of the audience, both during the episodes and the "battle" between the costumed actors outside, both companies could tell they had a hit.

The show debuted in syndication on September 5, 1983 in the UK and September 26 in the United States, and it immediately changed the game. Because *He-Man* was so successful, other animation studios began taking their wares to syndication directly, eschewing the standard route of a major network's Saturday morning programming block.

According to Scheimer, "Advertisers loved it, because with no significant children's programming off-network, they had been relegated to the Saturday morning ghetto. It became apparent that this was a much better market for us, both financially and creatively."[9]

But animators weren't the only ones paying attention. Within the next two years, Mattel's cross-media formula would be repeated by its competitors, such as Hasbro, and He-Man's popularity would be under siege by the likes of Snake Eyes and Optimus Prime. Until then, however, the success of *He-Man and the Masters of the Universe* was unparalleled.

Predictably, the series raised the ire of Action for Children's Television. The group's founder, Peggy Charren, filed a complaint with the FCC on October 11 of that year. The complaint concerned the several children's cartoons which had been broadcast in 1983, notably *He-Man*, that were based off of pre-existing commercial properties. The others that were named were a one-off Care Bears TV special, which had been played that spring, and the first *GI Joe* miniseries, which debuted weeks after *He-Man*.

These TV series and specials were not spin-offs of films or other TV shows, Charren argued. Instead, the desire to sell more toys "precipitated the development of the program-length commercials.... What makes matters worse is that most of the products are being advertised on children's television as well, making it hard to distinguish between product and programming."[10]

That night, both Charren and Filmation president Scheimer were guests on *Nightline* with Ted Koppel, along with *Schoolhouse Rock* producer Squire Rushnell, and a lawyer from the FCC. During the program, Scheimer defended his company's work on the *He-Man* cartoon and took offense to the allegations made in Charren's complaint. After *Fat Albert* was mentioned as one of the best children's programs, Scheimer said, "The care and sensitivity that we bring to *Fat Albert* is brought to this show. It is not a commercial. It is a show. The fact is that we took these toys, and we worked delicately and laboriously to make sure that we injected love, family, humor, and a whole cast of characters that weren't even existent in the toys."[11]

Scheimer stuck to his guns throughout the program and emerged unscathed. Even the FCC representative on the program noted that Charren's complaint didn't stand a chance under the Present Reagan's FCC chairperson, Mark Fowler.

Unfortunately, the ACT were not the only ones speaking out against "program-length commercials" like *He-Man*. The American Academy of Pediatrics formed a task force to focus on children and television, and its chairman, Dr. William H. Dietz, began speaking out shortly thereafter. "They sell a product while claiming to be entertainment, and I think that's unconscionable," Dietz said. "It is unfair and deceptive advertising. It is unethical to do that, in my opinion."[12] Timothy E. Wirth, chairman of the telecommunication subcommittee of the House of Representatives, voiced his agreement. He was echoed in the Senate by Frank Lautenberg.

The director of Yale's Family Television Research and Consultation Center, Dr. Jerome Singer, added his voice to the group of concerned specialists. He cautioned, "Children do not have the elaborate knowledge that adults have about the nature of the commercial world, the nature of advertising, the nature of product appeals."[13]

The existential crisis of children's entertainment aside, the series was also continually under fire for its perceived violence. It was also, strangely, accused of being not violent enough on at least one occasion.

In 1985, Jane Welch wrote an op-ed for the *Washington Post* crying out that "'He-Man' is really a plot to turn young hildren [sic] into bleeding hearts" for focusing on non-lethal conflict resolution. "He's forever tossing a bad guy into a convenient puddle, or bringing some bad-tempered monster to the way of Truth and Goodness," she complained. The character of Teela was also leading children astray for refusing to be helpless damsel in distress, according to Welch: "Young Americans might begin to think that men and women are equals."[14]

This apparently serious article was titled "'He-Man' is a Wimp Master." It was not dignified with a response by Filmation.

Despite any controversy, or perhaps because of it, *He-Man and the Masters of the Universe* was a hit. The show's success translated to toy stores, as Mattel had hoped, and the sales more than doubled between the figures' debut and when the cartoon aired.

The show not only benefited Mattel and Filmation, it also changed the paradigms of advertising and children's entertainment. However, an even bigger change came in the characters. He-Man and Skeletor had entered the cultural lexicon, making an impact they never could have from the toy line alone. Concepts original to the cartoon series, such as the catchphrase, "By the power of Grayskull," quickly became recognizable around the world.

As the 65 episodes of the first season were winding to a close, Filmation was already hard at work on the second. The standard for most shows at the time was a shorter second season, so the new episodes could be interspersed with reruns of the previous episodes. It was a time before cheap and commonplace home video releases, so broadcasters expected audiences to not catch every episode during the first run, or they may be waiting for a favorite episode to come back up in the rotation.

Animators had also considered another movie-length exploit for He-Man, maybe one focusing on his origin. But this was dropped when the orders came in: based on the show's strength, initial orders of 39 second season episodes were expanded to a full 65. Depending on each local TV station, however, the new episodes may have been spread out over two years instead of just one.

A full second season gave the writers many more opportunities to branch out. Filmation's Larry DiTillio updated the story bible and the writers began to focus on deepening character relationships and broadening the mythos. Episodes were centered on He-Man and Skeletor less, letting secondary characters like Cringer and Prince Adam's mother, Queen Marlena, take center stage. New characters based off of the most recent action figures, like Fisto and Whiplash, began to appear regularly. Even with the completed footage from season one the animators could reuse, a whole second season was just as daunting as the first.

Filmation hired on new writers, such as a young J. Michael Straczynski, who would later gain fame as the lead writer and showrunner for the sci-fi series *Babylon 5*, and win a BAFTA Award for his screenplay *Changeling*.

Straczynski was known for answering questions from He-Man fans back in the early days of the internet, and many of such interactions are catalogued on the He-Man.org website.[15] As he explained it, he got into writing for *He-Man* by being a fan. "I'd seen the first season," he wrote, "and just for the heck of it, wrote a spec script. Sent it to the producer. Cold. No agent, no contacts, no nuthin'." Filmation bought his script, and then another from him just a week later. He was added on as a regular staff writer.

"Overall, I enjoyed the experience," Straczynski said of his He-Man days. "I tried in general to write stories that were more adult in nature ... alternating those with comic episodes just for fun."

When the second season came to a close, the decision was made to put a cap on *He-Man*. Filmation decided that the series had reached the point of diminishing returns: they could not make any more money by producing new episodes than they could by selling the old ones. At 130 episodes, or one episode for every other weekday in a year, there were still plenty of *He-Man* to be syndicated and remain fairly fresh. With no definitive first story or concluding episode, these same stories could continue on forever. Skeletor would always be out there, looking to cause trouble. He-Man would always be there to stop him.

After touting the show's demographic breakdown on more than one occasion, with young girls reportedly making up 30 percent of the viewing audience, Scheimer and the Filmation crew saw the opportunity to tailor a new adventure program for girls.

They began work on the *She-Ra: Princess of Power* series during the second season of *He-Man*, looking for a program they could have more control creative over. The characters would be created jointly between the company and Mattel, who then produced the action figures based on the agreed-upon designs. In order to capitalize on the ongoing success of *He-Man*, the new heroine was tied as closely as possible to the old hero: She-Ra would be his long-lost twin sister.

In March of 1985, *The Secret of the Sword* was released to theaters. The feature-length introduction to She-Ra was actually the first five episodes of her cartoon series, with some additional editing to smooth out the transitions. As an actual five-part story, the plot hung together better than what had been released to theaters before *He-Man and the Masters of the Universe* debuted on the small screen. That looser collection of episodes had since been released on home video under the title *He-Man: The Greatest Adventure of All*.

Secret of the Sword was also a crossover with the previous series, as Castle Grayskull's Sorceress sent He-Man from Eternia to another planet called Etheria. This new locale is more lush and magical than Eternia, but one that has been conquered by an evil alien race called the Horde. Prince Adam's sister, Adora, is revealed to have been abducted as a child. She was brainwashed by the Horde's leader, Hordak, so she is now the tough and true-believer Force Captain of the ruling aliens. He-Man is able to snap her out of it and give her the Sword of Protection, a counterpart to his Sword of Power, which allows her to transform into She-Ra. After a brief visit to her birth parents, the King and Queen of Eternia, she decides to return to Etheria to use her super-powered identity to aid the rebellion against the Horde.

Throughout She-Ra's full 65 episode season, and a second of 28 spread across 1986 and 1987, He-Man would pop in for the occasional team-up. The two had a Christmas special in 1985, as well. But for the most part, she was left to stand on her own.

She-Ra: Princess of Power, a female-centric adventure series, surprised some by its success. Though there were other "girl's shows" on the air, none really featured fight scenes. And by this point in the '80s, she had competition from other popular cross-media franchise shows targeted at boys, such as *Transformers* and even *He-Man* himself, but her ratings stayed high.

Filmation tweaked their approach from the He-Man cartoon, keeping the moral of each episode, but lightening some violence and including more love stories in the plots. There was a softness to the character; She-Ra resolved threats in a more non-violent fashion than her twin brother, and her superpowers were portrayed as gentler as well. Unlike He-Man, for example, she could talk to animals.

Making a capable female protagonist as a role model for young girls was something Scheimer felt strongly about. "I was motivated to have strong women and girls on our shows," he said. "[*She-Ra*] wasn't meant to have a political message of feminism to it directly, but it was meant to show that women and girls could do the same types of things boys and men did if they wanted to."[16] The creators' intentions aside, the character is fondly remembered by women and men of all backgrounds. Decades later, she is still just as recognizable as He-Man.

Between the two massive seasons, not to mention the specials and crossovers, there are almost too many episodes of *He-Man and the Masters of the Universe* to pick favorites from. Even the two "Best of" DVDs available can't settle fan's debates of which episode is truly better than any other. Any viewer's mileage may vary.

Below is a breakdown of several key episodes of *He-Man*, included for popularity or notoriety, or for something more noteworthy from behind the scenes. It is certainly not meant to be a comprehensive list.

"The Shaping Staff": Season One, 1983

The second episode produced, yet shown a little later in the season, "The Shaping Staff" is the first episode of *He-Man* written by scribe Paul Dini. It begins abruptly, opening on He-Man smashing robots and hurtling a subterranean octopus-like monster over the nearest mountain.

It's all for training. He is merely breaking in Man-At-Arms' newest inventions.

Transforming back into Prince Adam, he hurries back to the palace for dinner. He arrives late, as usual, and clumsily knocks over a coatrack, which distracts Orko in the middle of one of his tricks. Queen Marlena says, "I think Adam inherited from me what we Earthlings call a sense of humor." This is the first mention in the series of the Queen coming from Earth as an astronaut. It's an idea that comes and goes throughout the mythos, after first appearing in a DC Comics story.

Orko's magic act is soon interrupted again, this time by a woman named Majestra. She is also a magician, and her white bob of hair resembles that of Sabrina the Teenage Witch from her Filmation series. Majestra performs a trick for the royal family, making King Randor disappear in a "Cabinet of Wonders." When the king reappears and suddenly invites this new magician to stay at the palace, Orko is suspicious.

He floats after the king and Majestra down to the dungeon, where they find the real King Randor. The two figures in the doorway reveal themselves as Skeletor's henchmen, Evil-Lyn and Beast Man, who had taken other appearances through the power of the Shaping Staff. The cabinet trick was used to swap out the real king for the fake one. Evil-Lyn displays the staff's power again by transforming King Randor into a goat. When they discover Orko eavesdropping, he is turned into a cricket. Their plan is to have Beast Man, as the king, command the royal guards to march on Castle Grayskull and annex it into Skeletor's new puppet kingdom.

Even as a cricket, Orko is able to warn Prince Adam. He turns into He-Man, and confronts the two imposters alongside Teela. Evil-Lyn turns her into a frog, and He-Man becomes a golden statue of himself. He is brought along to Grayskull as a present for Skeletor.

The skull-faced villain is already at the castle, using his magic powers to create an evil doppelgänger of He-Man, whom he dubs "Faker." Unlike the Faker action figures, he looks exactly like He-Man in every way, save his white, glowing eyes. It would be his only appearance on the show in any form. Faker calls up to the Sorceress inside the Castle, drawing her outside so Evil-Lyn can use the shaping staff to transform her into a tree.

Although one is made of wood and the other is encased in gold, the Sorceress and He-Man still share a telepathic bond and are able to hatch a plan. She disrupts the shaping staff's spell over He-Man, allowing him to break free and attack the villains. In a tussle with his evil magic-clone,

He-Man sidesteps a headlong tackle and Faker is sent plummeting off of a cliff.

According to Lou Scheimer, Faker's demise wasn't caught by Filmation executives until it was almost too late. Reviewing the footage, he said, "it almost looked like He-Man had caused him to fall, and, when I saw that, we brought in the writer and the director and reworked the scene with some new dialogue, so it was clear that He-Man wasn't the cause of Faker's death."[17]

He-Man is able to break the shaping staff, reversing all the spells Evil-Lyn had cast with it. Teela, Orko, and the rest are all back to normal. Still, the evil witch tries one last spell on He-Man, using one splintered end of the staff. It backfires, transforming her into a small, snake-like monster, with slithers away with the rest of the retreating villains.

"A Tale of Two Cities": Season One, 1983

It should first be noted that this episode has absolutely nothing to do with the novel by Charles Dickens. Instead, the script by Richard Pardee has He-Man caught between two warring Eternian cities when he saves a princess. To make it, Filmation borrowed heavily from "Tarzan and the City of Gold," an episode of their *Tarzan, Lord of the Jungle* series from 1976.

Adam and Cringer spot a princess, Rhea, being pursued through the forest by gray flying Gargon creatures. She is easily rescued once they transform into He-Man and Battle Cat, and the heroes pledge to return her safely to her city of Operon. The Gargons, Rhea explains, are the soldiers of Balina, the queen of the rival city of Targa, which isn't far away. A storm has been brewing, and as Battle Cat leads Rhea across a makeshift bridge, lightning downs a tree, which strikes He-Man's head. Unconscious, the hero falls into the river and is swept toward Targa. When fished out by the Gargons, it is revealed that He-Man has lost his memory.

A main character developing amnesia is a tale as old as time in both superhero comic books, which He-Man was inspired by, and in daily TV soap operas, whose release pattern the syndicated cartoon mimicked. Memory loss had already been touched upon in the Paul Dini episode "Quest for He-Man" earlier in the season.

In Targa, He-Man is believed to be a spy from Operon and imprisoned. In the dungeons he meets Garn, a fellow prisoner who has been forced to fight for the queen's amusement in the arena. Garn calls himself the strongest man on Eternia, and says he has won nearly enough battles to win his freedom from Queen Balina. He-Man, unaware that he is the most powerful man in the universe, doesn't know better than to be impressed.

Garn, Balina and her wicked magician sidekick Draka, and the other residents of Targa, are all of African descent. This is noteworthy for the era, when there was not much integration of races on animated TV shows. Filmation produced the *Fat Albert* series, starring African American characters, and the company frequently worked to include more diversity in their shows. The Eternia of the toy line, however, was awfully Caucasian for the most part. One recurring black character who was created for the cartoon, the royal archaeologist Melaktha, appeared in several episodes in a non-fighting capacity. Mattel finally included the first black Masters of the Universe figure, the heroic Clamp Champ, in 1986. Because of such a late inclusion, he would not appear on the *He-Man* cartoon. For this reason, Garn is a notable character in the Filmation mythos.

The Gargons have captured Princess Rhea and trapped Battle Cat outside the city. Queen Balina pits Garn against the amnesiac hero in the gladiator arena, and another blow to the head restores He-Man's memories. After winning freedom for both him and Garn, they find Battle Cat and hurry back to Targa to free the princess. As Garn seeks vengeance against his captors, He-Man stays his hand and tells him Balina and Draka will face justice in the courts of Eternia.

The representation of black characters in "A Tale of Two Cities" is not without its problems. By having He-Man, a noble foreigner, be responsible for solving the issues of a black culture, the story does play into the uncomfortable "white savior" trope. He-Man also tells Garn, an abused slave, to trust the courts to find him justice; in the more idyllic world of Eternia, however, viewers could believe the justice system would work fairly for a recently freed slave. On the whole, though, race is a non-starter in this episode. Queen Balina and Draka are just as villainous as Skeletor and Evil-Lyn, and Garn is just as mighty and heroic as He-Man's Caucasian allies. The costumes and design of Targa are more African tribal inspired, just as He-Man's is influenced by an understanding of Nordic barbarian looks. With what we see of the culture and characters, it's a shame they never appear again.

At the story's close, Garn is crowned the new king of Targa by Rhea's father. He thanks He-Man for showing him that "with great strength goes great responsibility." Like the episode's title, this turn of phrase was likely recognizable to audiences.

"Doubled Edged Sword": Season One, 1984

One of Lou Scheimer and the Filmation crew's favorite episodes was the first season's "Double Edged Sword." The episode's story allowed the company to nudge the fourth wall and address the concerns of parents and organizations like Action for Children's Television.

The kingdom of Eternos is facing an energy crisis. Teela, Adam, and Man-At-Arms travel to the Sands of Time desert in order to retrieve a new piece of Eternium, a very rare and powerful mineral that can fuel their generators. A piece has recently been unearthed by Chad, a young boy who dreams of joining the Royal Guard, his hover-wheelchair bound grandfather, and the boy's pet bee/elephant/silkworm creature called Burbie. Mer-Man and Trap Jaw also hear about the discovery, and rush to steal the Eternium to impress Skeletor.

In a skirmish with the villains, Chad is amazed by the skill with which his pacifist grandfather handles a shield and laser pistol. Angered, Mer-Man commands a giant sea monster from a small desert lake to attack them. Teela and He-Man intervene, and Chad is even more thrilled to see his heroes in violent, glorious battle.

Trap Jaw proceeds to take a bite of the mineral, giving him incredible power that makes him a match even for He-Man. The power is temporary, though, and in an effort to keep the villain from taking another bite, Chad's pet Burbie steals it away in its mouth. It accidentally ingests some, and then falls to the ground. Eternium is incredibly poisonous to someone who isn't a magical creature like Trap Jaw, it turns out. Beginning to cry, Chad tells He-Man his pet is dying. He-Man agrees to take them to Castle Grayskull to see if the Sorceress's powers can cure it.

This was not the first time Filmation had based a story around the death of a pet. In 1973, the company produced an episode of *Star Trek: The Animated Series* called "Yesteryear," in which the character Mr. Spock goes back to time to protect his younger self during a difficult experience in a desert. His childhood pet I Chaya, a large bear-like creature, is wounded and the young Spock makes the difficult decision to let the animal die instead of being treated with medicine to live on, in pain for the rest of its life. Dealing with serious issues in a mature fashion earned the episode, and Filmation, an Emmy nomination.

Though the stories are similar, the punch is pulled in "Double Edged Sword." The magic of Grayskull is able to cure Burbie, so Chad learns a valuable lesson without needing to sacrifice anything.

Instead of an on-screen death, the episode is best known for the story

Chad's grandfather tells while they wait outside of Castle Grayskull. While the boy weeps, he says he never thought his pet could be hurt. War, he thought, was all fun and games. His grandfather says, "I know how you feel, Chad. I used to be a soldier." He tells the story of his experiences in wartime, how he used to be thrilled by combat and eagerly fired at a group of enemy orcs he'd spotted on the top of a cliff. His lasers knocked loose a rock fall. As the mountain fell onto him, he was crushed and became paralyzed. Many of his fellow soldiers, he said, did not survive.

The boy is so moved by his grandfather's story that, even though his pet survives the experience, he's changed his mind about the glory of war. Enough Eternium survived to power the palace, and Chad now doesn't want to grow up to become a soldier.

"The Arena": Season Two, 1984

This episode is notable for the amount of violence and warfare it contains. By far the most action-packed episode in the series, Filmation allowed itself to make such a violent episode as long as the story was all about how wrong violence is.

The story itself concerns Om, an immensely powerful alien being who has evolved beyond a physical form. As a glowing ball of light in space, Om comes across a space probe launched by Man-At-Arms and arranges a visit to Eternia to learn of their ways. This meeting happens during another elaborate attack by Skeletor. This time, the skull-faced villain has hired a mercenary army of goblins to counter Eternia's royal guards.

Skeletor attacks as Man-At-Arms, King Randor, and Orko are explaining the ways of their world to the alien visitor. He-Man and the heroes counter immediately, as Teela leads their soldiers on Sky Sleds, and Ram Man and Stratos appear to help out as well. Although the sequence makes liberal use of stock footage, it's much more prolonged and intense than the usual fare.

Ever curious, Om has merely been observing the pitched battle quietly before it intervenes. Every participant is suddenly frozen in place as the alien visitor declares the warfare "wasteful." Instead of allowing the mass violence to continue, Om says he will pick the mightiest warriors from each side, and let their one-on-one combat decide the victorious side.

At this point in the episode, the story may be sounding familiar to genre fans. "The Arena" is very informed by the Frederic Brown story

"Arena," though it is not listed as an adaptation. "Arena" is considered one of the greatest early sci-fi stories and has been adapted many times. Most will remember it from the first season episode of *Star Trek* also called "Arena," when Captain Kirk is forced into single combat with the hulking reptilian Gorn.

The champions Om selects are He-Man and Skeletor. He-Man, being the valiant hero, offers peace to his nemesis, but Skeletor will have none of it. The two battle it out, the Power Sword countering every spell the villain summons. Such a duel is exciting for viewers, as the two so rarely came into direct conflict with each other. Instead of sending minions like Beast Man after the hero, or simply running away when a plan failed, now Skeletor could finally make good on his boasts of defeating He-Man.

The two are evenly matched for a while, but Skeletor grows more and more frustrated. He magically grows an insect to an enormous size, but it does not obey him and attack He-Man. He blasts it with magic bolts to force its obedience.

"Skeletor, stop!" He-Man calls out. "You're enraging him!" But the villain carries on until his magical powers fizzle out. As Skeletor runs away from the creature, He-Man picks it up and tosses it away. His mortal enemy is saved.

With that, Om signals the end of the combat. When it asks, He-Man explains he did not allow his enemy to be destroyed because he values all life. Om agrees to teleport Skeletor and his goblin army back where they came from. The strange visitor then departs Eternia, certain the planet is not doomed as long as there are some who value compassion over cruelty and greed.

"Jacob and the Widgets": Season Two 1984

Though one of the lesser *He-Man* episodes, this second season episode is a perfect representation of the wish fulfillment the title character offers.

It begins with Teela taking a Wind Raider high above Eternia, testing a new rocket booster Man-At-Arms has developed. It is powered by Corodite, a mineral mined by the tiny, child-like Widgets. After the booster performs better than expected, Adam and Teela take the Widgets to the beach.

In the ocean, Mer-Man is testing out some new robot sea monsters by attacking a small fishing boat. Seeing this from the shore, Adam transforms into He-Man and swims out to the rescue. The two mechanical monsters are easily destroyed. The boat's sole occupant was Jacob, a curmudgeonly hermit who doesn't seem too grateful for He-Man saving his life. He has no friends or family, he explains, and he lived on his fishing boat, which was destroyed. The Widgets, astonished to hear Jacob could live alone, insist on taking him back to their fort and caring for him as he recovers from his near-death experience.

Meanwhile, a frustrated Mer-Man realized he will need Corodite to build stronger robot sea monsters. Abducting a Widget, he learns they keep their mineral hidden in their fort's mines. The villain begins to hatch a plan.

In the Widget fort, Jacob is making for a terrible houseguest. Unaccustomed to being cared for, he grumbles as they feed him. "It's taken years of practice to become a successful hermit," he says, "and now you Widgets are ruining everything!"

As Teela stops by the fort for a visit, Mer-Man bombs a cave wall separating the mine and ocean, and it begins to flood. Teela tries to stop him, and she's joined by Jacob, who has learned the value of friendship. The villain proves to be too much for either of them, especially underwater, and the Widgets fire a signal flare to call for He-Man's help.

When he arrives, He-Man gives Mer-Man the boot, but the water is still rising in the mine and threatening to flood the entire fort. "The tide is rising," He-Man muses, "but the moon controls the tide." Looking into the sky, he says, "I guess I'll have to control the moon."

And that's exactly what he does. Taking his nigh-invincibility and super-strength to the next level, he flies the super-charged Wind Raider into space and pushes the moon away. As the tide lowers and the water retreats, he flies back to Eternia to fire lasers and start a rockslide to block the hole in the cave wall. Then, back to space to put the moon back where it belongs. The day is saved, and Mer-Man is kicked so far across the ocean, he doesn't return to the show for the better half of season two.

He-Man's role as the Most Powerful Man in the Universe has never been portrayed more literally. Such an astounding act is exactly the sort of thing that endeared the character, and the entire *He-Man* show, to a generation of imaginative children.

"The Problem with Power": Season Two, 1984

No list of notable episodes or "Best of" collections are complete without "The Problem with Power." It is one of the series' highlights, and it was a story clearly taken seriously by all involved.

The episode opens in Snake Mountain, as Skeletor summons General Tataran, the goblin leader he'd partnered with previously in "The Arena." Skeletor has a new plan to defeat He-Man, and he says the key to it is the heartless nature of the General. Goblins have no heart, speaking metaphorically as well biologically, and so they have no heartbeat.

Later, Man-At-Arms is telling the Eternos royal family about the villain's latest scheme: he has enslaved the population of the village of Zak on the Crystal Sea, forcing them to build a massive structure for him. King Randor sends Man-At-Arms, Prince Adam, and Orko to investigate.

When the three arrive, Adam recognizes the structure as a Dimensional Gate. He transforms into He-Man to stop the construction. Meanwhile, Skeletor is shown ensuring the tower is made improperly, booby-trapping it to fall at the slightest touch. General Tataran is given a force field belt, similar to one seen in Filmation's *Star Trek: The Animated Series*, and then Skeletor casts a spell to make him appear human.

He-Man and his friends approach and demand the villagers be set free. Skeletor taunts the heroes, and then begins firing magic bolts at them. He-Man chases Skeletor around the leaning tower, and he is finally frustrated enough to try punching his way through it. Man-At-Arms spots an innocent bystander and tries to warn the hero, but it's too late. The tower collapses right onto the man. Nobody watching is aware the "innocent man" is secretly the General in his impenetrable force field belt.

The concept of collateral damage in such a colorful, good-versus-evil universe is appropriately jarring to the audience. He-Man frantically digs the body out, hears no heartbeat, and is devastated. The surprising emotional depth of this episode is sold by John Erwin's voice acting. Skeletor casts a spell on himself to appear human as well, and tells He-Man that he killed his brother. He incites the townspeople against the hero as he walks off, dejected.

Orko follows after him, trying to explain that it was just an accident, but He-Man will near nothing of it. Floating back to Man-At-Arms, Orko sees the General and Skeletor turning back into their normal forms, but he is captured before he can tell anyone.

Atop Castle Grayskull, He-Man raises the Power Sword and says, "Let the power return." He is transformed back into Prince Adam, and he drops the sword into the bottomless pit surrounding the castle.

In the meantime, Skeletor has begun rebuilding his Dimensional Gate. When she's told He-Man can't come to their aid this time, Teela volunteers for a very dangerous mission to blow up the gateway before the goblin army can come through. After she leaves, Orko escapes from the magic-proof cell beneath Snake Mountain and tells Adam what happened. The prince tries to fly a Sky Sled down after the sword, but the winds in the bottomless pit are too much. He falls into the web of a massive spider, where he finds the Power Sword.

Teela allows herself to be taken captive by the goblins to get close enough to destroy the structure with her bomb. In front of his gate, Skeletor overwhelms her with a magic bolt just as He-Man arrives. Teela's bomb, primed for explosion, falls to the ground along with her. After the hero lands to check on his fallen friend, Skeletor steals the Sky Sled and escapes. He-Man picks up Teela and runs away at superhuman speed as the bomb detonates. The Dimensional Gate collapses once more. Without it, the goblins who had come through already begin to fade away, returning to their own dimension.

The episode ends with He-Man carrying Teela as they walk slowly into the sunset, trading flirtatious quips about how Teela is perfectly capable of walking. It hits a romantic note, giving the audience the most definitive look at the relationship between the two characters. It is such a conclusive ending that though "The Problem with Power" aired midway through the second season, it is considered a series finale by many fans.

As the episodes of *He-Man and the Masters of the Universe* remained strong in syndication, the toy sales continued their stratospheric climb. By 1984, the release of the third wave of MOTU figures had brought in an estimated $111 million. The next wave of figures was set to have more toys and vehicles, and more flats of product were being sent out to stores to keep up with the outrageous demand. It would go on to bring in $250 million.

He-Man was a constant fixture in households, between TV and home video, toys, video games, magazines, and all manner of other merchandise. Every place Mattel brought their golden property, it managed to exceed beyond expectations. The characters had even been moved into the live-action domain with traveling stage shows.

There was only one place left to go: the larger world of big-budget blockbuster action films.

3

Golan-Globus:
Going Global

In the mid–1980s, a hot toy property did not automatically mean an easy sell for Hollywood producers. Properties based on action figures had just barely been allowed onto television by that point. And although there were no FCC regulations keeping them off of the big screen, there was still a stigma about things. Who knew if a toy-inspired movie would bring out the audiences who saw the cartoon at home, for free? Would adult audiences come to the theaters, as well? And who could say if such a movie would be any good in the first place?

Mattel would not be deterred. The company sided with producer Ed Pressman who, strangely enough, had just produced the live-action *Conan the Barbarian* film in 1982. As they'd done with Filmation, they would be putting up half of the expense for the film, and letting the film studio invest the rest. Pressman commissioned a script from David Odell, whose genre credits included Jim Henson's cult classic *The Dark Crystal* and 1984's adaptation of DC Comics' *Supergirl*. Mattel's executives had faith in the project, but were aware of how expensive a film could be when it was set on a planet as outlandish as Eternia. Odell was told to write with a smaller budget in mind, and Pressman began shopping the property around.

The company was interested in a finished film that grew their brand and stayed true to the characters. They would have an important veto power over the script and certain elements of design. Perhaps due to their highly successful partnership with Filmation over the cartoon series, executives were open to fresh takes and willing to hand over a great deal of creative control. They did, however, retain two pivotal rights: Mattel would choose the film's director, and they would choose who would become the human face of He-Man.

The man who would be He-Man was born Hans Dolph Lundgren in Stockholm, Sweden, 1957. A thin and sickly child, he was called "Little Hans," and suffered from severe allergies and asthma. At a young age, he came down with a viral respiratory tract disease that would restrict his breath until his face turned blue.

"One of my earliest blurry childhood memories is from a hospital in Stockholm," Lundgren recalled. "I remember the dim lights and the smells. Ether vapors, disinfectants, or whatever it may have been. I lay alone in my hospital room staring up at the ceiling."[1] He was four at the time, and it would be a long while until he was healthier. Growing up as the weakest boy in school was a surefire way to attract bullies.

His home life wasn't much better. Lundgren's father was a large, manic depressive man, prone to sudden bursts of anger and violence. The young Hans, like his mother, bore the brunt of his father's cruelty. Looking back on that difficult time, Lundgren said, "It may sound strange, but you can get used to physical abuse. You find strategies to survive and even retaliate. I fought back by trying not to scream, cry, or show any pain when he hit me. I wasn't always successful."[2]

Haunted by his upbringing, he grew up desperate to prove himself and driven to not be bullied again. By the age of seven, he'd begun studying judo and other martial arts.

This is not to say he neglected his schoolwork. After graduating high school with top marks, he studied abroad in the United States under scholarships, attending Washington State University and Clemson University in South Carolina. He completed his degree in chemical engineering back at Sweden's Royal Institute of Technology, and then got his Masters from Australia's University of Sydney. Even in the tough field of chemical engineering, Lundgren graduated at the top of his class.

He had grown tall over the years, and gained muscle mass from his training in the martial arts. Lundgren focused on a full-contact karate called Kyokushin, a style made famous by Japanese masters like Sonny Chiba. By 1979, he had earned a black belt and was the captain of the Swedish Kyokushin team for the Kyokushin Karate Organization's World Open Tournament. Still practicing into the early 1980s, he won two European Karate championships, and another in Australia.

While finishing his master's degree in Sydney, Lundgren utilized his intimidating stature as a club bouncer. That's where he met the statuesque singer and model, Grace Jones. Initially hiring on the imposing young chemical engineer as a bodyguard, the two quickly began dating.

Graduating at the top of his class earned Lundgren the incredibly prestigious Fullbright Scholarship to the Massachusetts Institute of Technology. All packed to move to Boston, he changed his plans when he and Jones became an item. Instead, he decided to move to New York with her.

Lundgren returned to bouncing, now at Manhattan's Limelight club, and spent his free time with the likes of Andy Warhol and others in the New York art scene. He tried his hand at modeling, but found himself too tall and muscular for many. Jones had turned to acting by this point, finding her breakthrough role in 1984's Schwarzenegger sequel, *Conan the Destroyer*. She became a Bond girl the next year in Roger Moore's *A View to a Kill*. As Lundgren had been taking some acting classes since they'd relocated, Jones arranged a small role for her boyfriend. He can be seen briefly in the film as an evil henchman. Still, it was a big budget film, and his character was credited with a name instead of simply "KGB Agent #2"; it was an impressive role for someone with no formal training.

He found himself bitten by the acting bug, and it didn't take him long to find his next gig. The film with his career-defining role was released just a few months later, at the tail end of 1985: *Rocky IV*. To an entire generation of filmgoers, he would always be known as Ivan Drago, the seemingly indestructible Russian boxer.

The character of Drago required minimal acting from Lundgren. He was not a brash or boastful opponent for Sylvester Stallone's Rocky Balboa, the way Carl Weathers' character Apollo Creed had been. In fact, the majority of speaking was done for him by various Soviet trainers or his wife, played by Brigitte Nielson. What the role did call for was an imposing physicality, something Lundgren brought in spades.

As for the character's fighting skills and strength, called "freakish" by a reporter in the film, Lundgren's casting may have been a little too perfect. In an incident that was reported during filming a boxing scene, Lundgren picked up Carl Weathers and threw him some three feet into the ring's corner. Weathers climbed out of the ring and threatened to quit.[3]

While filming another of the film's matches between Rocky and Drago, Stallone, who was also directing, suggested he and Lundgren should actually hit each other, instead of pulling punches for the camera, in order to get into the minds of their characters. "After the third take of taking body blows, I felt a burning in my chest, but ignored it," Stallone later recalled. Later that night, he was struggling to breathe and needed to be rushed to the emergency room. He stayed in intensive care for eight days. Stallone explained: "What had happened is he struck me so hard in the chest that my heart slammed against my breastbone and began to swell, so the beating became labored, and without medical attention the heart would've continued to swell until it stopped. Many people that have car accidents die like this when the steering wheel slams into their chest."[4] The car that caused this accident, however, was Dolph Lundgren's fist.

Rocky IV was patently ridiculous, with a story that introduced a robot sidekick and a script full of patriotic platitudes, including a speech from Rocky at the conclusion which is implied to have settled the Cold War. Still, the film was a runaway success. It was the most successful sports film for the next two decades, spawning more sequels for Stallone and making Dolph Lundgren a star.

And he was exactly what Mattel was looking for. Lundgren was a name-brand action hero who was new enough in the business to not scoff at playing an action figure. He was tall and blond and possessed the kind of musculature of their toys brought to life. As far as the toy company was concerned, they'd found their He-Man.

For their director, Mattel put their trust in Ed Pressman. The producer's brother ran Pressman Toys, a gaming company, who had once employed a young man named Gary Goddard.

Goddard was a California boy who found a calling in entertainment. This started early, as he was a musician in high school. He worked in the gaming industry, helping to design the board game Candy Land and even serving as the visual basis for King Kandy. Then, after a stint as an Imagineer for Disney, he formed Gary Goddard Productions in 1980. The company specialized in attractions for high-end hotels and theme parks. It would become Landmark Entertainment a few years later. The company led to work across various fields of entertainment, many of which were based on or tied into popular films or licensed characters. One of these jobs was creating a live show called "Conan: A Sword and Sorcery Spectacular" for Universal Studios.

The Conan show allowed Goddard to experiment more with directing, something he'd always been interested in. The show was considered groundbreaking, full of dramatic lighting and practical effects, and it turned a lot of heads.

He said, "I knew that Ed Pressman was looking for a director so I called him up and told him that I'd directed the Conan show."[5] Pressman and David Odell, who had finished his script, went to see a performance. Immediately thereafter, they called Goddard back and arranged a meeting.

This was not his first brush with Hollywood. Goddard had previously been commissioned to write a screenplay treatment based on the Marvel Comics heroine Dazzler, whom producers expected to be played by Bo

Derek of *10* fame. While his treatment was well-received, the film went nowhere. Producers kept Goddard on hand to co-write the project Derek did do: another Edgar Rice Burroughs adaptation called *Tarzan, the Ape Man.* The 1981 film, retelling the familiar Tarzan story from the perspective of Jane Parker, did not go over well. Though it made a decent return at the box office, it was widely panned and nominated for six Golden Raspberry awards that year. Derek "won" for Worst Actress, but the script by Goddard and Tim Rowe fortunately went home empty-handed.

The aspiring film director was well known to Mattel by this point, as well. After Gary Goddard Productions contributed to an aborted project called "The Peanut Butter Papers" for the toy company, they were kept in contact with to act as consultants. By the time Pressman brought up Goddard's name for a potential director, higher ups at Mattel, like Executive Vice President of Marketing Joe Morrison, recognized his name.

Ed Pressman was a supporter of first-time directors, so a lack of cinematic experience did not disqualify the young Goddard. Morrison and the other Mattel executives quickly signed off on him as well. With both a star and a director in place, not to mention their financing and a household name in He-Man, Mattel had everything they needed for a hit movie ... except for a film studio to make it.

Along with Pressman, the producer, Mattel executives like Morrison and John Weems, the Senior Vice President of Entertainment, began making the rounds. "Universal Studios was interested," Morrison said, "and then Cannon came to us and made an offer on the deal that we thought was the right thing to do at the right time."[6]

Cannon Films was famous, if not infamous, by that point. The film company was on a calculated and not terribly covert mission to become a big, respected studio in Hollywood. Their main tactic was a blitzkrieg of content; with 25 releases in 1985 alone, they produced a shockingly high number of films for a non-major studio. Many, if not most, were not well received critically or commercially. Regardless of quality or overall profitability, their movies were shown and their name was everywhere.

Signing with Cannon did not guarantee a masterpiece by any means, but they were a brand name that guaranteed a film could be completed quickly and on the cheap. Any heavy lifting in terms of marketing or appeal, Mattel figured, could be left to He-Man.

As for the studio, a live-action *Masters of the Universe* film would stick close to their genre and exploitation film roots while utilizing a larger budget than they were accustomed. The film, with its PG rating, would likely reach out to a broader audience than their standard ninja and vigilante films could. More than anything, they saw it, along with other films like *Superman IV: The Quest for Peace* (1987) and their Stallone vehicle *Over the Top* (1987), as their way to finally break into the world of Hollywood blockbusters and gain respect in the industry. They'd been seen as the quirky underdog studio for several years at that point, and they were ready to break into the big leagues.

Cannon Films was founded in 1967 by Dennis Friedland and Christopher C. Dewey, two film buffs in their 20s who kept the company afloat by releasing English-dubbed softcore pornographic films from Sweden. Scrappy and ambitious, the company turned their attention to exploitation films of other sorts. They released *Fando and Lis* in 1970, a cinematic footnote for being the first full-length film by eccentric auteur Alejandro Jodorowsky. It had to be extensively censored before release in the United States, and it was not greeted favorably.

The young studio's first, and possibly greatest, success came later that year in the form of *Joe*. The gritty and hyper-violent revenge drama starred Peter Boyle and captured the spirit of a troubled moment in American culture. Showcasing the frustrated divide between generations in the midst of the Vietnam War, the film pitted the titular blue collar conservative everyman against the perceived draft-dodging, drug-addled youth. It seemed to express the frustrations of much of the country, and gave enough violent wish fulfillment to make conservative filmgoers reportedly stand up and cheer in the theaters.

Cannon's film excelled at the box office. Off of its budget of just over $100,000, it took in nearly $20 million, making it one of the highest grossing movies of the year. It was received just as warmly by critics. Time magazine declared it "a film of Freudian anguish, biblical savagery and immense social and cinematic importance."[7] It even received an Oscar nomination for Best Original Screenplay.

Cannon was, unfortunately, unable to capitalize on such a shocking success. *Joe* was the company's first film which could not objectively be described at pornographic, and everything else they had in the works was not exactly in the mainstream's sensibilities. As the '70s wore on, Friedland and Dewey churned out domestic releases of risqué or exploitative foreign films, and the occasional softcore of their own design, such as *The Happy Hooker* (1975) and its sequel, *The Happy Hooker Goes to Washington* (1977). Business was not going well.

Their dealings with foreign filmmakers had brought them in contact with Israeli director Menahem Golan and his cousin/producing partner, Yoram Globus, on more than one occasion. The two had been making movies together since the mid–'60s, reaching the peak of Israel's film industry. Branching out to get their films distributed outside of their home country introduced them to Friedland and Dewey, who released their film *Lupo!* in the States in 1971.

Their second collaboration came in 1978 with the release of *Operation Thunderbolt*, based on the Israeli Defense Forces' real-life hostage rescue at Uganda's Entebbe Airport two years earlier. Golan directed, shooting an alternate version of every scene in English only for an American release through Cannon. This proved to be a wise decision. The film was a hit in their home country, and it also nabbed a nomination for the Academy Award's Best Foreign Language Film.

Shortly thereafter, Golan and Globus moved to the states and made an offer. At $.20 per share, the two would need to raise $500,000 to buy the company. That was $500,00 they didn't have. What they did have was the international contacts to sell films around the world. Author Andrew Yule chronicled this one-of-a-kind offer in his scathing exposé, *Hollywood a Go-Go*: "The cousins were convinced that the films in Cannon's vaults had been undersold in the international market, so they went to Friedland and Dewey with a typically outrageous proposal. Cannon should give them the rights to their catalogue in the foreign and ancillary markets for a 25% commission, this to cover the cost of buying Cannon."[8]

And so, through some curious accounting, Cannon Films was reborn.

Under new management, the company continued releasing exploitation titles. In 1980, Golan and Globus oversaw a larger production slate. There was a third *Happy Hooker* installment, the slasher films called *Schizoid* and *New Years Evil*, and other largely forgettable cash-in flicks. The expanded audience and resources allowed Golan and Globus to indulge in some dream projects. The first of such films was 1980's *The Apple*. Directed by Golan, it was low in budget yet epic in scope, a sci-fi disco opera full of biblical allegory and music industry satire, with not a hint of subtlety visible to audiences. While it was released to capitalize on musicals like *Grease* (1978) and *Xanadu* (1980), it was also fulfilling the filmmaker's dream to make a creation myth story. However, *The Apple* was laughed out of theaters. Famously, the studio handed out copies of the soundtrack at the film's premiere, most of which were thrown at the screen.[9]

The year 1981, however, saw the release of *Enter the Ninja*, starring a severely miscast Franco Nero as a heroic martial artist. A reasonably successful film, *Enter the Ninja* is better known for its impact on the cinematic culture of the early '80s: it introduced America to the ninja.

It was followed by dozens of riffs, knockoffs, and official Cannon Films sequels.

By this point, Golan and Globus were gaining a reputation not only as scrappy B-movie underdogs, but also as hyperbolizing self-promoters. The two were so often so eager to prove themselves as serious American filmmakers, they would advertise for movies that did not, and never would, exist. This method led to an extra dose of advertisement: by announcing a film set to star both Sean Connery and Roger Moore, for example, the company would get more press when the stars and their agents has to say there would be no movie teaming up the two James Bond actors. Cannon Films still ended up in the papers.

In late 1980, the company took out massive advertising space to promote their upcoming films. One title listed was *Death Wish II*, a sequel to the popular Charles Bronson revenge drama from the mid–'70s. There was no script for such a film. In fact, Cannon did not own the rights. When Dino De Laurentiis, the Italian producer who did own the rights to *Death Wish*, learned of this, he made a call to the Israeli upstarts.

As explained by Brian Garfield, author of the novel *Death Wish* was based on, "His lawyers explained to the people at Cannon that they could face a serious lawsuit for fraud (because they did not own any rights to *Death Wish*) or they could buy the rights from De Laurentiis, Landers-Roberts and me, for a price to be determined by us. Cannon, against the wall, gave in. Dino forced them to make the movie."[10]

The price tags for the film rights and the star, Charles Bronson, were less expensive than a lawsuit, but it made *Death Wish II* (1982) the most expensive Cannon film yet. When it turned a modest profit and put the company on Hollywood's radar, however, Golan and Globus discovered their unique business strategy: pre-sales and loads of hype.

Cannon Films were run by salesmen, and aggressive ones at that. Golan would sell a movie's rights to theater chains and video distributors around the world before that film was finished. Sometimes, before it was even started. By guaranteeing a certain amount of income up front, the company would attempt to off-set the costs of productions, marketing, and distribution. As the company amassed their stable of regular actors, such as Charles Bronson, and regular directors, such as Golan himself, they could put together a prospective poster full to sell foreign markets. Sometimes promising a bankable name would allow the company to sell a region. In other instances where the language barrier was too wide, Golan was able to sell a market based on the poster image alone.

This led to situations like 1983's *10 to Midnight*. On one visit to the

Cannes Film Festival to woo foreign distributors, a Cannon producer pitched an interesting sounding title to Golan: "10 to Midnight." With no film in production, or even preproduction, under such a title, the chairman still told everyone about the movie. Describing it as full of "great action and great danger and great revenge,"[11] he managed to pre-sell some international markets for the non-existent film. Then, Cannon simply had to acquire a script, in this case a cop-versus-serial-killer thriller titled "Bloody Sunday," and change the name. In other similar situations, the company would commission writers to fashion a full script based off a title, and maybe one actor, alone. In most cases, that would be enough.

Along with the foreign territories, Golan and Globus also targeted the burgeoning VHS market and new pay movie channels like HBO. In interviews, the moguls bragged about their no-frills approach to business; they did not spend money on expensive lunches or vacations, they claimed; they just worked. They also indulged in other cost-saving tricks that bordered on unethical and verged on illegal. For example, the longer they held onto their funds, even after it'd been spent, the more interest it could accrue. Most payments were made as late as possible. This led to a bad reputation in Hollywood among actors, writers, and crew members. Unions had to be called to threaten lawsuits on their behalves on more than one occasion.

As for the money these employees were meant to be paid, that was another story altogether. The cousins were dogged by rumors of mafia connections for years. There was seemingly no other way they could continue to produce so many films when few, if any, made a profit.

Their actual finances were less of a money laundering operation and more of a one-level pyramid scheme. Cannon's bookkeepers would claim over exaggerated expected profits for the first two years after any film's release. They would not need to claim any expenses for films in production, so they produced more and more to hide the failures when the real box office takes were announced. As long as they continued to produce more and more films, their very real losses were off-set by the hypothetical wins on paper. Any profits were quickly sent to accounts in tax haven countries to save every penny they could.[12]

The company's strategy was built around the hope of one *Star Wars*-level hit blockbuster. If something they made was successful enough, it could pay off all the building debt and hidden losses. And the more movies they made, the better their chances of making that one-of-a-kind hit. With each consecutive loss, they could do nothing else but make more movies.

After the modest and impactful hit of *Enter the Ninja*, Golan and

Globus were able to influence culture again on more than one occasion. The next came in 1984 with the dance film *Breakin'*.

Inspired by a German documentary about the urban fad of break-dancing, *Breakin'* struck a chord with young audiences. Its portrayal of rapping and the burgeoning hip hop culture was novel enough to garner attention, not to mention the astounding dance moves by real-life break-dancers/first-time actors Adolfo "Shabba Do" Quiñones and Michael "Boogaloo Shrimp" Chambers. The film debuted the same weekend as *Sixteen Candles*, and it managed to beat John Hughes' modern classic to the number one spot. Off of the Cannon-standard budget of barely over $1 million, its total box office gross was more than $38 million.

Thanks to the success of *Breakin'*, more Americans was exposed to rap music and hip hop dancing. Scant months later, Cannon cashed in with *Breakin' 2: Electric Boogaloo*. It was not as successful as its predecessor, but its title has gone down in pop culture history.

Around this time, the company began working with action star Chuck Norris. Norris had already starred in several action movies, like *A Force of One* and *Lone Wolf McQuade*, before teaming with Golan and Globus. With very few exceptions, he would only work with Cannon Films for the next decade.

Norris's first Cannon film was 1984's *Missing in Action*, a military fantasy piece about a former POW returning to Vietnam ten years after the war to free the prisoners who remained. It is notable for cashing in on the success of *Rambo: First Blood Part II* before that film even came out. While *Rambo* was still filming, Cannon was able to read its original treatment written by James Cameron. Thus "inspired," the filmmakers cranked theirs out fast enough to beat the Stallone film.[13] Widely panned by critics, *Missing in Action* still made great money at the box office. It was deemed successful enough to release its already-filmed prequel the next year, and shoot a third installment in 1988.

Of the nine Cannon films Norris made between 1984 and 1994, perhaps the most noteworthy would be 1986's *The Delta Force*. It was another from the "prisoner rescue military fantasy" genre made famous by *Rambo: First Blood Part II* and *Missing in Action*, not to mention others like *Uncommon Valor*, but this one did not revolve around a decade-old war.

The Delta Force was based on the hijacking of TWA Flight 847, which had occurred just months prior. However, instead of the two weeks of tense negotiations and complex international diplomacy, the Golan-directed film spun the real-world events into an over-the-top action spectacle. On the big screen, Chuck Norris's team of commandos eschewed reality to save the day with motorcycles capable of firing missiles. With every terrorist's death came a pithy one-liner. This was a different kind of exploitation film, and audiences ate it up.

With a substantially larger budget than previous Cannon fare, *The Delta Force* managed to turn a small profit for the studio. It did not, however, receive many positive reviews. Though Roger Ebert said it "tantalizes us with its parallels to real life,"[14] others found capitalizing on a very real, very recent tragedy tasteless. This was not a retelling of factual events, like *Operation Thunderbolt* had been. It was pure Hollywood revisionism. Variety's review called the film out for "rewriting" fresh history, "thereby turning itself into an exercise in wish fulfillment for those who favor force instead of diplomacy."[15]

But it wasn't all crowd-pleasers and cheap, trashy exploitation films. Golan and Globus were also looking for the respect and acceptance of the larger studios, and this led them to produce a surprising number of "art house" films as the 1980s progressed. The cousins worked with respected filmmakers like John Cassavetes in 1984 for the critically acclaimed *Love Streams*, and Norman Mailer for the much less loved *Tough Guys Don't Dance*. The company's release of Jean-Luc Godard's *King Lear*, the contract for which was a napkin the infamous director signed, similarly flopped. On the other hand, Cannon's production of the opera *Otello* won the Golden Globe for Best Foreign Language Film. They also produced two films for the Russian-American director Andrei Konchalovsky, including the multiple Oscar nominee *Runaway Train* and one of the hits of the 1987 Cannes Film Festival, *Shy People*.

Cannes became an obsession of Golan and Globus. The two producers were regulars at the festival, always showing up to hyperbolize their upcoming projects and debut the classier of their films. Still, the producers were never able to win the festival's coveted Palme d'Or award. The industry respect and mainstream credibility Cannon wanted were also not materializing. Try as they might, they were still being viewed as a B-movie studio.

In the interest of diversifying the company, along with ensuring their films were always shown, Golan and Globus began buying up theater chains. They began with foreign chains like Italy's Cannon Cinema Italia and Cannon Tuschinski Theatres, the biggest theater chain in the Netherlands. Next came Screen Entertainment of Britain, making Cannon "the largest motion picture exhibitor in the United Kingdom with 485 screens."[16] Along with the smaller theater chains they'd bought before, they controlled about 39 percent of the UK film market.

In the United States, the cousins bought Commonwealth Theatres, the sixth-largest chain of cinemas in the country. Whatever films their studio made, they were able to make sure they would not be kept off of the big screen all around the globe. This helped to add to the illusion of their success, and also to fulfill contracts which guaranteed a theatrical release for their stars.

Even as their budgets began creeping higher and they courted respected directors, they had not managed a big summer blockbuster. Their surprise hits like *Breakin'* were more due to economics of scale: if they had been more expensive to produce, such a return at the box office would not have been so impressive. And even the grosses from films like *Breakin'* were not enough to compete with the major studios. There was also the matter of consistency: for every successful movie, there were several that failed to launch. It was enough to make the financial experts of Hollywood begin to ask questions about their bookkeeping methods.

Still, the cousins worked to be taken seriously by the traditional movie studios they were trying to compete with. Those studios would release some lower budget fare and distribute for independently produced films, like Cannon did, but they would also fill their coffers with the revenue from a big-budget "tentpole" picture or two. If Golan and Globus wanted to make the profits of a big studio, and to be viewed as one themselves, they'd need to invest a staggering amount of money into their products.

While the occasional film budget stretched to $8 or $15 million toward the middle of the decade, Cannon Film's first attempt at a big-budget was 1985's *Lifeforce*. The sci-fi spectacle piece, directed by Tobe Hooper, cost a reported $25 million.

The film itself, based on a pulpy '70s novel called *The Space Vampires*, concerned an alien race of vampires brought back to Earth by astronauts. The story slowly evolves from sci-fi to horror to a full-blown global disaster crisis, with occasional dashes of outright comedy, over the course of its two-hour running time. The strange roller coaster path of its tone, along with some impressive special effects, were enough to win over some critics. Unfortunately, the R-rated film opened against Ron Howard's feel-good *Cocoon* in an already dismal year for ticket sales. *Lifeforce* flopped hard.

With $25 million budgets, successes needed to be bigger and failures cut deeper; Cannon would be suffering from *Lifeforce* for years to come.

Taking another shot at their career-making blockbuster, Golan and Globus turned to Sylvester Stallone. Though the star was apparently uninterested in working with the studio, he came around when the producers offered to pay him a record-setting $12 million for his involvement. Their desperation showing, Cannon Films was now paying one actor more than the entire budgets had been for most of their best-grossing films.

Golan directed the resulting film, 1987's *Over the Top*. The melodramatic sports picture starred Stallone as a truck driver trying to gain custody of his alienated son while also winning the World Armwrestling Championship. Despite a soundtrack full of popular rock bands and a script co-written by Stallone and Academy Award winner Stirling Silliphant, it wasn't a hit inspirational sports movie like *Rocky* had been. It barely made back more than half of its budget.

By this point, newspapers had begun running stories about the company's disappointments and cash flow problems. With every Cannon Films disappointment came another round of speculation about just how long the company could stay solvent while trying to compete with the major studios.

How Cannon funded its pictures, most of which did not perform well, had become the subject of much discussion in Hollywood circles. Many experts in the industry began accusing Golan and Globus of being too optimistic in their reporting of revenue. Gordon Crawford, senior vice present of Capital Guardian Research, went on record saying, "They keep reporting higher earnings on pictures that nobody goes to see."[17]

Mid–1986, Cannon Films disclosed that the Securities and Exchange Commission were beginning an informal inquiry into their accounting and business practices.

"Bankruptcy" was the word being whispered about the company even as they signed their deal with Mattel to make *Masters of the Universe*. Golan and Globus had other big projects in the works at the time, including their deal with DC Comics and Warner Brothers to produce the fourth installment in the Christopher Reeve *Superman* franchise. There would be other smaller budget releases as well, more sequels for *Death Wish* and *Missing in Action*, the occasional arthouse fare like *Street Smart*, and a line of films based on familiar, public domain fairy tales already adapted by Disney, called *Cannon Movie Tales*.

A successful *Masters of the Universe* film would be exactly what Golan and Globus needed to keep their company moving forward. Between name brand recognition, content that skewed toward children, and a story that incorporated time-tested elements of the Monomyth, the film would have everything required to be a big, hit, franchise movie. All they needed to do was get it finished before their company collapsed.

4

Pre-Production's Quest

With the ink on the contracts still wet, Gary Goddard got down to work. The script provided by David Odell was seen as a good starting place, but not exactly the *Masters of the Universe* story the new director wanted to tell.

In an effort to keep production costs down and ensure relevant point-of-view characters for the audience, Odell's script took place almost entirely on Earth. Kevin and Julie, a sweet high school couple, were part of the story from day one. As Goddard remembers that early draft, the script opened "with a very beat-up, bedraggled He-Man pounding on the back door of Julie's house and her finding this guy who's a strange heroic warrior."[1]

What proceeded was a fish out of water story with He-Man, Teela, and Man-At-Arms stuck on earth. There were several ridiculous interactions with the locals, including brushes with a trigger-happy police officer and some angry bikers.[2] It had the makings of a fun, economical romp, but it was not in line with the epic fantasy tale Goddard had pitched to the producer, Ed Pressman.

Instead, Goddard wanted to make a live-action comic book, something with super-powerful heroes and tortured, maniacal villains, with a struggle reaching across worlds for the fate of the universe itself. To accomplish this sense of epic scale, he began pushing for the planet Eternia to play a bigger role. An alien planet offered up so much more storytelling potential, especially one as full of magic and futuristic technology as Eternia.

While setting the entire film on an alien world would be impossible for *Masters'* set budget of $17 million, Goddard said, "I felt we needed to see Eternia.... I said without something like this, how do we give a sense that Eternia is real, and how do we make this more than a bunch of costumed characters running around on Earth?"[3]

The producers were convinced and the script was revised. The story was now bookended by two sequences on Eternia to establish the grand, cosmic scope and be resolved in a battle unlike anything on earth. Cannon hired young screenwriter Stephen Tolkin to revise Goddard's new draft and smooth out the differences between it and the Odell version they'd signed off on. Despite the many changes by Tolkin and Goddard, neither were listed as writers in the final credits. The script would go through many more revisions throughout preproduction, and even afterwards, but Goddard was now convinced the film was on the right path.

The next step was finding the right crew available to bring this vision to life. "I tried to bring the best to the project," the director said. "It wasn't easy, as this was a Cannon film and budgets were tight."[4]

Richard Edlund, who had won Academy Awards for his work on the *Star Wars* films, had recently left Industrial Light and Magic to form his own effects company, Boss Film Corp. Goddard quickly scooped him and his crew up to handle the special effects for *Masters*. The young company signed on during an early draft of the script which called for a modest number of SFX shots. Their workload would be increased as production rolled on.

Another early addition to the crew was Ralph McQuarrie, a cinematic sci-fi designer made legendary by his contributions to the *Star Wars* franchise. In 1975, he had illustrated the first scenes from George Lucas's space opera to sell the project to Hollywood producers, making him responsible for the iconic designs of characters like Darth Vader, C-3PO, and Chewbacca. McQuarrie's time on *Masters of the Universe* was brief, but he did provide the designs for the sleek and faceless Air Centurion costume. His illustrations for characters like He-Man and Teela were deemed too faithful to the toys to be practical in live action, and most of his stunningly intricate sci-fi vehicles were outside of their budgetary possibilities. Still, McQuarrie left his mark on the production.

Goddard also sought the involvement of John De Cuir. De Cuir was Hollywood design royalty by the mid–'80s, after having won Academy Awards for classics like *The King and I* and *Cleopatra* and was still working on then-recent films like 1984's *Ghostbusters*. As a set designer, he was instrumental in the first stages of *Masters*.

Another Academy Award winner brought onboard was editor Anne Coates. She had won in 1963 for *Lawrence of Arabia*, and had since been nominated twice more, for *Becket* (1963) and *The Elephant Man* (1980). Coates would be instrumental in the latter phases of production to bring the film together as a whole.

Not all appointments worked out perfectly, though. The first director of photography would eventually be replaced early in filming, and the first production designer was also not working out. Geoffrey Kirkland, fresh off of successful films like *War Games* (1983) and *The Right Stuff* (1983), did not share Goddard's design sensibilities. While the director wanted a sci-fi, comic book vision, the dry, British Kirkland brought a more "intellectual" interpretation.

As Goddard remembers it: "I said, 'You know, I don't think you're really getting this.' And he said, 'Well I hate this f---ing stuff.'"[5]

Kirkland left the project and recommended his replacement be William Stout, the film's storyboard artist. Stout had gotten his start on *Tarzan of the Apes* newspaper comic strips and bootleg album covers. From there he progressed to Hollywood, where he filled a number of design jobs. He provided concept art for films like *Buck Rogers in the 25th Century* (1979), drew storyboards for *Raiders of the Lost Ark* (1981), and served as production designer for *The Return of the Living Dead* (1985).

Stout was also already a regular to Cannon Films, having just finished working on their remake of *Invaders from Mars* (1986). He had already pitched some designs for Eternian sets and costumes which had gone over well with Goddard.

Stout was also uniquely qualified for the job based on his friendship with Don Glut, the man Mattel had originally hired to flesh out the world

One of several design illustrations for the look of the cinematic Castle Grayskull completed by production designer William Stout. (Courtesy William Stout.)

of their Masters of the Universe toy line. He was familiar with the concepts and stories of each character, though he had never seen the TV series. As such, his take on these characters could be trusted to be authentic but not overly devout to the previous incarnation.

In Stout, Goddard found someone who envisioned Eternia the same way he did. "Gary and I shared the same vision," Stout said. "Because of our mutual interests (like Jack Kirby comics, for example) we communicated in a very fast shorthand that each of us understood. That made everything we did work much faster and easier."[6]

The works of Kirby, the famous comic book artist, influenced much of the production. While the studio didn't allow Goddard to hire him as a conceptual artist, and ultimately removed a "thank you" for him in the final credits, he and Stout often looked to his artistic style for inspiration. Jack "the King" Kirby is best known for his collaboration with writer Stan Lee to create Marvel Comics superheroes like the Avengers and the Uncanny X-Men. The filmmakers found their creative bearing in the characters and stories Kirby was famous for: Skeletor would be an obsessive, tragic despot in the style of Dr. Doom; He-Man would be the blond, noble, super-powerful type like Thor; and their battles would span all time and space, like those of the Fantastic Four.

After the film's release, more Kirby parallels were noted by comic book creator John Byrne. Much of *Masters*, he reported to *Comic Book News*, echoed Kirby's "Fourth World" stories for DC Comics. His characters in comics like *New Gods* traveled through "boom tubes," which are similar to the portals the film's Cosmic Key would open, The Sorceress was similar to Kirby's character The Highfather, Skeletor resembled the evil Darkseid, and so on. Goddard would reply to Byrne's assertion, and his letter confirming the film's homages was printed in the back matter of an issue of Byrne's *Next Men* series.[7]

As Goddard continued to revise the script, the designers were hard at work finding the correct vision for Eternia. To do so, William Stout recruited more talent from the world of comic books, namely Jean Giraud, the French artist known as Moebius. Renowned for his paintings and comics like *Blueberry*, Moebius had relocated to Southern California to provide design work for Hollywood movies like *Alien* and *Tron*. Stout, a former comic book artist, had met him at a party at cartoonist Sergio Aragonés' home years before and the two had remained close friends.

Moebius was hired and assigned to some of the more difficult-to-realize concepts. Many designs from the toys and cartoon, like animal themed vehicles and often skimpy costumes, could not be readily adapted into the new medium. There was a lot of work left to do.

However, Cannon Films kept the designers from getting too carried away. As costs began to be tallied, many of the sequences set on Eternia were forced to be cut. There was no room in the budget to fully realize Goddard's vision of Skeletor's lair on Snake Mountain, or the Eternian palace and capital city. The director had to scramble to find a way to bring this alien world to life while not being able to show much of it.

"I convinced them to build ONE BIG SET that would stand for Eternia, and OPEN there and CLOSE there," he said, "some 30 minutes or more would be shot on that set and give the film some sense of size and scope."[8] This workaround would be the throne room of Eternia. It was moved from the royal palace to Castle Grayskull itself to better condense the story.

Grayskull would still need to be shown from the outside, though. Its finalized design would be incorporated as matte painting, and shown only once, so no other sets or models would be required. A glimpse of Eternia could be permitted, but no cities could be shown or additional sets built. The script still contained a quick action scene as He-Man fights Skeletor's troopers outside of the castle. Despite location scouting for earthbound places that looks otherworldly, such as caverns in Iceland,[9] the budget won out again. Goddard was disappointed with the end result: the Vasquez Rocks, a spot just north of Los Angeles. The broad, jagged rock formations would be recognizable to most filmgoers after being featured in *Star Trek*, *The Twilight Zone*, and many, many other productions.

With one recognizable location, and most of the film taking place in actual suburban California, the design crew doubled down on the throne room set and Eternian characters. They could still make *Masters of the Universe* the unique live-action comic book they'd dreamed of.

Throughout preproduction, the Mattel executives supported Goddard and encouraged his crew's creativity. After the liberties taken by Filmation ended up benefiting the toy line, they had learned to welcome some originality. There were, however, several hard and fast rules. Chiefly: He-Man could not kill. He couldn't even treat anyone badly.

The director argued that the audience's expectations were different for live-action. He reminded the executives that he was hired to make an action movie, and encouraged them to view other recent successful '80s action movies, like *The Terminator*: "I said, 'You know this is a live-action movie, and he's the hero and he has to "kill" people and generally be a bit of a bad-ass.'"[10] Mattel, the makers of children's toys, was unconvinced.

A compromise was reached: Skeletor's troopers would be clad in armor from head to toe, giving them a robotic appearance, but whether they were alive or not would never be disclosed on camera. The extent of He-Man's violence would be left to the discretion of each individual viewer. This also meant our hero could smash, slash, and blast his way through as many of them as the filmmakers wanted him to. And, because they might be robots, there would be no blood.

Keeping things bloodless was a core concern of Mattel's. This is best expressed by a page from Goddard's draft of the script included in Dark Horse Books' 2015 hardcover *The Art of He-Man and the Masters of the Universe*. In the scene it depicts, Skeletor is sending his minions through a portal to Earth, where He-Man and his companions have fled to. "Kill the refugees from Eternia and bring me their heads," the super-villain is commanding. This line of dialogue is singled out, and in the margins, a Mattel representative has scribbled, "No killing! No heads!" and then suggested the alternative dialogue of "*Eliminate* He-Man and his allies...'"

Further down the page, the script calls for Skeletor to pluck a severed head from a pike beside him and feed it to a monster called an "Oggor." This section is circled and marked with a simple "NO!"[11]

Mattel stayed protective of their characters and their depictions, especially of their fates. In a scene succeeding the one described above, Skeletor was to punish his henchmen for failing on their mission to Earth. He would pick one cowering villain to be made an example of, and disintegrate him with an "energizing dissolve" effect. It would be a pivotal moment for Skeletor as a character, displaying just how ruthless, unforgiving, and terrifying a nemesis he really is. It would also boost the body count, killing off an actual character in an child-friendly, bloodless fashion.

Goddard had selected Beast Man for sacrifice, but again, Mattel stepped in. As he appeared regularly on the Filmation cartoon and was one of the original Masters of the Universe figures, the company declared him too important to the franchise to be killed off. Frustrated with so many "safe" characters, the filmmakers decided to create some of their own. Instead of dealing with the hassles of adapting everyone into the new medium from the realm of plastic, their new characters could be designed for the screen first. Mattel, who was looking to tie their next wave of He-Man figures to the film, agreed. One of the new characters, the reptilian mercenary Saurod, would be the henchman eradicated by Skeletor. And he even got an action figure made in his honor.

Other characters were added, replaced, or removed out of a different kind of necessity. Almost immediately, the film's budget and the available technology of the time made certain fan-favorite aspects of the Masters of the Universe mythos off-limits.

Battle Cat was the first to go. As Goddard likes to remind fans, "these were the pre-digital days of film making"[12] and realizing such a character through purely practical means was virtually impossible. The only options would be to bring in a real lion and attempt to dye its fur to match the toy, or use stop-motion technology. If the filmmakers could get Battle Cat to show up, the budget ensured it would be for a very brief cameo. The crew had little faith the stop-motion would look good, or the character's appearance would do anything besides stand out like a sore thumb. He was quickly dropped.

As *Masters'* sequences on Eternia were streamlined, many other regular characters were left out. With no palace seen, or even mentioned, King Randor and Queen Marlena disappeared. With no Battle Cat, there was no call for his secret identity from the Filmation cartoons, Cringer. There was also no more Prince Adam for He-Man to transform into.

Many fans have speculated that these changes meant *Masters of the Universe* intentionally ignored the *He-Man and the Masters of the Universe* series, and the filmmakers based it entirely on the toy line and early mini-comics, where there was no Prince Adam identity. Goddard and the crew, however, say this is a result of the film's action-packed plotline. With Eternia at war, there was no call for He-Man to transform back into Adam. The planet's royalty were likely in hiding, and not all characters, like Battle Cat, were there when our heroes made their trip to Earth. By not addressing the characters or concepts at all, the director had "left it open for a sequel to bring them all into the story."[13]

The most noticeable absence from the film was Orko, the fan-favorite comic relief from the Filmation cartoons. He had become a major character to the franchise, joining Prince Adam and King Randor as characters appearing first in the cartoon and then becoming an action figure, instead of vice versa. Early on, it was decided Orko would be impossible to translate based on his appearance alone.

The character, who was only a few feet tall and fully covered in his robes and giant hat, could be achieved through puppetry, but he would require wires to float and electronics to move. There would need to be a voice actor, and the difficulty of having the live actors interacting with the prop. Of these potential difficulties, Goddard said, "I made the conscious decision to not saddle myself with those things. Because I think a film is only as good as its weakest element, its Achilles heel. And I just knew that an Orko character hanging on wires, it would have been a nightmare."[14]

Instead of dropping the character altogether, as the production had done with Battle Cat and the others, they devised a stand-in. "I created Gwildor to provide an Orko-like comedy relief character, but one that would not need to be on wires in every scene," Goddard said.[15] Gwildor was another short, funny, robed character, but one who did not have expensive-to-realize magical powers.

Though he would fit the part of the funny character, he was also more pivotal to the plot. Gwildor, a member of a dwarfish race called Thenorians, would be a master locksmith and inventor. His creation, the Cosmic Key, would set the plot in motion and serve as the film's MacGuffin; the Key allows Skeletor to control of Castle Grayskull, and it is responsible for the heroes' trips to and from Earth.

The inclusion of Gwildor also let the film echo the standard formula of the cartoon series. The common inciting incident of *He-Man and the Masters of the Universe* episodes was He-Man and the other heroes encountering a new character or a new object of power. Then, He-Man and Skeletor would fight over this new element to decide if it would be used for good or evil. In *Masters*, Gwildor and his Cosmic Key filled in those spots nicely.

As the script went through revisions, designers like William Stout began butting heads with Mattel. "They didn't want me to change a thing in regards to any of their characters, which was ridiculous," Stout said.[16] The toymakers wanted to keep their trademark characters as recognizable as possible, and the filmmakers wanted adaptations that would look more natural on the big screen. But the toymakers were the ones writing the checks.

The look of He-Man quickly emerged as the most difficult challenge. Several designers and concept artists, including Ralph McQuarrie, gave their interpretations of the character, but nothing was able to strike the balance between Goddard's vision and Mattel's demands.

Stout handed the project off to his friend Moebius in the hopes of getting something completely unique. He was not disappointed. The illustrations returned from the French cartoonist took the director's "He-Man at war" concept to the next level. The character's signature bits of armor, his wrist gauntlets and boots, appeared homespun and nearly haphazard. Moebius theorized the armor was made by He-Man himself, from bits of wreckage he'd salvaged from the battlefield. Though Mattel vetoed most of the innovations, Stout has called the costume that made it on-screen a watered-down version of what Moebius submitted.

While he constantly fought the toy company for more updated and

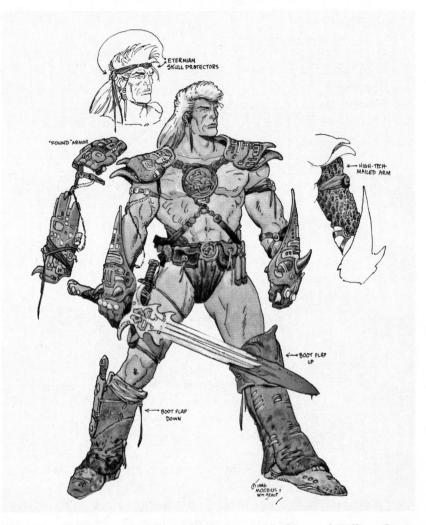

Big screen He-Man, as envisioned by designers Moebius and William Stout. (Courtesy William Stout.)

practical designs for characters, Goddard's main concern with the toy-accurate He-Man costumes Mattel was pushing for was the amount of bare skin that would be left exposed on Dolph Lundgren. In the compromise worked out based on the Moebius design though, the director said: "They allowed me to add the shoulder epaulets and straps, and the cape, along with the knee level boots, which at least put SOME clothing on him and which gave him a more rounded look."[17]

The finished He-Man costume design was accepted by the crew but not by the star. In a 2010 interview, William Stout recalled an incident during the fitting. Lundgren was rejecting the knee-high boots and telling costume designer Julie Weiss he'd only wear the smaller kickboxing boots he'd brought along. Stout was called in. "I told him they looked terrific," he said, "except for the fact that they made him look rather effeminate." Immediately, Lundgren changed his mind. "The boots were never an issue again."[18]

Gary Goddard had some reservations about Mattel's choice for He-Man, as well. Even as he recognized the buzz surrounding Lundgren and agreed he matched the image of the character perfectly, he expressed concerns over the thickness of the actor's Swedish accent. In addition, it had become very evident that *Masters* would only be Lundgren's second real role. He would be learning a lot throughout the production, and he would lean on what he'd picked up from Sylvester Stallone, whom Goddard speculated the young actor was emulating.

Despite rumors of a tension between the two, Goddard has said, "Dolph looks the part and he gave it his all."[19] He worked with an acting coach and dialogue coach throughout the film's short preproduction, along with the weight lifting and health regiments, and his work with stunt and fight coordinators. To this day, the director will be the first to praise Lundgren's work ethic. He's also been very forthcoming about his meeting with the producers about hiring a voice actor to dub the star's lines.

Citing Lundgren's accent as too difficult for audiences and a likely distraction, Goddard pushed for the live-action He-Man to speak more clearly. Even as the Mattel executives objected, the filmmaker sought out voice actors to prove his point. "We found an actor that could've dubbed him and it was a perfect match," Goddard recalled. "I think the film would have been better had I been allowed to dub him, but Cannon said no. 'We paid for Dolph Lundgren and we want his voice.'"[20]

The actor's contract also specified he was allowed three attempts to record his own lines. On that third take, the producers decided Lundgren's accent was clear enough for American audiences.

Though Goddard still harbored doubts, the film's choice for He-Man proved to be ironclad. Next, he turned his attention to the rest of the cast.

For He-Man's rival, the villainous Skeletor, the director had found his perfect actor in Frank Langella. The New York stage actor specialized in Broadway fare but was already no stranger to the big screen. In 1970, his first film role in *Diary of a Mad Housewife* won him an award from the National Board of Review, and garnered another nomination for New Star of the Year at the Golden Globes.

Langella's career bounced back and forth between stage and screen. He won his first Tony Award in 1975 before taking on the role of Count Dracula on Broadway and then its 1979 film adaptation. His turn as the Count became the best known role in his early career in both mediums; the live show earned him another Tony nomination, and the film netted him a Saturn Award nomination for Best Actor.

When the mid–'80s came around, Frank Langella had won another Tony and cemented himself as a respected character actor on TV, film, and the stage. "I had seen Frank in the Broadway production of *Amadeus* and I never forgot it," Goddard said.[21] With an inexperienced actor in the lead and a production lacking credibility in the eyes of the industry, Langella was exactly the kind of actor the director needed. The filmmakers never had any doubt he'd be able to act through the mask or makeup a character like Skeletor required. And so the first-time director approached the venerated stage actor to play a super-villain in a movie based on an action figure.

"I didn't even blink," Langella has since said. "I couldn't wait to play him."[22]

The actor had been made well aware of the franchise by his four-year-old son, whom Langella said would run around the house with a plastic Power Sword yelling, "I have the power!" The boy's favorite character, as luck would have it, was Skeletor.

Once he'd signed, Goddard began working surreptitiously behind the scenes to congeal the story around the villain. More of the story's focus was devoted to Skeletor, to give Langella more time on camera. The director trusted him to carry more emotional weight than the untested Lundgren. Skeletor's entrance into Grayskull was moved to the front of the film, replacing a brief scene in the script where a wounded Eternian solider looks up from the battlefield to see the villain's ship flying overhead, toward the castle. By allowing the villain to deliver the important exposition, Lundgren was now left to shine in the action scenes instead. Opening on Skeletor's victory march, along with the many cutaways to him while He-Man is on Earth, even seemed to make the characters more dynamic character in the final cut.

Langella was also kept fully involved with the creative decisions surrounding his character. He worked with William Stout's costume designers to find a cape that would flow just right for his melodramatic movements, and his skull-like facial prosthetics went through several revisions until they found one that would work best for the actor's expressions. His input to the character was deemed "invaluable" by Stout.

SKELETOR   MOTU ·6·1986·

The look of the live-action Skeletor, as agreed upon by director Goddard, actor Langella, and the folks at Mattel. (Courtesy William Stout.)

Goddard also worked with him to rewrite the character's dialogue. Given Langella's talent and stage experience, Skeletor became a tragic villain in the classical sense, one consumed by his desire to rule the universe as much as much as by his need to defeat He-Man. His Skeletor would roar Shakespeare-esque monologues, like "I must possess all or I possess nothing," alongside actual quotes from the Bard.

Langella's Skeletor would be complimented by the casting of Meg Foster as Evil-Lyn. Foster had first turned heads in the 1979 TV miniseries adaptation of *The Scarlet Letter*, and again in *Ticket to Heaven*, a Canadian drama about cult indoctrination which was ranked one of the top ten films of 1981 by the National Board of Review of Motion Pictures. Her take of Evil-Lyn was the devoted, then spurned right-hand woman, and her naturally ice-blue eyes made her transition into a supernatural character seamless. The bizarre psycho-sexual tension between her and Langella, provide some of the filmmakers' favorite moments in *Masters of the Uni-*

verse. According to Goddard, the two on screen together provides "the real moments of power and real emotion" in the film.[23]

Goddard also looked for an experienced, dependable actor to play along-side Lundgren as a hero. He found this in Jon Cypher, a TV actor who typically played roles as doctors, policemen, and other authority figures. He was best known to audiences in the 1980s as Fletcher Daniels, the chief of police on the long-running *Hill Street Blues*. The director approached him to play Duncan, Man-At-Arms to the Eternian Royal Guard.

Cypher signed on, though he was shooting the final season of *Hill Street Blues* at the time and that led to a hectic schedule. He expressed some concern to the director that the part seemed thin in the script he was given, and Goddard promised to expand the role and make the character more three-dimensional. As the actor remembers it, "Gary was true to his word and, in fact, I actually rewrote one of the scenes and Gary liked it and added it on the very day I brought it in."[24]

Unlike Langella, Cypher was no fan of the franchise and didn't do much research. This seems to work in his advantage, though; his Man-At-Arms is earnest and earthy, very flesh-and-blood compared to alien mercenaries and robot soldiers. That extra bit of humanity made all the difference in the fantasy film.

Casting began for the role of his daughter, Teela. Goddard and his casting director, Vicky Thomas, put out the call but struggled to find the right, effortless fit for the character. "I must have seen a hundred different women for Teela," he said, "and what I wanted to know was could they act and could they hold a sword? Could they hold a blaster and not look out of place? And by the way, we had no time, there was no time for training on this film. This was a Cannon film."[25]

As he grew frustrated with the process, the director remembered Chelsea Field. The former *Solid Gold* dancer was attempting to break into acting, and Goddard had been impressed with her physicality when she auditioned for his live Conan show at Universal Studios. He had Thomas call her in for an audition. And then another. And then another.

Field speculated she had returned ten different times, reading for the part and tumbling over sofas with her pretend laser gun for producers. Only later did it occur to her why she had to jump through so many figurative and imaginary hoops for the role: Goddard was still trying to convince the producers about her. As she explained, "back then, going from being a professional dancer into acting was so, so difficult. The perception was that dancers made terrible actors."[26] So she returned again and again, swinging her make-believe swords until Goddard was able to offer her the part.

MAN·AT·ARMS   TEELA

The redesigned costumes for Man-At-Arms and his daughter Teela, who would be portrayed by Jon Cypher and Chelsea Field, respectively. (Courtesy William Stout.)

In the script, the part of the Sorceress was minor. Already captured by Skeletor before the film began, she would have little screen time. Her presence, however, would be felt throughout the story, as our Eternian characters constantly speak about her or swear by her. Goddard's production needed someone stately enough to deserve such reverence.

They found their Sorceress of Grayskull in English-born character actress Christina Pickles. She got her start in the early '70s, holding down lengthy runs on soap operas *Guiding Light* and *Another World*, along with bit parts in forgettable TV movies or horror dreck like Oliver Stone's *Seizure* (1974). In 1982, she began her role as Helen Rosenthal on the hospital drama *St. Elsewhere.* Pickles' compassion and dignified poise came through in the character, earning her Primetime Emmy nominations for

Outstanding Supporting Actress in a Drama Series in 1983, 1985, and 1986 before her casting in *Masters of the Universe*. The TV series was still going strong during the production of the film.

For the two human "point of view" characters the producers felt *Masters* required, the filmmakers looked for youthful actors who could exude the right kind of all-American wholesomeness.

The first was Robert Duncan McNeill, an up-and-coming graduate of Julliard. McNeill had already appeared on the daytime soap opera *All My Children* and in a West German TV movie by the time he auditioned. He was deemed a worthy fit for Kevin Corrigan, the Earthling character who carried much of the movie's emotional weight.

To play Kevin's girlfriend, Vicky Thomas suggested Courtney Cox. Goddard was unimpressed with the young actress' first audition, thinking that, in her makeup and mature outfit, she would appear too old for the part. Thomas convinced the director to give her another shot, and told Cox to return with no makeup, in a simple pair of blue jeans, and to just be herself. The second interview convinced Goddard that Cox would make the perfect sweet, vulnerable teenager for his movie.[27]

Contrary to popular belief, *Masters of the Universe* would not be Courtney Cox's first acting role after her appearance in the music video for Bruce Springsteen's "Dancing in the Dark." The video was released in 1984, some three years before *Masters* would be released, but she was still known as "The Girl from the Springsteen Video" at that point. In the meantime, Cox had made appearances in TV movies and guest spots on shows like *The Love Boat* and *Murder, She Wrote*. She was a regular cast member on another show, the very short-lived superhero comedy-adventure series *Misfits of Science* (1985).

Her first film role, though in a much smaller capacity, was released just months before *Masters*. Albert Pyun's *Down Twisted*, another Cannon film, claimed the honor of the actress' first big screen appearance. However, the low budget crime thriller received overwhelmingly negative reviews in its brief theatrical run and was not released on home video for several more years. *Masters of the Universe* would be her first major role, and her first widely released movie.

The last key human role was that of Detective Lubic, the stern and skeptical policeman the Eternians encountered on Earth. It would be a part requiring an overbearing demeanor and comic timing, as the character is continually thwarted and befuddled. As such, the casting of James Tolkan was absolutely spot-on.

By 1987, Tolkan had transformed from a character actor to a one-man

Hollywood trope. After one-off appearances on TV series and bit parts in films, his breakthrough came as Principal Strickland in *Back to the Future* (1985). With his bald head and aggressive line readings, he was the perfect authority figure actor for the '80s; Tolkan was stern and direct, never tolerating "slackers" and other misfit young people. His appearance in the next year's blockbuster *Top Gun* would play to his strengths as well. In the role of Detective Lubic, he could play the same style of character, but provide more laughs and even end up as a hero.

With the film's human faces found, Goddard turned back to the assorted aliens and monsters *Masters* required. Though the characters all required extensive makeup and costuming, no corners were cut with the actors who would be unrecognizable.

The perennial He-Man villain Beast Man, named "Beastman" in the credits, was played by muscleman Tony Carroll. The part of Saurod, the lizard-man mercenary, went to Pons Maar, the actor and puppeteer responsible for characters in *Return to Oz* (1985) and the Dominos mascot The Noid. He was cast after playing the character Fu in the 1986 film *The Golden Child*.

Another new character, Karg, was played by the voice actor Robert Towers. No stranger to costume work, Towers had played Captain Crook in McDonalds' commercials for the better part of a decade, and he had worked with Goddard previously on the live Conan show. His short stature would come in hand to play Skeletor's new lieutenant.

As cumbersome as the Karg suit could be, Towers joined the chorus of voices praising the designs of Stout and his crew. "I LOVED my costume," he said. "It was so great, with the little daggers and the hook and the cape. I was really inspired by it."[28]

For the part of his creation, Gwildor, Goddard recruited one of the best-known little person actors. Billy Barty had been acting since the 1930s, when he co-starred with Mickey Rooney in short comedy films, and continued to appear in movies and on TV regularly up to when *Masters* was filmed in to the mid–'80s. He was best known for gag roles due to his height, but he also had a good career in sci-fi and fantasy genre films. Barty had appeared as leprechauns, a munchkin in *The Wizard of Oz*, a dwarf in *Legend*, and as the title character in Cannon Films' musical *Rumpelstiltskin* the same year he played the eccentric Thenorian locksmith.

Nearly everyone on set had a fond memory about working with Barty. As Stout described it, "every day there'd be a tug on my coat and it was Billy. And he had a new joke for me. Every single day. He was just a great guy to work with."[29]

Gwildor's look was designed by Claudio Mazzoli, and it proved to be just as complex as any done by Stout or Moebius. Like the other actors, it took several hours of makeup every day to turn Barty into Gwildor, but he stayed in good spirits as production moved along.

The makeup effects for *Masters of the Universe* was provided by Michael Westmore, one of the premiere makeup artists in Hollywood. By the time production started, Westmore had already won an Academy Award and four Emmys. He would go on to win another five. His expert attention to detail and the way he based prosthetic moldings off of the actors' likenesses proved to be the key component to the convincing alien and monster effects in the finished film.

Anthony De Longis was hired to fill many roles in the production. The multi-talented actor, stuntman, and fight coordinator had come highly recommended to Goddard based on his skills with a sword. *Masters'* stunt coordinator, Walter Scott, first had De Longis train Lundgren for the film's sword battles. The Power Sword prop was large and unwieldy, nicknamed "The Buick Slayer," but the training went well.

"I trained Dolph for a month giving him a solid one and two handed broadsword vocabulary," De Longis said. "He's a terrific athlete and a trained kick boxer so he had terrific natural skills."[30] Lundgren had a solid grasp on the techniques, but the rushed shooting schedule didn't leave time for extensively choreographed action sequences. Most were thrown together the day of shooting.

De Longis stood in for Frank Langella as a fight double, dueling with Lundgren at the film's climax. He was also cast as Blade, another of Skeletor's mercenaries. The character quickly became a fan favorite.

Blade gave He-Man a more evenly matched physical opponent, one he could duel with more than once throughout the film. This way, the film could provide plenty of action and swordfights while saving the one-on-one conflict with Skeletor for the finale. Casting De Longis, the fight choreographer, as the character He-Man would battle the most in the film was a good way to ensure these fights could be pulled off without a hitch.

Playing one of Skeletor's henchmen typically required a bulky costume and hours in a makeup chair in order to pull off an otherworldly appearance. De Longis convinced the filmmakers to let him shave his head instead. "I was always a fan of Yul Bryner, so I didn't mind," he shrugged.[31] As he drove to Whittier, California, for the weeks of night shooting, he could be seen buzzing down his scalp with an electric razor.

This humanoid, but more "edgy" look was accentuated by an eye patch and a metallic chinstrap headpiece, complete with spikes protruding from the earpieces. In fact, most parts on his costume were covered with knives, blades, or other sharp objects. Combined with the chainmail and rubber pieces beneath, the ensemble weighed upward of 55 pounds. De Longis talked Stout's costume crew into removing the outfit's sleeves to let his skin breathe a little more. This also likely assisted his mobility for the complex sword maneuvers he would need to do. Between the exertion of the role and the weight of the costume, he ended most shooting days by pouring the accumulated sweat out of his boots.

De Longis was also hired for another special skill of his. As a renowned expert with a whip, his character was called upon to punish He-Man in front of Skeletor's throne. After demonstrating his prowess for the filmmakers, he showed up to that day of filming and was handed a simple black hilt. The whip itself, he was told, would be added later with computer effects. That scene is one of the more memorable of the film, but De Longis has expressed his disappointment with the effects in several interviews.

One final costuming and design issue, the one that caused the most backlash from the filmmakers and audiences alike, was the look of Skeletor's troopers. As they needed those cannon fodder characters to appear anonymous and without personality, so the audience wouldn't feel bad when He-Man destroyed them, the designs all began to skew into very familiar territory.

"I fought hard not to have them look like *Star Wars* Stormtroopers painted glossy black but I sadly lost that battle," William Stout reflected.[32] The idea of fully armored, nameless soldiers had been done so well in the *Star Wars* films, and the public consciousness grabbed into their image so thoroughly, it was hard to get around it. The production used the familiar-seeming design by Mazzoli, and the similarities were pointed out by audiences immediately.

Goddard has defended the look of the troopers on many occasions. Their appearance, he's said, was the only way to give the troopers an ambiguous appearance, allowing them to be either living or robotic underneath. As he describes it, this was just another part of the compromise he reached with Mattel.

The score was another aspect of *Masters of the Universe* that was immediately compared to *Star Wars*. The film's original music was composed by Bill Conti, a "master Songmaker" if there ever was one. Incredibly prolific, Conti was scoring multiple films, TV movies, and TV shows every year throughout the '70s and '80s. His big break came in 1976 when he scored the blockbuster hit *Rocky* (1976). He would go on to provide the music for every successive *Rocky* installment, ironically save *Rocky IV*, which starred future He-Man Dolph Lundgren.

Like many contributors to the film, Conti brought his impressive pedigree to a cinematic endeavor viewed with skepticism in Hollywood. He had been nominated for several awards by 1987, including Golden Globes for *Rocky*, *An Unmarried Woman* (1978) and the James Bond film *For Your Eyes Only* (1981); he was nominated for Academy Awards for *Rocky* and *For Your Eyes Only*, and won the Oscar for Best Original Score in 1983 for *The Right Stuff*.

Conti's bombastic themes would prove to be a perfect fit for *Masters*, though they sounded a bit familiar to most audiences.

As preproduction hurried along, work began on building the sets. The Earthbound spots the script called for would be filmed practically, using existing locations and buildings in Whittier, California. In the revised, budget-friendly final script, there were only two indoor Eternian sites that needed to be built.

The first was Gwidor's home. Designed by Claudio Mazzoli, the set was built to Billy Barty's scale, causing for cramped shooting conditions. The large, single room was intricately furnished. Every surface was covered with tiny techno gadgets that blinked or beeped or whirled. As evidence of his calling as a locksmith, the front door was lined with several kinds of sci-fi locks. In a last minute moment of inspiration on the day of filming, Gary Goddard sent someone out to buy a simple sliding chain lock. The cute little visual joke was added for the set's one scene.

The set was barely finished by the time its big day for filming came around. After all the needed shots were finished for the scene, the script called for Gwildor's home to be destroyed as Karg leads Skeletor's troops inside. For added realism, the little set was actually wrecked by the exploding door.

The production's main point of pride came from the Eternian throne room set. As most of the Eternia scenes had to take place in that one room, Goddard and company worked to ensure that room was as impressive as possible.

The set was designed by William Stout, though he was inspired by sketches from his friend Moebius. "This was the seat of power for the entire universe," he explained. "I reasoned that power is neither good nor bad—it's what you make of it and how you use it. So, above the floor level were what I called the Space Gods, giant bronze statues of those who had used the power based in that room for good. Below floor level was the dark side, demonic creatures that represented power used for bad or evil."[33]

As envisioned, Stout's throne room was truly epic. The assembled crew worked all throughout preproduction, and well into the process of filming, to bring it to life. Production needed to be arranged around the set's completion, saving the many throne room scenes for last to give the carpenters and set dressers enough time. It would prove to be worth the wait.

The set was constructed at Culver Studios in Culver City, California, then known as Laird International Studios, a spot which holds a special place in Hollywood lore. Years before, it was the home of RKO Studios, where cinematic classics like *Citizen Kane* and *King Kong* had been shot. Inside the famous studio, the production had selected the two largest soundstages and demolished the wall separating them. The resulting space was rumored to be the biggest Hollywood set in 40 years.

Inside, a tiered network of platforms, staircases, and walkways were constructed around columns and archways. While such a complex design would look interesting, even regal on screen, Stout had primarily laid the room out to make the most interesting sword fight possible. For the climactic duel between hero and villain, the production designer had envisioned something classical and swashbuckling, like an Errol Flynn film, so the characters could battle their way across the throne room.

Stationed along the walls were the towering Space God statues, which were alternately called the Elders of Technology or the Gods of Technology by Goddard, to reinforce the mixture of magic and sci-fi science on Eternia. Around them hung long banners of deep, rich purple trimmed with golden patterns. Space for several large chasms were left on the set's floor; these spots would be enhanced with matte paintings to show the demonic side of the Castle. In several shots of the film, massive carved skulls and descending staircases would be visible beneath the throne room. From angles focusing on the floor level, the pits still gave off a volcanic red glow.

Against the far wall of the set were two massive golden doors, complete with swirling, intricate symbols. These doors were originally designed for Skeletor's base on Snake Mountain, but were repurposed when those scenes were scrapped.

The opposite wall sported the large, circular portal that would open at the film's climax. In front of it was a raised platform with a sci-fi contraption, where Skeletor would imprison the Sorceress of Grayskull to siphon off her magical powers. Front and center was the throne itself, a seat which seemed both ostentatious and ancient at once. Though surrounded by flashy technology, the chair was fitted between two small stone columns, each covered with faded hieroglyphics. The Laird Studio set received plenty of visitors as the crew was finishing their work. Stout called the awed reactions one of the biggest thrills of his job on *Masters*: "Everybody in The Biz came by to see it and have a picture taken seated on the throne to all the power in the universe!"[34]

Even the filmmakers themselves were impressed with the final product. The set painters had seemingly transformed the plywood walkways into marble, and the other minute details were all perfectly realized to add to the verisimilitude. The set would be one of the most expensive aspects of *Masters of the Universe*, but it was executed in such a way that it appeared even more costly than it was.

When looking back on the highlights of his time making *Masters*, Goddard thought of his first time stepping foot into that finished set. He also mentioned filming the epic opening sequence in the throne room, as Skeletor marches toward the throne, flanked by Evil-Lyn and dozens of his troopers, victorious at last. "That was a great moment," he smiled.[35]

As filming progressed and the movie began to take shape, things were far from certain. In fact, Cannon Film's financial situation seemed more perilous with each passing day. The studio's own stockholders had filed a class action lawsuit, accusing Golan and Globus of cooking their books

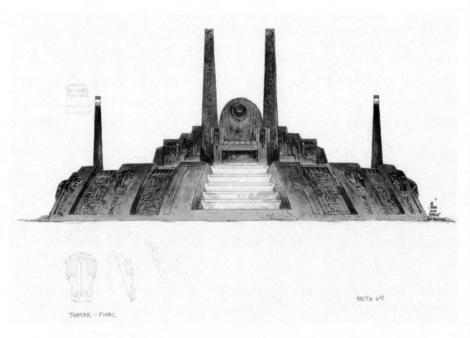

"The throne to all the power in the universe!" (Courtesy William Stout.)

and misrepresenting the strength of the company. "This action followed those of two individual shareholders a few weeks earlier, reported in the Wall Street Journal. Those individuals had bought Cannon stock at $44 and seemed to be claiming they had been mislead by financial information Cannon had put out."[36]

Next, the studio announced that the SEC's informal inquiry into the company's finances had turned into a full-fledged investigation. The government would be digging deep into Cannon's finances, accounting, reported earnings, taxes, and nearly every other facet of the company. Such news drove their shares even lower than before, and the money needed to continue production on *Masters* became bound up in red tape.

Mattel, for their part, did not appear to have much faith in the project. Their executives seemed more interested in selling toys and keeping their trademark hero as family-friendly as possible. They kept a close eye on the constantly evolving script and suggested more action figure tie-ins.

With toy executives leaning over one shoulder, and the troubled accountants from Cannon on the other, Gary Goddard buckled down to make his movie. Slowly, even painfully, *Masters of the Universe* began to come to life.

5

A Battle Fought in the Stars, Now ... Comes to Earth

In the Beginning...

We open with the Cannon film logo, which is, appropriately enough, a symbol coming together briefly and then falling apart dramatically. Next we're given a list of names on a plain blue background, which doesn't exactly fit the windy sounds that serve as soundtrack. But that's okay. It's building.

Next begins an expository voiceover, an unnamed narrator explaining the location and foreshadowing the plot. This is a popular trope of many sci-fi/fantasy movies aiming for an epic scope. It also serves as a convenient introduction as the film itself, once it starts up, wastes very little time on explanations.

This particular introduction is spoken as we fade in on a matte painting of Castle Grayskull, the centermost point of Eternia, a planet at the center of the galaxy. As we get closer, we see the intricacies of the castle's design. It's gothic, temple-like, but hedged with blinking lights. Technology and mysticism, if not outright magic, living in perfect harmony.

A mere speck in the left eye socket of the titular skull of Grayskull, we are first shown the Sorceress. She stands in her home, this castle, seemingly miles above the surface of the planet. The tiny homes and dwarfed spires twinkle below her, but she's looking upward, into the night sky. Something is happening up there, some colors warbling into existence. Is this the ancient, cosmic power the Sorceress is tasked with protecting? No. It's just the credits.

Bill Conti's soaring, bombastic theme has often been unfavorably compared to the brassy anthems in the *Star Wars* films. Hearing it like this, as actors names fly around space, it's easier to think of one of John Williams's other classic scores—1978's *Superman*. The film's theme, complete with its subconscious associations, does its job. Immediately, the viewer knows they are in for a grand space opera, complete with one immensely powerful protagonist.

To these sounds, the names of actors and crew are propelled through a space rainbow. After one last name, Gary Goddard, the film begins with a literal bang. An explosion rips through space, ending our credits.

And We're Off

"The whole idea here was to set a mood," said Goddard. "We started, really, from the villain's point of view, and got a lot of exposition out of the way."[1]

We're treated to a brief view of Eternia, an alien landscape brought to life on the Vasquez Rocks outside Escondido, California. The aftermath of a battle is visible in the smoldering sci-fi wreckage. Surrendering Grayskull guards are being herded by black armored figures. The war is over, and from the looks of it, the bad guys won.

Inside Castle Grayskull, a massive throne room has been similarly overrun by these "crack troops." One more man in black marches along the impossibly long walkway. The dark, ominous score is punctuated by the sound of his staff striking the ground. Here we have the man in charge. He demands a report from his second-in-command, Evil-Lyn. He-Man, we're told, is leading the resistance. The Sorceress has been captured. Their side has won, she says. Grayskull is theirs.

"No," Skeletor turns, correcting her harshly. "Mine."

Goddard has called *Masters of the Universe* a labor of love, and it's overwhelmingly obvious in this scene. The score is booming and epic, the lighting is pitch-perfect to bring the costumes and makeup to life, and the throne room set is both huge and minutely detailed. We can see tier after tier of staircases descending into the depths of Grayskull, along with gigantic statues stretching up into the distance above. This is far from the only example of such an attention to detail from the production.

A sizeable chunk of the magic on screen is centered on Frank Langella as Skeletor. He has disappeared into the character, swirling his cape and growling his pompous dialogue. Though he is clearly enjoying the inherent camp of the project, Langella also provides moments of genuine creepiness.

In this first sequence, Skeletor and Evil-Lyn, as played by Meg Foster, deliver their exposition, by occasionally staring directly into the camera. Breaking the fourth wall like this is certainly unorthodox, but guaranteed to deliver chills to the children in the audience. Sure, this is a kiddie movie, but there is a surprising edge to the family-friendly entertainment.

Enter He-Man

"People of Eternia," Skeletor announces to the planet, "the war is over. My forces are victorious!"

The villain's face is broadcast into the skies surrounding Grayskull by the holo-spheres, witnessed by handfuls of surrendering castle guards. And someone else, too.

He-Man stands atop the slanted rocks with the Power Sword, here called the Sword of Grayskull, in hand. The cartoon character has become battle-hardened, his hair mussed, his bare muscles soot-smudged. His costume is familiar enough, but not exactly the same as it appears on the action figures. While just as exposing, the boots are taller, the chest piece covers less, and his trunks aren't furry, like a barbarian's. He has a flowing cape in royal purple. At once, it's more utilitarian and more gaudy.

Surveying the wreckage, He-Man spots a small group of Skeletor's troops leading away a prisoner, a small figure trapped in a net. With this, he leaps into action.

He also leaps into one of the most awkwardly edited sequences of the film.

On the whole, *Masters of the Universe* is smooth and competently made, especially for a first-time director. But the following brief scene is difficult to follow.

The shots of He-Man looking over the battlefield and the shots of him fighting these troopers were clearly filmed far apart. Where he's looking doesn't match up with the camera angles we're shown, so when he jumps into frame, it's seemingly from out of nowhere.

Much of the ensuing fight is filmed in close-ups, focusing on the clash of sword against rifle barrel, He-Man's chest as he turns, his grimacing face. At its best moments, it's confusing. At worst, it's fuel for the camp crowds, the viewers looking for "so bad it's good."

He-Man shows no mercy, flinging a knife at one trooper, slashing another across the torso with his sword, gunning down several more. As the film never explicitly states these soldiers are robots, the violence can be a bit surprising at first.

Though he doesn't seem to need it, He-Man receives assistance. The last few crack troops are shot by Teela and her father, Man-At-Arms. These two are dressed in variations on the Grayskull guard uniforms we've spotted in battlefield backgrounds. The design has been streamlined since the cartoon, and it's all in shades of blue instead of Filmation's gold and green.

Gwildor

That small figure in the net is calling out for help. Our reunited friends hurry over to set him free. This is Gwildor, who introduces himself as a locksmith, inventor, and member of a race called Thenorians. "Any foe of Skeletor is a friend of ours," Man-At-Arms tells him.

When asked why he is so important to Skeletor's forces, Gwildor invites He-Man and the others back to his workshop. Here Gwildor reveals his greatest invention, a small device covered with buttons and spiky tuning forks: the Cosmic Key.

The Cosmic Key, Gwildor explains, can allow travel to any place by manipulating the "gravitonic tones" that bind the universe together. Immediately, He-Man sees where this is going. "And that's how Skeletor's troops got into the city and surprised us," he finishes his new ally's sentence.

Gwildor hurries to explain. It was stolen by Skeletor's lieutenant Evil-Lyn. The villains have the Cosmic Key, but Gwildor still has its prototype.

"You little worm," Teela spits. "Don't you realize what you've done?"

She's calmed by He-Man, but this isn't the only instance of Teela's bigotry toward Thenorians in the film. It's a small character quirk, but a puzzling one for a children's movie. In her defense, Gwildor doesn't seem too broken up about his part in the capture of Castle Grayskull.

Alarms are sounded. Skeletor's troops have found them.

Outside we see one of Skeletor's major henchmen, Karg, leading a group of black armored troopers. Gwildor pulls a lever and beckons his new friends to hurry through this secret passage into "the caverns beneath Grayskull." If these caverns and passages exist, it's unsure why Skeletor needed a Cosmic Key in the first place.

Following He-Man into the passage, Gwildor pauses. "I don't like adventures," he says to himself. Goddard added this line as a *Lord of the Rings* reference.[2] Upon speaking it, the small, hermitic character rushes off with his new tall, brave friends on a journey that will take him very far away. He might even just save the day.

Take a Deep Breath

At this point, about 11 minutes into the film's running time, it's worth noting how fast it's moving.

It's common for genre films of this nature to begin with an action scene, but *Masters of the Universe* goes far beyond a standard set piece. Aided by the ominous score, the film already has a great deal of momentum behind it. This first extended sequence of *Masters* could even be confused for the third act of another film, one which has already established all it needs to and it now simply focusing on the action.

We're given that brief voiceover introduction and then we are thrown headfirst into a civil war. Even if the viewer is familiar with these characters from cartoons or action figures, that still does little to explain why Eternia is in this state. And so we're simply along for the ride. We're piecing together the backstory when we're given clues and we're rooting for He-Man because he looks like the hero. The story's mechanisms and plot holes fall away. This is simply entertainment.

Passage through the caverns beneath Grayskull has delivered our heroes to the castle's throne room, which now appears to have been emptied of Skeletor's troops. He-Man and the others are apprehensive, but still move in to free the Sorceress from the energy field Skeletor has trapped her in.

While Gwildor attempts to use the Key to open a "doorway" through the force field, the Sorceress tells He-Man just how bad the situation is. Skeletor is stealing her powers. "I can withstand him until moonrise," she says, "until the Great Eye opens on the universe." Our heroes have been given a deadline but, for the viewers, it's a wobbly one. We're not told how long an Eternian day is. Again, we're not given the time to consider that.

The rattling of armor alerts our heroes to Skeletor's return. The black-clad troops file in with Skeletor and Evil-Lyn. Man-At-Arms and Teela take up defensive positions, as He-Man stands defiant beside the Sorceress. Behind the dais, Man-At-Arms shouts at the villain, asking if he dares to threaten the Sorceress's life.

"I dare anything! I am Skeletor!" This is one of those lines of dialogue that might've scared off most actors, but Langella is eating up the melodrama. His performance grows more gloriously unhinged throughout the film.

Evil-Lyn hears Gwildor using his prototype key, and the shootout begins. The massive throne room set allows for plenty of creative camera movements, sweeping in and around the squadron of crack troops as they fire away. Sparks explode whenever one is shot. Evil-Lyn has pulled back to a safer position, but Skeletor stands in the midst of the battle, too obsessed to be anywhere else.

Man-At-Arms, the tactician, realizes the battle isn't going to end well. He tells Gwildor to stop working on freeing the Sorceress and to get them a doorway out of the throne room. Gwildor hits keys at random and presses the big red "Energizer" button.

In the corner of the throne room, balls of light swirl together and we watch the flat surface of the film dip inward. A misty vortex is formed. Begrudgingly, He-Man follows his companions toward the portal. As the shootout continues, an errant shot hits Gwildor's Cosmic Key and it drops to the ground.

He-Man grabs Gwildor and jumps into the portal while the troops lunge for the Key. As the portal begins to fade, a claw on a grappling line is fired back out into the throne room, grasping the Key and retracting it back toward our heroes. The door closes.

"Find them," Skeletor screams. The villains' Cosmic Key can trace the prototype whenever it is used. The next time the Key is activated, they will know where they are.

"He-Man lives and possesses that Key," Skeletor says to the camera. "I must possess all or I possess nothing."

Coming to Earth

Lightning strikes in a sunny, verdant forest, and we begin to see a familiar swirling of light. Another portal has been opened. Our heroes are flung through the "doorway" onto a muddy riverbank.

"We could be anywhere," Gwildor says. "Any planet in the galaxy! Any planet in a thousand galaxies!" They can find their way back to Eternia with the help of the Cosmic Key ... which seems to have been misplaced in their journey.

In this scene, we can practically hear the film relaxing. After an action-fraught first sequence, the story finally has a chance to settle into itself. The characters' definition shapes up. Man-At-Arms is the team's realist, the seasoned and unflappable veteran. Teela is the fiery one, always first to let loose with her tongue or her laser pistol. Gwildor, the comedy-maker, is another of cinema's absent-minded inventors.

He-Man, our hero, is conspicuously bland. He's peaceful, smiling at

Gwildor's antics, and fast to calm the hot-headed Teela. As an icon of machismo and alpha male might, he almost seems censored. Due to the cartoon's violent reputation with concerned parents, Mattel was clearly cautious to not make him appear too warlike.

This temporary respite also allows more lightness to creep into the film. The first sequence held firm to its portrayal of a planet at war. The tone was grim, the protagonists seemed outnumbered and overwhelmed. Now Gwildor clears his clogged gill-slits, spraying the group with muddy water for a moment of comedy. They group then ventures off to marvel at their first alien life form: a cow.

But the clock is ticking down. To enact their next suicide mission to free the Sorceress, they first need to find the lost Key. The team splits up to scout the area.

Meet Our Earthlings

Nearby we see the sign for Robby's Ribs, a local fast food joint.[3]

Inside is Julie, a bright eyed teenager wearing a waitress's red checkered shirt and neckerchief. She smiles as she hands over a bucket of fried chicken to a customer off-screen.

Julie, we learn, has suffered a family tragedy. Her parents died recently when her father's plane crashed. Julie blames herself, in a not-quite-sensible teenage way, because she wasn't there with them. Instead, she lied about needing to study so she could spend time with her rock 'n' roll boyfriend, Kevin. Now she's packing up, quitting her fast food job, and moving to New Jersey.

She removes her apron and walks to the back of the store. A coworker follows her, gnawing idly on a fried chicken leg. "If you break up with Kevin Corrigan," she tells Julie, "you will regret it for the rest of your life."

Behind a swinging saloon door, Julie is unbuttoning her uniform shirt. Though only shown from the shoulders up, and even in a movie alongside a nearly naked Dolph Lundgren, this image is surprisingly intimate. Julie, as a character, is stripped raw.

A horn sounds outside the restaurant. Kevin Corrigan has arrived. Julie has to catch a bus to the airport that night, but they have some time to kill. On her last night in town, Kevin asks his girlfriend to come listen to his band's sound check. He's just that type of guy.

Cultural Differences

Teela and her father have converged in the woods near Robby's. The two Eternians spot Gwildor hiding in nearby bushes, using his grappling claw to steal food from a nearby convertible. They confront him and accept their share of the bounty.

Teela speaks through a full mouth: "I wonder why they put their food on these little white sticks..."

"Those are rib bones," Man-At-Arms says, unperturbed. He continues to munch while his daughter and Gwildor freeze.

"You mean this used to be an animal?" she asks, coughing. Man-At-Arms smiles and takes another bite. His companions have lost their appetites.

"What a barbaric world," Teela says, throwing down her half-eaten barbecue.

This scene is the perfect example of a major theme of the rest of the film–The fish out of water. These Eternians bumble through 1980s Earth, misunderstanding social mores and standing out like sore thumbs. They also learn from these Earthlings, even as they endeavor to protect them from the evil that will follow them from their home planet. Where He-Man is, Skeletor can't be far behind.

While it's entertaining to watch aliens be confounded by what the viewer considers ordinary, it's also a one-way mirror. We infer that Eternians, and Thenorians, for that matter, don't eat meat. But what do they eat?

Masters of the Universe is admirable for its sense of scope and perspective. We're shown world-building in ways both grand, like the throne room shootouts, and subtle, like expressions in throwaway dialogue. For example, the characters have their own measurements for time and distance, *chromots* and *metrons*, respectively. While this does wonders for immersion, it also brings up more questions than it answers. We have no idea how long a chromot is, or how far a metron[4] is.

We hear characters saying, "Thank the Sorceress," as if she's a religious or political figure. And she very well may be both. While previous incarnations of the *Masters* franchise did portray a king of Eternia, there is no reference to one onscreen. Grayskull is a proper castle, complete with a throne room, and we're told the only person who belongs there is the Sorceress. Is she merely a figurehead, or something more? It makes one curious what, exactly, Skeletor's claim to the throne is.

Twilight's gloom is approaching the small California town. On the way to his sound check, Kevin has driven Julie to the cemetery so she can say goodbye to her parents. They stand in front of the graves and Julie's voice cracks as she elaborates on her feelings of guilt. "God, I wish ... I wish I could change things," she whispers into the shoulder of Kevin's leather jacket.

"But you can't. That only happens in fairy tales."

Kevin helps her away from the gravesite and, on cue, the cemetery's lampposts flash into life, spreading a golden light around them. A beeping noise gets their attention, leading them from the path toward a small smoking crater. Inside, they find the Cosmic Key. These two innocent kids are walking directly into a fairy tale or, as their Eternian counterparts would think, just an average day. But those are cultural differences for you.

Awkward Relationships

Across the cosmos, Evil-Lyn has been alerted by the Earth kids playing with the prototype Cosmic Key. They can't locate them too closely just yet; the readings are still only narrowed down to the closest "parsec-eon."

The Cosmic Key was always intended to be a device for not only traveling to different planets, but also to different times. While this plot element is used much later in the film, it was never clearly established beforehand. The Key is always used for transportation, getting Skeletor into Castle Grayskull or He-Man to Earth. This throwaway line, saying our renegade heroes were tracked down to the parsec (unit of distance) and eon (unit of time), is the closest we get to foreshadowing the final scene.

By now, Julie is awkwardly standing by as Kevin sets up for his band's big gig at the local high school. Once his keyboard is sound-checked, he begins to fiddle with the Cosmic Key once again. He happens across the Energizer button and, as the two of them marvel at the lightshow the Key produces, Skeletor's forces are able to zero in on them.

Sensing a trap, Skeletor ordered Evil-Lyn to round up an advance team of mercenaries to investigate before sending a battalion of his soldiers. He stands by as she introduces each member of the team:

Blade, a one-eyed, bald humanoid in spiky body armor, is introduced first. He was intended to be a physical equal for He-Man, especially as a swordsman. Though the Power Sword has always been an important element to the character of He-Man, he almost never engaged in a sword fight on the *He-Man and the Masters of the Universe* cartoon. The live-action filmmakers were interested in correcting that oversight.

The reptilian Saurod is introduced next. Possibly the film's most visually striking character, this first moment on screen shows off the detail of the costume and makeup. As expert puppeteer Pons Maar arches and sways his neck, a sac in his throat inflates like a frog's. It's a tiny moment that came from a lot of hard work by the film's designers and costumers.

Next is the only previously established character, Beast Man, now called The Beastman. He was one of the first Masters of the Universe action figures made and has been present in every incarnation of the concept. Mattel wanted as many familiar characters as possible in the film, an idea Goddard bristled at. While most established characters did not make the cut, Beastman earned himself a fairly prominent role.

The last in this "elite commando unit" is Karg, the gray-skinned, hook-handed lieutenant who earlier lead the raid of Gwildor's workshop. Karg is portrayed as being a figure of authority, second only to Evil-Lyn. He will be leading this "curious quartet," as Skeletor calls them.

The evil, black-cloaked figure marches in front of them, issuing his demands. He wants the Key but, even more so, he wants He-Man. "Now," he says, "you are to go through to this world where they are hiding, find the Key, do what you wish with the others but bring He-Man back alive. Understand?"

It's almost uncomfortable how similar this scene is to one in the *Star Wars* sequel, *The Empire Strikes Back* (1982). In it, Darth Vader, another melodramatically evil figure in a black cape, marches in front of his assembled team of bounty hunters, issuing his orders for the capture of Han Solo and the crew of the *Millennium Falcon*. It's easy for films like these, epic comic book-y space operas, to fall into the same tropes and repeated motifs, but these sequences almost mirror each other. It's hard to believe this wasn't intentional.[5]

Masters of the Universe certainly has an awkward relationship with *Star Wars*, but that's not the only awkward relationship on screen. As the film progresses, we are privy to more of the strange bond between Evil-Lyn and Skeletor. The two are never implicitly stated to be lovers—this is a kids' movie, after all—but there is a sinister sexual tension between the two of them. The relationship warps throughout the running time, as Evil-Lyn seems nearly worshipful of her leader at the beginning, but she slowly grows resentful as she watches the obsession with destroying He-Man consume him. It's a subtle character arc, another tiny detail which adds so much to the film's re-watch value.

Return of the Action

Back in the high school gym, Kevin is still amazed by the Cosmic Key, which he's convinced is a new high-tech Japanese synthesizer. He wants to drive it over to show his friend Charlie, the owner of the local music shop. Julie volunteers to stay behind in the school.

Kevin hesitates for a second, but then rushes off. She'll have the place to herself, he says, except for school's janitor, Carl.

As soon as she's alone, there's a noise from behind the gym's door. In the hallway, the Key's doorway is opening. The mercenaries and a handful of black armored troopers are hurrying into our world. In classic horror movie fashion, Julie walks slowly toward the door.

"Carl?" she asks hopefully. "Is that you?"

Carl is thrown through the doorway and the mercenaries enter. Julie shrieks. As she runs off to hide behind the stage, they open fire. Sparks fly. Speakers explode. A fire catches.

"No, no, take her alive!" Karg orders. "She may know where the Key is!"

The four creatures hunt as Julie struggles to scurry away. Julie manages to splash ammonia in Beastman's eyes and, as he's blinded, escape through the door to the outside. The gymnasium is left in flames behind her.

According to Goddard, "The challenge here was to make it look like a girl like this could actually escape these four attacking villains and make it look realistic, so you wouldn't think they look foolish. And I think we did that in the cutting."[6]

This sequence underwent many changes before filming. David Odell's first script only included two mercenaries, Beastman and Saurod. The two were to chase Julie through the entire high school, until she manages to trap Saurod under a bookshelf in the library and blind Beastman with sulfuric acid from the science lab. The finished product makes Skeletor's minions more menacing, and Julie's escape more difficult. In the film, the Earthling barely makes it out alive.

Tracking the Key nearby, He-Man hears Julie's screams. She's running down alley, banging on doors and shouting for anyone to help. Night has fallen, and the mist is mixing with nearby sign's neon lights to make everything look slightly surreal. Julie ducks under a fence into a junk yard. Blade easily slices through the fence with one of his swords and the mercenaries follow.

Inside, He-Man catches Julie and tries to calm her. Hearing her talking about "monsters," a realization flashes in his eyes. He-Man says he'll take care of it. "Protect yourself," he says, handing her a pistol. And then he walks off to take care of it.

The film has had plenty of action so far. The characters are constantly running or shooting or narrowly escaping, but this is the first full-on fight scene since the brief confrontation when He-Man saved Gwildor.

The ensuing junk yard fight is much better shot and edited than that first example, thankfully. He-Man sneaks through the maze of wooden crates, attacking the troopers and mercenaries. It's a complicated scene, involving many unique characters, air cannons, and special effects, and it all comes together beautifully.

After a shootout, and brief-but-satisfying sword fight with Blade, He-Man once again receives assistance when he doesn't particularly seem to need it. After single-handedly taking on about a dozen combatants, Teela and Man-At-Arms again show up, guns a-blazing. Karg orders the retreat, and the remains of his team pulls back to transport to Eternia.

A Brief Note on Asexuality

Alerted by the fire trucks' sirens, Kevin hurries back to the high school as the blaze is still being extinguished. As he asks about Julie, who he left there "just ten minutes ago," he falls under the overbearing gaze of tough guy Detective Lubic. We're told vandalism, possibly even arson, is suspected.

Blocks away, Julie recognizes He-Man's description of the Cosmic Key and says it's with her boyfriend.

"He's in terrible danger," He-Man tells her. He introduces Teela and Man-At-Arms and asks if his friends had any luck in their search.

"Not as much as you, apparently," says Teela, staring daggers at the young Earthling wrapped in He-Man's cape.

This throwaway line is a reference to the character's flirtation in the minicomics. Any romance was merely implied in the Filmation series, of course, as it was a children's cartoon. If anything, their relationship in that incarnation was closer to confused love triangle between Clark Kent, Lois Lane and Superman, as it also involved He-Man's secret identity, Prince Adam.

This exchange also is notable for being the only instance in which He-Man is not treated like an utter eunuch.

Although He-Man is muscular, barely dressed and, objectively, rather attractive, the idea of his sexuality never once factors into the story. There's never a whisper of attraction from suburban damsel-in-distress Julie and, when boyfriend Kevin joins the group, there's never a second of jealousy when He-Man sees him rescuing her. One can assume that, just as Mattel insisted, "He-Man can't kill," they also added, "He-Man can't be sexualized." A quick eyebrow-raise from Teela is all we get.

But the moment ends and the film carries on. Gwildor arrives, bearing another moment of lightness and "native transportation"—a pink Cadillac equipped with new sci-fi gadgets.

Again with the Darkness...

In Castle Grayskull, Evil-Lyn is kneeling before Skeletor. He grasps her head with both hands, peering in close as they whisper.

"The people wait for He-Man," she says, her pale eyes gleaming. "They believe that he will return to lead them. For you to rule completely, he must be destroyed."

"He-Man.... If I kill him, I make him a martyr ... a saint ... no. I want him broken."

This *Macbeth*-style interaction is interrupted by the banging of the throne room's doors. The advance team has returned. And He-Man is not with them.

Stammering, Karg reports that they found the Key, but could not capture it. They battled the Eternians but were "outnumbered," so they've returned for a larger invasion force.

He-Man is still free. He still lives. The four mercenaries cower as Skeletor rises to his feet. They all know the penalty for failure.

They beg for another chance, and this time Skeletor speaks an actual Shakespeare quote—"I am not in a giving vein this day," from *Richard III*. He extends his hand and purple lightning arches out, striking Saurod. The reptilian henchman writhes and screams as he's slowly dissolved.

"It would be a pity to let their talents go to waste," Evil-Lyn says, taking her place at Skeletor's side. He grabs her arm and pushes her out toward the remaining mercenaries.

"Save your pity for yourself, if you fail!"

Confusion washes over Evil-Lyn's face as Skeletor tells her she's in charge of the team now. Just like that, Evil-Lyn's spot of privilege and confidence is taken away. Their relationship has pivoted; from here we can watch the disillusion grow in Meg Foster's performance as Skeletor's obsession pushes his right-hand woman further away.

In a film unafraid to flirt with darkness, this is by far the most grim sequence in its running time. As Gary Goddard wrestled with both Mattel and Cannon for every ounce of creative control he could, this shows us where that leeway went. He has created a story with stakes, where characters can die even if the hero can't kill them, and where the villain is cartoony but still utterly evil.

Evil-Lyn's team arrives near the junk yard. Inside the fence, she uses an Eternian "scanner" to view the past, watching for the ambush Karg spoke of. All she sees is He-Man.

"Outnumbered?" She smirks. "Outclassed is more like it."

Troopers report activity from the Key. They trace it to Julie's house, where Lubic drove Kevin. The paranoid detective soon loses interest in the missing Julie or any possible arson her boyfriend may have committed. He is more interested in the Cosmic Key. The device may not be a Japanese synthesizer, Lubic says. It may be part of some Communist plot. He takes the Key back to Charlie's music shop to ask some questions, leaving Kevin at the house.

Tropes of the 1980s

Movies are best interpreted when viewed in the context of their original release date. *Masters of the Universe* hit theaters in the fall of 1987 and, like most films of the era, the decade's motifs were quite strong.

One common trope of science-fiction / fantasy films of the time was "coming to Earth." Appropriate budgets were not always available, or the filmmaking technology was not always advanced enough to express the future or an alien world. As a result, there would often be "bookend" scenes at the beginning and end of the film, or merely an introduction taking place in these fantastic locales before the action relocates to the then-modern day.

Masters was constructed with these limitations in mind. By setting so many scenes inside Grayskull's throne room, the story could bounce back and forth between Earth and Eternia more often. This gave the fantasy world more screen-time than it did in films like *The Terminator* (1984), *Star Trek IV: The Voyage Home* (1986), and *Howard the Duck* (1986).

The film also comments on the popular mindsets of the time. Detective Lubic is the voice of the '80s establishment, paranoid about the rise of cults or Communist sabotage striking the small, idyllic California town.[7] Later in the film, he's seen leading his police squad around, swearing he just saw an invading army. He's portrayed as both eager for and ultimately unprepared for war.

Perhaps the greatest '80s trope found in *Masters of the Universe* is the story's reverence for music. Music is quite literally magic, the glue binding the universe together. And the instrument best identified with 1980s music, the synthesizer keyboard, is also a lynchpin. The Cosmic Key functions as a keyboard, the instrument our teenage musician Kevin plays, allowing him to eventually save the day through rock 'n' roll.

These elements can "date" any film, but it can also allow it to work as a time capsule. In a story about interplanetary travel, even travel across time, we need a concrete locations in both space and time. Looking at Teela's aerobics-style spandex costume or hearing Kevin insist Gwildor's Cosmic Key is a Japanese synthesizer, there can be no doubt that we're looking at the 1980s.

The Gang's All Here

As Evil-Lyn and the remaining mercenaries storm Julie's house, Kevin is alone and cleaning the kitchen. As Beastman approaches, he throws the only thing within reach—a paper towel. This does not work as well as Julie's ammonia did.

When he is subdued, Evil-Lyn applies another Eternian gadget—the Collar of Aldruber. With it in place, Kevin is calm and docile, hypnotized, his eyes dilated, speaking with a voice that sounds auto-tuned. Shown a hologram of the Cosmic Key, he tells Evil-Lyn it was taken by Lubic only minutes before.

"We should be able to track the Key from the air," Blade says. Evil-Lyn agrees and the team returns to the hovering transport in the front yard. They leave Kevin behind, the collar still in place.

Gwildor's modified "land-boat" pulls up moments later. He-Man and our heroes storm in, finding only destruction and the collared Kevin. When Man-At-Arms frees him, Kevin blinks away the Collar's effects and mistakes our Eternians for the evil crew representing Skeletor.

Julie tries to calm him by saying these strangers are her friends.

"Your friends?!" he sputters. "Will somebody tell me what the hell is going on here?"

An awkward introduction follows.

Just past halfway through the film's running time, the gang is all together. All the characters have been introduced and maneuvered into place. All expositions and introductions finished, we're ready for a massive battle or two and an action-packed third act.

Kevin is clearly not on board with the plan, but he tells He-Man that Lubic said he was heading to Charlie's music store to ask more questions about this mysterious Cosmic Key and its possible Soviet connections.

Our heroes reach Charlie's before Evil-Lyn's forces and Lubic is there, revolver in hand, demanding answers from these strangely dressed visitors. "How come I get the feeling I've been looking for you all night?" he asks, poking a finger at He-Man's bare chest.

As He-Man's attempts diplomacy, Teela kicks the gun out of Lubic's hands and snatches the Key away. Skeletor's forces are closing in. The clock is ticking down to Eternian moonrise, when the balance of cosmic power is set to shift. Gwildor is set to work on the Key, trying to find their coordinates home. Teela leads him and the humans into the back of the music shop, Lubic at gunpoint, as He-Man and Man-At-Arms fortify the storefront to prepare for battle.

Live-Action Comic Book

Evil-Lyn's flying transport has landed in the middle of the deserted, idyllic downtown. She tells Beastman to rally the troops and attack the music shop on her signal. Blade and Karg follow her off to prepare for a secret side mission.

Inside Charlie's, He-Man and Man-At-Arms have hunkered down behind a stack of amplifiers and keyboards. In the back room, Teela paces anxiously as Gwildor tinkers with the Cosmic Key, muttering to himself about the distances and melodies.

Beastman's black-clad troopers smash through the shop's windows and everyone starts shooting. The troops and musical instruments alike explode in showers of sparks. Our heroes are well-defended, but there are so many of them rushing in. He-Man and Man-At-Arms quip calmly as they toss grenades and dive for cover.

The entire music shop shootout is expertly filmed. The atmosphere is tense and imposing, letting the viewer know that their favorite action figures are better than these faceless soldiers, but they are still in danger of being overwhelmed. The camera shows us multiple perspectives in such an enclosed space, and the sparks erupting from the troopers look fantastic. In a movie so reverent of music, the destruction happening in Charlie's music shop is framed as especially monstrous.

In the back room, Gwildor explains the workings of the Cosmic Key to Kevin. The Thenorian is working hard on those coordinates, but he tells Teela he has no idea how long it will take him.

"I'd give all the chalconite in Fribillian if I could only spend two units with a master Songmaker!" he exclaims in frustration.

The Cosmic Key was better explained in earlier versions of the script. Each gravatonic tone Gwildor punches into the Key is a part of a time-space coordinate. By combining the right notes in the right order, the melody opens a doorway to the exact second and exact square foot he wants. Determining these notes is an exact science, and for a person like Gwildor, it requires a great deal of calculations. A master Songmaker, however, simply feels the music of the universe. They can complete the precise melody instinctively. Someone with such a magical power would make their path back to Eternia much easier.

Teela tosses the revolver to Kevin and hurries up to the front of the shop to assist He-Man and her father. Her addition to the music shop shootout makes a noticeable difference. Commenting on the need for a "woman's touch," she stands from behind their barricade of amplifiers and mows down a batch of troops in a shower of sparks.

She pops back down behind the barricade and, smirking at the camera, says, "Woman-At-Arms." *Masters* is occasionally awkward with its attempts at humor, but this is by far the most cringe-worthy.

In the back of the store, Julie looks out the window, where she sees a vision of her late mother standing in the alleyway fog. She quietly slips out the back door.

"Mother?" she asks. "But the plane...?"

"Oh, I'm so sorry you had to go through all that Julie," the woman tells her. "But we had to disappear! We're doing very important, very secret work...."

Gary Goddard has spoken many times about his intention of making *Masters of the Universe* as a "live-action comic book," and this plot twist is a prime example of the supernatural soap opera that entails. A character's parents faking their death while working on, apparently, top secret government work isn't far removed from the funny books. A very similar story is told a few years later in *Amazing Spider-Man* issue 366, in which Peter Parker's long-dead parents return with stories about being secret agents. They're later revealed to be robots. Just like that story, all is not as it appears in the alley behind Charlie's music shop.

Julie runs back into the store, snatching the Cosmic Key and bringing it to her "mother," who is then revealed to be Evil-Lyn.

A Low-Budget Invasion

With the Key in Evil-Lyn's hands, Beastman pulls his forces out of the music shop. The shootout moves to the back alley, where Skeletor's troops fire on our heroes, preventing them from chasing down Evil-Lyn and getting the Key back.

The squadron marches back to the parked transport. Evil-Lyn cradles the Key like a child, carefully typing in the coordinates for Eternia.

Finally able to pursue, He-Man and his friends are hurrying down the empty downtown streets when the wind whips up. A ghostly blue light is projected on them. They've seen this before—the formation of one of the Key's portals. The group scrambles to hide.

A marching, ominous theme swells as Skeletor's forces emerge into planet Earth. For all their comparisons to the Stormtroopers of *Star Wars*, those white-armored bad guys never looked as fascistic as these ones do. They march in perfect formation, holding their weapons in identical postures, their superior officers wearing capes to signify rank. The Air Centurions, troopers on flying discs, soar overhead. It's a massive military presence.

Finally, Skeletor arrives in his huge personal transport. He is seated on a throne inlaid with images of skulls and snakes, in front of a red glowing dish. "Contact Evil-Lyn," he growls, not looking particularly pleased with the mission's success.

A blue light projects on her face as she smiles faintly, reporting in. "I have the Key, my lord," Evil-Lyn says, clearly proud.

"And He-Man?" Skeletor cuts her off.

"He has eluded us."

"That will be all," he grunts, ending the transmission. As the blue light fades from Evil-Lyn, we can see her expression sinking. This moment may be it, the final slight that pushes her too far.

Back at Charlie's, Detective Lubic has acquired a shotgun but knows he needs backup. "It's an invasion," he proclaims.

It is and it isn't. There is clearly a military force assaulting the town, but almost nobody seems the wiser. The streets are empty. The shops are closed. This is played for chuckles at Lubic's expense later, but it's also a symptom of the budgetary restrictions of the project. We can have an invasion, but it can't become an invasion movie.

Curiously, no version of the script called for the town to be aware of Skeletor's incursion. Odell made mention of bystanders hiding behind their cars and running in terror. One brief scene was cut from the finished script that would have a young neighbor boy watching the mercenaries land their flying ship and break into Julie's. He watches excitedly, ignoring the unnamed "sci-fi fantasy cartoon show" on the television. When he tells his mother about the aliens and flying saucers, she turns off the TV and says, "I think you watch too much of this garbage, Jimmy."[8]

The Air Centurions chase our heroes through alleyways until He-Man steals one of their flying discs. He battles more Centurions in the air above the town, in a potentially exciting sequence which just never quite works out. The technology to make this look good doesn't seem to be available just yet. Or if it is, Cannon Films didn't provide the money or time to make it happen. It's worth noting a similar sequence is pulled off beautifully in another famously troubled production, 1991's *Highlander II: The Quickening.*

A Turn for the Worse

As He-Man uses Gwildor's grappling device to steal the Cosmic Key from Evil-Lyn, the rest of our heroes hurry through an apparently abandoned building to take shelter on the rooftop. Kevin and Julie huddle in the corner. Teela expresses concern for He-Man, as he should've joined them by now, and Gwildor explains to Man-At-Arms how his calculations for their return trip have been progressing.

All the while, Skeletor's massive flagship has been silently rising behind them.

"I only have two numbers left," Gwildor explains. "Once we get the Key back, we'll be gone within two pretons!"

"I think not, Gwildor!" booms Skeletor's voice. Our heroes whirl around and fire their blasters. Skeletor raises his hand and the bolts are harmlessly dissolved in his force field.

He is clearly growing more powerful as the story progresses, as his energy field saps the magic from the Sorceress back on Eternia, reducing her to a feeble old woman. He demands Man-At-Arms and Teela drop their weapons and, Teela a bit more reluctantly than her father, they comply. Given the budget, the rooftops around them are filling with a surprising number of armored trooper extras.

"I would never knowingly serve the lord of Snake Mountain," Gwildor proclaims. "Wait until He-Man arrives. He'll see to you."

He-Man, the villain gloats, is expected.

Skeletor's troopers circle our heroes and, at that moment, He-Man's flying disc follows the last Air Centurion up and over the rooftop. Shock dawns on his face as he sees all those soldiers waiting for him. It was a trap.

Julie rushes forward to warn He-Man. Skeletor raises his hand, and a purple lightning arcs from him fingertips. He-Man's flying disc is struck, along with Julie's exposed leg. Skeletor blasts again, hitting the Cosmic Key once it tumbles loose as He-Man crashes to the rooftop.

The troopers swarm He-Man. He fights through them, drawing his sword, just really cleaning house. Teela and Man-At-Arms begin to struggle, but are quickly reduced to hostages once more. Our hero, however, if having no such issues. In any other movie, this would be a serious issue.

Time and time again throughout the runtime of *Masters of the Universe*, it's proven that no one is greater than He-Man. In this scene, scary robot soldiers dog-pile on him and he throws them off by flexing. Having an invincible protagonist is the surest way to spoil any sense of danger in the narrative. But then again, this is He-Man. This is the melodrama of Good Vs. Evil on a cosmic, sci-fi / sword-and-sorcery scale. Of course he's stronger than the bad guys. He's the Most Powerful Man in the Universe.

In the end, He-Man has only one weakness, and it's one Skeletor knows to exploit. "One more move," he shouts from his floating ship, "and your friends will not live to see another day!"

And that's that.

He-Man allows himself to be shackled by the troopers under Evil-Lyn's command. The mercenary Blade beams excitedly as he collects He-Man's massive sword, and our heroes wish each other "Good journey" as He-Man is led away.

Man-At-Arms, Teela, and Gwildor are left to rot in this "primitive and tasteless planet" alongside Kevin and the injured Julie. Their prototype Cosmic Key is left behind, but Skeletor's magic has wiped Eternia coordinates. They're stranded.

What Exactly Is Going On Here?

Masters of the Universe moves quickly and avoids being bogged down by building the worlds and mythologies of the cartoon and toy line. It does, however, occasionally skip over establishing some important information.

"This is *our* fight," He-Man tells Skeletor on the rooftop, one of many references to the two's animosity. However, there's no explanation in the film of how this came about. We can infer that He-Man is the guardian of Castle Grayskull, but for all the focus given to Skeletor, we get very little of his motivation. He wants to rule the universe. Why exactly this is, or how he managed to amass his followers and robot army, aren't even hinted at.

In addition, we see very little of Eternia. We are shown the majestic throne room of Grayskull and the smoldering battlefields on those sideways rocks, but nothing of everyday life. We don't see the average Eternians that Skeletor addresses in the film's opening. We don't know how they feel about Skeletor, or about the Sorceress, who the main cast of heroes seem to treat as both a ruler and a deity. As we are without context, it's possible to view Skeletor as a liberator overthrowing a theocracy. Instead, we're supposed to embrace the simplicity of the narrative—Shirtless guy is good, skull-faced guy is bad.

A simple workaround for the light story-telling is to watch *Masters of the Universe* as a sequel to *He-Man and the Masters of the Universe*, the Filmation cartoon show. However, many fervent fans of the show never accepted the film as canon. There were too many differences, namely the lack of characters like Battle Cat and Orko, the assorted redesigns of costumes and characters, and the vastly different tone Goddard brought to this version.

In most of the films which followed *Masters*, audiences were treated to origin tales or rehashes of familiar stories from other media. Skewing closer to the source material in 1987 would have likely placated fans but, at the time, it's unclear if Hollywood would've known that. Much of what was learned from the making of this first action figure adaptation was what not to do.

Goddard and the screenwriters, Odell and Tolkin, may have been instructed to avoid the simplistic motivations and backstories of these characters. They may have also decided to sidestep these elements to focus on the action, even as a way of broadening appeal. The filmmakers were discovering how this new subgenre could work as they made the movie.

As Simple as Music

Back on Earth, the invasion is over. As soon as the Cosmic Key's massive portal fades, Detective Lubic is shown leading a group of cops around the empty streets. "They were here, I'm telling you," he shouts. "It was the damnedest thing you ever saw."

Left alone, Man-At-Arms, Teela, and Gwildor follow our Earthlings down to a small fountain. Everyone is concerned for Julie, as she's become feverish since struck with Skeletor's magic. The spot of her leg is a sizzling mass of blood and strange green pustules. The poison is already in her bloodstream, they tell Kevin. Only their Sorceress can heal her now, but the path back to Eternia is all but impossible.

"You see, Kevin," Gwildor gently explains, "opening a dimensional door is relatively easy. But the tones, Kevin. The tones that were stored in this Cosmic Key were completely erased."

Kevin brainstorms for a moment and then whistles the melody played by the Key whenever they've pressed the Energizer button. Gwildor and the Eternians watch in awe; remembering a catchy tune is as magical to them as their run-of-the-mill dimensional doors seem to us. A Songmaker is tantamount to wizardry.

Even with the praise heaped on him, Kevin's confidence falters when, on the bench beside him, Julie shifts and whimpers in pain. He's nothing special, he tells his new friends. "There's a million of me."

The Kevin Corrigan at the start of the third act is light-years from the Kevin Corrigan we meet in the first act. Initially introduced as a self-centered character, we watch the concern for Julie and his new friends blossom throughout the story. Our action figure characters are larger than life, Lubic is played for laughs, and Julie is a kind girl who misses her parents; Kevin is the only heroic character with an arc.

The villains, namely Skeletor and Evil-Lyn, are a different story. Goddard directed his focus from the less dynamic character, He-Man, and the less trained actor, Lundgren, to keep the camera on Langella's Skeletor as much as possible. The focus on Kevin is a less obvious creative choice, but his development helps make these new, original Earthling characters more interesting.

Gwildor hatches a scheme. Using spare Eternia technology Man-At-Arms and Teela have on them, they'll be able to jump-start the Key. As for coordinates, they now have a master Songmaker to supply the tones. Kevin rushes off to steal a keyboard from Charlie's demolished music shop. It's up to him, up to the magic of synthesizer-based '80s music, to save the day.

The Sad, True Story of Pig-Boy, Contest Winner

Back on Eternia, the villains march into Castle Grayskull triumphant. He-Man is there, bound as their captive. They march him down the long walkway to the throne. Skeletor is the lead, and he doesn't even pause mid-step to snatch his tall snakehead staff from a tiny green minion, a character seen only in this brief shot. Blink and you'll miss him.

Meet Pig-Boy.

As *Masters of the Universe* was in pre-production, Mattel announced a contest for one lucky fan to win a part in the film. Children across the country saw the toy advertisements and rushed to fill out the entry forms. Soon a winner was announced: eight-year-old Richard Szponder from Chicago, Illinois.

As Mattel finalized the paperwork with Szponder's family, Goddard and the crew began scrambling to find a way to fit him in. No such roles had been prepared. There were no parts for children in this children's movie.

In the DVD commentary, Goddard laughs when the character makes his appearance. "The way the contest came down," he explains, "by the time we got to the final sequences, when this kid was actually flown out to be in the movie, we are essentially in Eternia. So the only way for the kid to appear in Eternia, based on the way the script was written, was to put him in some kind of character makeup or costume."[9]

"Prior to arriving in California, I had no idea how they would fit me into the film," Szponder said in a 2010 interview. "During one of our first visits to the studio, we were taken on a tour where I was shown concept drawings for the Pigboy character."[10]

At a point in the production when time, money, and tempers were running short, this contest was a promise that needed to be fulfilled. Mattel paid for the Szponder family to be flown out to California for nine days, along with various sightseeing trips to keep everyone else occupied while Richard was on set. Limousines were hired. A tutor was brought on to keep the boy current on his schoolwork.

Just as it was for Billy Barty and the other actor working in costumes, it took several hours each day to transform Szponder into Pig-Boy. Adhesives used to attach the mask left his face burning for days.

"Being in full makeup and costume probably made the whole experience easier," he said. "I don't remember being particularly nervous, and I do remember that everyone on set seemed excited to have me there. They were all very encouraging and helpful and treated me like a professional."

Pig-Boy can first be spotted in the background of the scene early on as he brings Skeletor's staff to the throne. After his close-up, however, he disappears.

"When the scene was filmed," Szponder said, "Skeletor grabbed the staff from me, turned to look at me, and shouted, 'Now leave!' I then scurried off. When I first saw the film in the theater, I actually missed my scene. I was expecting something much more significant than what ended up in the film."

The young would-be actor still recalls his disappointment that day in the theater. "What was even more disappointing, though, was when the film was first aired on television. The portion of the scene where I appeared was cut altogether!"

Brutality

He-Man is shackled in the throne room before a gloating Skeletor. The mercenary Blade hands over He-Man's sword, eliciting a look of shock from the Sorceress, who has become withered and drained from the force field. The Sword of Grayskull is sheathed in a blinking gizmo next to the throne. Moonrise, the final component of this techno-mystical ceremony, is imminent. "Our lifelong battle is ending at last," Skeletor proclaims, "in the only way it could."

But acquiring all the powers of the universe isn't enough for the villain. He orders the holo-spheres activated again, so that when the power is bestowed upon him, the planet can watch He-Man kneel to him.

He-Man, understandably, refuses.

That's when Blade moves behind him, activating a glowing red laser whip. Skeletor watches with delight as his enemy is flogged.

The scene was filmed with De Longis only holding the handle while the laser whip was inserted in post-production. "They wanted to show off their special effects," he's since stated. "Frankly, I prefer real skills done in real time. I think it provides a character credibility and offers the audience more emotional investment and ultimately a more satisfying moviegoing experience."[11]

The laser whip sequence is considered one of the most memorable points in the film. Like the Air Centurion set-piece earlier, it's a fun, high concept sci-fi idea, but the execution falters. The arc of the bright red laser whip doesn't match the movements of De Longis's arm at several moments, and when Lundgren moves to react to the "impact" of the whip, it doesn't seem to match up either.

On Eternia, the clock is counting down. "The moon rises to its apex," one of Skeletor's robot troops announces.

"Ah! Do you hear?" In a tight close-up, Skeletor taunts the captive, bloodied He-Man. "The alpha and the omega. Death and rebirth. And as you die, so will I be reborn!"

Equality in Cosmic Power

The giant circular window behind the throne whirs open to show the night sky. Skeletor turns to face it triumphantly.

The great eye of the universe is opening, shown as balls of glowing golden energy flying down into the throne room. They spiral around Skeletor before being absorbed into his pale skull face. He describes the feeling to his audience as his body begins to glow with golden power.

"Of what consequence are you now?" he says, spitting his laughter. "This planet, these people ... they are nothing to me! The universe is power! Pure, unstoppable power! And I am that force, I am that power!"

Although we can assume he's speaking to He-Man, he seems to be addressing the entire throne room. As power-mad as Skeletor has always seemed, he's now proclaiming himself a god. Evil-Lyn visibly gulps.

Goddard seems to have turned Frank Langella loose in this scene. Skeletor comes into his own with some delicious chewing of scenery, interspersed with reaction shots of his overwhelmed cronies.

"I actually didn't want to cut away from him at all," Goddard said. "I think he did a brilliant performance. The cut-aways I reluctantly agreed to. The studio felt we needed them, but I really felt this was a scene we could stay with Frank for the whole performance."[12]

That golden glow surrounding Skeletor becomes a blinding flash of light. Everyone covers their eyes except for Evil-Lyn. When the light fades, Skeletor has changed. His dark robes have been replaced by shiny golden armor. His hood has become a tall, ostentatious helmet covered with spines, spikes, horns and a pair of bat wings.

For all his transformations and newfound power, he's still the same petty Skeletor. "Now, kneel!" he screams at the captive He-Man. That cosmic power blasts from his eyes, striking He-Man's bare chest.

That golden energy suggests something. Gold is the color of power, not of good or evil. Castle Grayskull, as we're told by the opening narration, is at the direct center of the darkness and the light of the universe. Just as the massive throne room shows both the statues of the benevolent "Gods of Technology" and the dark, sinister-looking pits and sub-levels, this cosmic power is similarly neutral. The banners hanging throughout, which have typically been the same dark, regal purple as He-Man's cape, are now that same shiny gold color.

Skeletor has finally won. He is now free to use all the powers of the universe for his nefarious purposes.

Coming to Eternia

Back on Earth, Gwildor's plan is coming together. Kevin plays the melody on a keyboard as blue electrical energy arcs around the Cosmic Key. As the light flashes, the beginning moments of their dimensional portal, the persistent Detective Lubic jumps out with a shotgun. He threatens arrest. Teela pulls out her blaster. Lubic reaches for Kevin as he frantically plays the keyboards...

Meanwhile, Skeletor is taunting He-Man, asking where his friends are, when his friends arrive. A lightning-crackling portal flashes in the throne room, and suddenly there is a chunk of Earth around our returning heroes, including portions of sidewalk, brick facade, Cadillac, and a very bewildered detective Lubic.

Much of this sequence changed from the original script, as well. Initially, He-Man was not taken back to Earth as Skeletor's captive. He was stranded on Earth with his friends, only to come back to save the day as everyone might expect. Perhaps this level of predictability is what caused these changes. Instead, the audience is shown He-Man being brutalized, so his lowest point comes from torture and humiliation instead of simple powerlessness.

Instead, the heroes and the Earthlings appear right in the thick of the action for their rescue mission. Skeletor's forces open fire on them. They take cover behind their borrowed Earthling structures to shoot back.

He-Man, realizing Skeletor won't keep his pledge to let the others live, breaks free rather easily. Though his back has become bloodied from Blade's lashes, it suddenly appears he's been playing possum this whole time. He escapes as soon as he realizes he can and begins smashing his way through the robotic troopers. Skeletor blasts at him with his extra powerful golden lightning, but it becomes evident that even now the two aren't equals.

As the shootout rages, our Earthlings join in. Protecting the injured Julie, Kevin is seen brandishing an Eternian pistol. Lubic calls the troopers "Pinkos" and begins dispatching them with his shotgun. Though the odds are clearly against them, perhaps due to the element of surprise, our heroes are gaining the upper hand. Again, it's unclear whether He-Man actually needs any of the "cover action" Man-At-Arms and the others are providing. He seems to be taking out the bulk of the army on his own.

Evil-Lyn, Karg and Beastman are seen backing toward the door before flat-out leaving. The production team didn't view this as a cowardly retreat. It was more of them washing their hands of Skeletor and his mad war. Evil-Lyn had been spurned one time too many.

He-Man is battling his way through the troopers to get to Skeletor, and his Power Sword. Overwhelmed in the midst of the robots, mercenaries, and laser crossfire, he takes cover behind one of those towering statues and decides to push it over, scattering the villains. He-Man was typically shown as absurdly super-strong in the cartoons, strong enough to push moon out of their orbits even, and this live-action moment is a remnant of that.

Duel

He-Man rushes past Skeletor to collect the sword of Grayskull from the contraption beside the throne. Skeletor blasts at him, and He-Man is shown struggling briefly as the golden lighten strikes him. But he doesn't let go of that hilt.

He soon pulls the sword free with a flash of light, and holds it over his head to shout the trademark, "I have the power!" The music swells. The lights glare and people watch in awe.

But he doesn't give the full catchphrase, *"By the power of Grayskull, I have the power,"* only the last bit. In previous versions of the *Masters* script, He-Man swears by the power of Grayskull on several occasions. For example, on the rooftops after the Air Centurion sequence, the hero was meant to draw his glowing sword and say, "By the power of Greyskull, [sic] I challenge you, Skeletor. Here and now."[13] It's unclear why this well-known phrase was removed by the time filming rolled around.

"Let this be our final battle!" Skeletor shouts and, in one blinding instant, his staff connects with He-Man's sword. Blue and yellow glows emanate from the weapons and, sudden, those are the only lights left in the room. Everything else fades away.

The change in lighting isn't the only difference. The room seems to have cleared out, giving the two more room for their duel. There's no tripping over blasted robot bodies. The camera work has altered as well. Gone are the smooth, sweeping dolly shots, replaced now with jerky steadicam and close-ups. Things suddenly look much more like a music video from the era.

The man inside Skeletor's golden armor has changed as well. Filling in for Langella is the Blade actor and *Master's* fight choreographer, Anthony De Longis.

De Longis recalled filming this sequence in a 2010 interview. He had been working with Dolph Lundgren to make the fight appear even between the hero and villain. "I designed some practical but very complex and flowing attacks and defenses," he said, "to give Skeletor's character credibility by pitting He-Man against a worthy opponent."

But this did not work out as planned. The choreography had begun before the design for Skeletor's armor had been finalized, and the size of the helmet wasn't revealed to De Longis until the day of filming. "I couldn't wield the staff around my head or even efficiently around my body without clipping the projecting horns," he said.[14]

The fight needed to be reworked on the spot, as production could not waste a single moment at this point. This sequence was the very last to be filmed.

In the end, He-Man breaks Skeletor's staff, severing his connection to his cosmic power. He-Man, ever heroic, hesitates, unwilling to kill his adversary. Skeletor, ever villainous, takes advantage by attacking him with a hidden sword of his own. By now the two have edged close to one of Grayskull's many bottomless pits. Through no fault of the virtuous He-Man, Skeletor slips over the edge. Just like the death of the Filmation Faker character in "The Shaping Staff," care was taken to make sure He-Man's hands are unbloodied in the end.

In the throne room, the lights come back on. The crackling force field around the Sorceress fades, and she is seen at her proper young age once more. The rest of He-Man's allies cautiously peek over the top of that pink Cadillac. "Victory!" they shout.

Exhausted, the hero nods in agreement. "Victory."

Cue the Happy Ending

There's a dissolve, indicating an undisclosed amount of time has passed. Castle Grayskull's throne room has been repaired to its former glory. Man-At-Arms' Eternian guards stand throughout as He-Man leads Kevin and Julie to the throne. The Sorceress is seated at her rightful place, surrounded by Man-At-Arms, Teela, Gwildor, and Detective Lubic. A woman in a shimmering toga is standing at his side. He has decided to stay.

"What am I going to go back there for?" he asks the incredulous Kevin. "And look what I got here, I got a castle, I got a view, I got clean air, I got a beautiful woman.... It's some kind of retirement, eh?"

The Sorceress gives Julie a small token of their planet's affection—a glowing blue ball surrounded by a golden ring. The two humans look around, eyes growing misty. Hugs are exchanged. "Don't say 'goodbye,'" Teela tells Julie. "Say 'good journey.'"

According to Gary Goddard, much of this scene ended up on the cutting room floor. Despite the longer sequence being well received by test audiences, the studio wanted to wrap up this epilogue quickly. "Essentially," he said, "Julie has a 'moment' with each of her Eternian companions, leading to her departure. That scene got cut in half—and I think—we lost the heart of the moment."[15]

This scene was clearly a favorite of Goddard's. In the DVD commentary he refers to it as "a little homage to *Wizard of Oz*." Visually, it does resemble the scene when Dorothy prepares to board the hot air balloon back to Kansas. Gwildor's wild red hair is even adorned with bows and ribbons like the Cowardly Lion's was. But the scene is brief. Julie, our "Dorothy," speaks each companion's name but isn't allowed the time to share what important life lessons they've taught her.

He-Man calls for the portal to Earth to be opened. Gwildor approaches, the Cosmic Key in hand. "Are you sure you don't want to go back in your planet's history?" he asks them. Though never stated before this on screen, the Key is also a time machine.

Our Earthlings politely refuse, simply wanting to go home. The doorway opens in the middle of the throne room and Kevin and Julie make their way toward it. The Eternians call out a last "Good journey" as they step into the light. Suddenly, Julie turns back to shout, "No, wait Gwildor! Send us back, back before..." as the portal's whooshing sounds drown her voice out.

The lights flash and fade, the music rescinds to birdsong, and Julie wakes up in her own bed. Everything is in place, not packed up for her move, not trashed by Skeletor's troopers. She sits up in bed, wearing a large, white, full-length nightdress as a visual symbol of our return to innocence.

It's easy to spot Goddard's allusion to the *Wizard of Oz* in this epilogue, but the messages don't quite sync up. In that classic 1939 musical, Dorothy returns home to the drab sepia-toned Kansas farmhouse to realize how good her life was before she went off on a magical adventure. In *Masters of the Universe*, however, Julie's life had been pretty awful before the adventure. She's sent back in time to correct something that was done before the film even started. We only get a happy ending because of He-Man.

Her mother and father are downstairs in the kitchen. They seem surprised when she rushes in, hugging them and sobbing with joy. She's returned to the infamous day, the day she lied to spend time with Kevin, leading to her parents' tragic plane crash. She grabs their plane keys and flight logs, backing toward the door. "I love you!" she cries happily and rushes outside.

In the middle of the street, Kevin Corrigan is waiting for her. He remembers the films events, too. It wasn't a dream.

They look down at the glowing blue ball in his hands. "Eternia," Julie breathes.

In the ball, an image appears. We see the tall, gothic facade of Castle Grayskull and then, overtop of it, He-Man lifting his sword triumphantly and calling out, "I have the power!"

But Don't Forget About...

After the credits, out of steaming, bubbling muck at the bottom of the pits of Grayskull, Skeletor's gleaming white head pops up.

"I'll be back!" he promises the viewers with an evil grin.

6

The Terror
of Post-Production

The finished product very nearly wasn't finished.

Almost immediately, the film's crew found themselves behind schedule. Even with the more mundane locations on Earth and the reduced budget Cannon Films had planned for, *Masters of the Universe* would be a special effects driven movie. Especially in the mid–1980s, this was a costly and laborious process that took plenty of time. There was also the matter of set and costume designs, needed to represent the alien and varied nature of the Eternian creatures and characters. Sci-fi/fantasy films with such a scope required a year of pre-production work, minimum, before the camera even began rolling. *Masters* was given two months.

Complicating matters further, the script still wasn't finalized when filming began. Director Gary Goddard had expanded the film's story to include Eternian settings as well as those on Earth, but how much they'd have the time to film, let alone the money to design, was up in the air. As everyone involved began feeling the crunch, many ideas were left by the wayside. The story was streamlined to make filming move faster, and an entire sequence or two were dropped.

Early into production, Goddard scrapped a plan for He-Man and his friends to take a more circuitous route back into Castle Grayskull for the finale. Instead of the hotwired Cosmic Key sending the group directly into the throne room, they would appear outside the castle's walls. After spotting Snake Mountain in the distance, the group would utilize the network of caves beneath Grayskull to sneak back inside, as they had in the first act. It would not be an easy trip this time. The caverns were due to be full of Snake Men, who had joined with Skeletor's forces once he'd taken control of the planet. As Goddard recalled the sequence: "The heroes are dragged into the tunnels and a lot of action takes place amid the tension of them trying to escape from the caverns."[1]

After defeating the Snake Men, the group of heroes would find themselves in Grayskull's dungeon, where more members of He-Man's resistance had been imprisoned by Skeletor. This would include new characters to be used in future toy lines, named in the script as Wizaroid, Blastar, Mandroid, Nettor, and Mirroman. Also due to be included, as a treat for fans, He-Man's sister She-Ra. "I was disappointed when She-Ra was cut," said production designer William Stout.[2] He had designed a new costume for her, which Goddard and many on the crew were excited to see on screen.

These last-minute additions would bolster He-Man's crew when they engaged Skeletor's troops in the throne room, and make for a more epic battle scene. The scenes and characters were cut from the script as filming was beginning, which took some weight off of the production teams. Their removal likely improved the pacing of the finished product, as well. With no detours or important characters added late into the story, the heroes show up quickly to save He-Man and keep the plot moving along smoothly. This also kept the movie from appearing like too much of a toy commercial.

Another alteration to the script cost the film a reference to the franchise's other incarnations. In the depths of Castle Grayskull, Earthlings Kevin and Julie would've been shown an American flag. They would've been told that Eternians were descended from the NASA astronauts who came to the planet in their future. This would be shocking for the characters but familiar to audiences who had already seen this explained in the comic books, or the Paul Dini written *He-Man and the Masters of the Universe* episode "Teela's Quest." Goddard was not overly fond of the American flag reveal, saying he'd already seen such a thing done on *Star Trek*.

Introducing the element of time travel at this point could have established the full power of the Cosmic Key for the film's conclusion. This scene was likely dropped later in production, as it appears in Marvel's Star Comics adaptation.

Such cuts and alterations were necessary to keep production costs down and shorten filming time. Losing the American flag and the battle with the Snake Men helped things, but it wouldn't be enough.

Pre-production was still underway as filming began. In order to give Stout and his production team time to complete their costumes and set construction, Goddard began filming the Earth sequences first. They

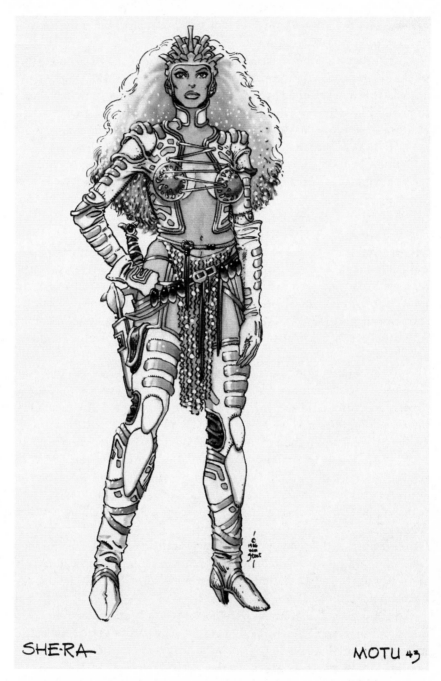

SHE·RA   MOTU 43

William Stout's design for a live-action She-Ra. She was omitted from the film to the disappointment of all. (Courtesy William Stout.)

started where He-Man and his allies landed in the forest, as it required no sets. Everything in the massive throne room set was saved for last, and it was still barely completed in time. "I was designing to the last week of shooting," Stout lamented.[3]

The two months' head start the designers had was not nearly enough, but it was more than was allotted for the special effects. The SFX cinematographer Richard Edlund, Academy Award winner and founder of Boss Film Corp., estimated their working time at seven weeks.

According to Edlund, Cannon Films had grossly underestimated the budget for such an effects-heavy film. The script revisions almost doubled the number of SFX shots Boss Film Corp. had signed up for. This, in turn, pushed the budget higher. "Well, it was originally placed as a $15 million production," Edlund said, "but it went about half-again over that."[4]

With a rising budget and a production struggling to keep up with their deadlines, Golan and Globus began turning up the pressure on their first-time director.

Cannon Films was under pressure, as well. Goddard said he later learned that, as they were filming, the company was mere months away from filing for Chapter 11 bankruptcy.[5] Every delay in filming, every extra SFX shot, every move that wasn't pinching pennies or cutting corners were moves that were costing money Golan and Globus didn't have to spend. All they wanted was a finished product to release, fast, to make enough money to continue rolling along.

Desperation was also mounting for Mattel. They started the wheels of a live-action He-Man film in 1985, when the franchise was still in its golden age, but that age was quickly coming to an end. On the air, Filmation's *He-Man and the Masters of the Universe* cartoon was only airing in reruns. The episodes were under siege from competitors like *Transformers* and *GI Joe*, other cross-media brands who had learned their tricks from the Most Powerful Man in the Universe. Ratings were beginning to slide.

Comparatively, toy sales were in an all-out freefall. As the toy lines expanded to include more figures and more expensive vehicles and play-sets with each successive wave, Mattel had begun shipping more and more figures to toy stores, anticipating the demand would continue its exponential growth. In *Mastering the Universe*, Roger Sweet blamed the downfall of the brand on "all of those product-loaded pallets that were dumped on all of those toy store shelves."[6]

After years of under-shipping their toy lines, causing an often frenzied demand, the company overcorrected just as disinterest was setting in, or perhaps causing that colder response. Suddenly, there was too much

He-Man on the shelves. Stores began cutting prices just to get some free space for other merchandise. Needless to say, this volume-driven method was not winning the company any friends in the world of retail. While they were struggling and losing money to sell off their Masters of the Universe stock, the demand for toys like Teenage Mutant Ninja Turtles were rising.

Toy stores weren't the only ones growing frustrated with Mattel's sales tactics. Parents, even the ones who never considered the Filmation cartoon to be mere marketing, began complaining about the waves of Masters of the Universe adding more and more figures along with the expensive playsets. There were more toys for children to clamor for, and the costs were adding up to the adults holding the checkbooks.

This was pushed even further in 1986 when the company rebranded its '70s novelty item "Slime." One playset for the He-Man wave of that year was Hordak's Slime Pit, a spooky and fairly cheap set-up where kids could trap a figure in place and dump the bright green gunk over their heads. Each playset came with a can of Slime to use. The Slime, however, was not available for sale on its own. If children wanted more, they would need to have their folks buy a new Slime Pit, or buy two new Masters of the Universe figures at $6 each to get a "free" can. The Slime was treated as an extraneous add-in to the figures instead of the thing consumers really wanted.

As the grown-ups grumbled, marketing experts began to chime in. Michael Kamins, an assistant marketing professor at USC, said "They're positioning it as a bonus, clouding the issue. It's not really a bonus, and as a strategy, it's manipulative. You only need a can of Slime, and you have to buy two figures to get it."[7]

For all the money Mattel made on their "free" Slime, they ended up paying plenty out, as well. After accidents occurred while children played with the goop, "many Slime-soiled carpets were bought at Mattel's expense."[8] Paying to replace carpets didn't endear the company with parents, though. For many, they'd had just about enough of He-Man.

After an amazing sales year in 1986, grossing over $400 million, in 1987, sales plummeted to just $7 million.[9]

With a laugh, Goddard recalled the day Mattel executives showed up at the set. They frantically pulled the director into a room and told him about the disastrous toy sales. Now, everything depended to the film being successful; if he made them a hit action movie, they'd see the bump in their sales of the next Masters of the Universe wave, and He-Man would be saved. Goddard took the opportunity to remind the executives of their stringent rules.

"And I said, 'Well, we're doing the best we can. But you know, we're also trying to obey all these rules...' And one of them goes, 'We don't care what you do! We don't care what you do! Have him kill people! Have blood, guts, gore, sex! Do whatever you have to, just make sure this movie is a hit!'"[10]

As the young director did his best, Mattel's ambitions were also being stymied on another front. According to Mattel's Joe Morrison, "What was it like dealing with Cannon? Those guys were crazy. And they were running out of money."[11]

According to some, the 50 / 50 deal worked out between the two companies called for Mattel to pay for their half of production first. This amount covered much of the preproduction and the beginning of filming. It didn't last long. As William Stout remembered, "So Mattel said, 'Okay, it's time for you to kick in that second half,' and Cannon said, 'No.'"[12]

Morrison disputed this. "Contrary to some beliefs," he said, "Mattel never put up any money for the film. But what we did do was this: I can't remember the exact figure overall, but it was either a million or a half-million that Cannon paid us as a rights fee. But whatever it was, they had only paid us half up front."[13] When funds were running short and things began to grind to a halt, the executives had to waive payments for the rights fee so Cannon could have enough money to continue.

Whatever assistance Mattel had given, the film's future was far from certain. "There were shooting weeks when the crew threatened to stop because money was not in the bank to cover their checks," Goddard said. He would call Golan and Globus and plead with the crew to wait until the end of the day before quitting, "and in the end—the money did come through."[14] With the crew growing disillusioned, Goddard tried his best to keep the cast from learning about the film's rocky financial footing. The last thing he wanted was his actors, several of whom were fairly untrained, worrying about getting paid instead of focusing on their performances.

The money Cannon Films was spending on *Masters of the Universe* is another issue altogether. Just as the studio used the occasional profitable film to cover its losses on the others, it would also use money earmarked on other projects for whatever else needed funds.

Cash for all projects were communal in nature, treated like a pot the producers could dip their hands into as required. Because of this, listed budgets for Cannon movies vary slightly from source to source. These vagaries in accounting were also exacerbated by more substantial communication breakdowns. At times even Globus would not be aware of the film projects his cousin was financing from the studio's communal pot. The numbers were all a bit squirrelly, which was another factor that led to the SEC's investigation.[15]

Much of the money in the company's coffers at this point came from Warner Brothers. Looking for another bankable name for their next attempt at a surefire blockbuster, Cannon Films paid Ilya and Alexander Salkind to sublet their cinematic rights to the Superman character. After the disastrous reception of Salkind's last two Superman projects, 1983's Richard Pryor vehicle *Superman III* and 1984's *Supergirl*, the producers were happy to get money without needing to risk making another installment themselves. Instead, Cannon would pay them for the privilege of taking such a risk. And if, by chance, "the public had grown tired of the series, Cannon would absorb any losses."[16] The deal, worth $5 million, was happily signed over one of Golan and Globus's infamous trips to Cannes.

Recent box office dentings aside, Superman was still a respected and marketable brand name. Cannon's own Superman film could draw on the worldwide recognition, but the producers knew they'd need the "real" Superman to lend their installment credibility. Christopher Reeve had hung up his tights by this point, so dissatisfied with the production of *Superman III* he dropped out of a planned cameo in *Supergirl*. But living in the Man of Steel's shadow was tough, and he was having trouble finding the funding for a gritty journalist film he wanted to make. Cannon talked him into reprising his most famous role by promising to fund the dream project, 1987's *Street Smart*, and by allowing him a great deal of creative control over *Superman IV*'s script. He was given a "Story By" credit, as he ensured the film would revolve around the important real-world problem of nuclear proliferation.

Warner Brothers paid out $40 million to Cannon to make the film, and the Superman project immediately began a nosedive. The cash was grabbed up by the 30 other movies in production until less than half was left to go toward what it was intended for. By generous estimates, the budget for *Superman IV: The Quest for Peace* became $17 million.

The impact was immediately felt. Experienced crew members were fired and replaced with cheap, inexperienced Israelis. The money for special effects was slashed, leaving visible wires for flight and the same blue screen shots repeated over and over throughout. Filming was restricted to the Cannon-owned Elstree Studios, north of London, and the production took a short trip up the M1 in an attempt to make Milton Keyes double as New York City.

Everyone involved was growing frustrated, but none more so than Christopher Reeve. He could see the "important" film he set out to make falling apart as its budget evaporated. Despite everything Warner Brothers had contributed, suddenly the filmmakers couldn't afford to do much of anything. "They're coach tourists who want first-class service," Reeve said of Golan and Globus. "They'll nickel-and-dime you on paper clips."[17]

Though the actual accounting numbers aren't available to confirm, it has been generally accepted that much of *Superman IV*'s money went toward keeping *Masters of the Universe* afloat. It's impossible to know for sure, as Cannon Films was going bankrupt and they had so many films in the works at the time, but *Masters* was the only other bigger budget production at that same time. They would be released within two weeks of each other.

Masters of the Universe was in the last phase of filming, the sequences inside of the massive Eternian throne room set, when the threats began. Golan and Globus told the crew to begin wrapping things up. The production would be coming to a close, Cannon said, whether they were done filming or not.

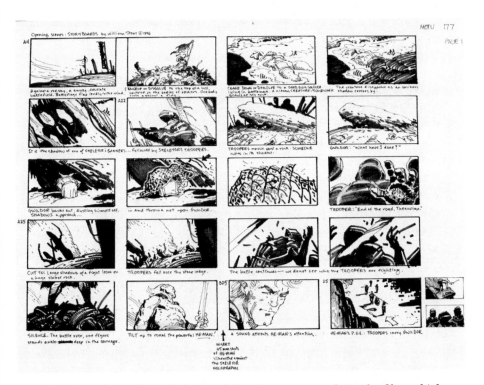

William Stout's storyboards from a deleted sequence early in the film, which would've been the first introduction to He-Man. (Courtesy William Stout.)

The only thing remaining was the climactic battle itself. Things had already been streamlined by Man-At-Arms, Teela, Gwildor, and the humans appearing in the middle of the throne room, but more trimming needed to be done to finish in time. The crew did their best to rush through the effects-heavy shoot-out scene. In an effort to hurry things along, Goddard devised a big show of strength from He-Man, something genuinely super-heroic to make up for less screen time spent on the battle. The Most Powerful Man in the Universe would now push over one of the giant throne room statues, scattering Skeletor's troops. It would work as an impressive moment, hopefully wowing the audience enough to not mind the story skipping ahead to He-Man and Skeletor's climactic duel.

Their "final battle," as Langella's Skeletor proclaims it, had already gone through several changes. In earlier drafts of the script, Odell had the two battle their way out of the throne room, onto a landing pad, and then onto the rooftops of the capital city of Eternos. In another draft, as evidenced by the depiction in the Star Comics adaptation,[18] the two wind up on the roof of Castle Grayskull. Standing atop the skull of Grayskull, Skeletor kneels and feigns surrender, only to hurl He-Man over the side. The hero clings for dear life as Skeletor cries out, "Now I am master of the universe!"

Suddenly, Skeletor is struck by a rock. In the panel itself, it's difficult to trace the origin of this action. The way the motion and impact lines of Mike Zeck's artwork merge, it could be a chunk of Grayskull, broken free by He-Man and thrown upward. The panel before, it does appear our hero's hand is grasping for something. More likely, however, is that the rock was thrown from behind. Evil-Lyn, the spurned second-in-command, is visible behind Skeletor, in the perfect position to throw. This would certainly complete her character arc as witnessed in the film: after giving everything to Skeletor and finding herself an eternal runner-up to his ambition, instead of taking the henchmen and escaping, she sucker-punches him once he's finally gotten everything he wanted.

As Skeletor falls forward, down the face of Grayskull, He-Man reaches out and catches him. He-Man hangs there, holding his enemy, and says that now that the war is over, perhaps they can make peace between them. "Keep your peace!" Skeletor responds. "Keep your mercy!" And he lets himself fall into the pits below Grayskull's jaw-bridge.

It's clear to see why this climax was changed in the script stage of the project. A fight across the top of Castle Grayskull would require another large set, complete with a blue screen backdrop to portray the alien night sky of Eternia. Having the characters hanging from the side of a massive building would cause problems of its own, as well. In the finished film, we only get one view of the castle from the outside, and it's clearly a matte painting. All of the Grayskull scenes take place inside the castle, in that one soundstage. Even for a production that was less cash-strapped than *Masters*, such a sequence would be very difficult.

Early on, Goddard changed the finale to be resolved inside the throne room to save money and design time. As Skeletor's master plan now revolved around "the Great Eye of the galaxy" and the circular portal behind Grayskull's throne, that became the instrument of his demise. After the one-on-one fight with He-Man, Skeletor would be pushed back through the portal and consumed by the powers of the universe he was trying to master.

As the filmmakers' clock was counting down, this elaborate annihilation for their villain was jettisoned. There wasn't much time to find a replacement, though.

By this point, Cannon had given the production a one-day notice. Get the shots finished and turn out the lights, because the set was getting shut down. The problem was there was much more than one day's left of material to film. The crew hunkered down and tried to get as much done as they would be allowed to.

"I knew we were running short on time," the director recalled. "I told the [director of photography], 'I want you to basically kill the lights on the soundstage and just let them fade to darkness.'" The new idea to save time would be to film the fight under dimmer lighting, not showing off the massive throne room set and the dozens of extras in armor. The camera would not require such timely set-ups and the crew could film more in less time. As Goddard envisioned it, He-Man's Power Sword meets Skeletor's Havoc Staff, and "the power [of the clash] is so much that it saps the power from everything and then we're in this dark void, and that's where I can do whatever I got to do to get us to the end."[19]

As the lights faded, effects were added for the sword to shine a blinding blue-white while Skeletor's staff crackled with his stolen cosmic energy. Abbreviating the action called for an additional special effects shot, another one Boss Film hadn't signed up for. The budget ticked upward slightly once again.

Fight choreographer Anthony De Longis, who was standing in for Frank Langella as Skeletor's fight double, worked with Lundgren to throw together a quick routine. In the dark, in Skeletor's bulky golden costume and vision-restricting helmet, De Longis struggled to make the action look good. "I literally couldn't see the stairs or the ground where I was fighting," he said. Between the leather-soled boots and a slippery film left on the ground from the smoke machines, "it was like fighting on an ice precipice."[20]

The set was kept dim and misty, illuminated by a spinning color wheel in the background. The expensive throne room was barely visible in the sequence. The two fighters did not utilize much of the soundstage's space, either. "It's a shame," Stout said, "because I had really designed that set for sword fighting. I made sure there were ups and downs and over and unders and all kinds of ways it could be used to get most out of this battle."[21]

But there simply wasn't the time. After filming "random battle footage" for about three hours, the *Masters of the Universe* was shut down.

"They weren't going to let us shoot the final battle," the director said. "How can you have an ending without that final battle between He-Man and Skeletor?"[22]

Goddard's completed footage showed He-Man battling Skeletor in the darkened room. Then the hero gets the upper hand and cuts through the golden Havoc Staff. That was it. The film would pick back up in the throne room with a restored Sorceress and there would be no mention of Skeletor. There was no actual resolution to their epic confrontation between good and evil. The people from Cannon Films appeared to be more concerned with getting the film released than finished.

According to Goddard, "At one point, the Cannon guys, Golan and Globus, said, 'It doesn't matter. It doesn't matter, you know? They'll fight. They'll just fight, and then we'll just fade out.'"[23]

Not giving up, the young director kept after the studio to let him finish the picture. After three or four months they acquiesced, but with a condition: Goddard would need to put up the money. "I can laugh now but it was not so funny then," he said.[24]

A new finale was devised, something they could shoot in one day's time. It would be quick and not particularly elegant, but it could tie all of the footage together and have the hero dispatch the villain.

According to Goddard: "Cannon still owed me $100,000 per my contract. The shoot was going to cost just a little over that. They said, 'You put up $50k from your salary and we will match it.' I couldn't believe it. I said, 'This is YOUR movie—and there is NO ENDING.' But they were serious so I said yes. So they kept 50K of my salary, matched it, and we got that day I needed to finish the movie."[25]

The cameras quickly rolled for the one last sequence, Skeletor drained of his cosmic power and attempting to trick He-Man into letting his guard down. There would be no time or resources for the villain to be sucked out of the circular portal, so Goddard settled for having him fall into one of the giant pits in the throne room. They had been there the whole time via matte paintings, so it was a fairly seamless correction. It did lead to another unfortunate *Star Wars* comparison, though, as Skeletor's fall looks a lot like that of The Emperor in 1983's *Return of the Jedi*.

With the additional day of filming finished, Cannon had enough to cut together into a full, complete film that Goddard was happy to put his name on. "I was just pleased that we ended up with a beginning, middle and end," Stout said. "That was kind of a shock to me, because I wasn't sure we had that."[26]

However cash-strapped, Cannon Film's self-promotional machines raged on. Golan and Globus advertised *Masters of the Universe* at the Cannes Film Festival that year with large banners, as proud of it as they were of the more artistic faire they were debuting, including *Barfly* and *Tough Guys Don't Dance*. Whenever asked, and frequently when they weren't, the producers said *Masters* would be "the Star Wars of the '80s."[27] Other marketing Cannon investigated, such as corporate tie-ins with Sunshine Hydrox cookies and Burger King, never materialized. Still, the film prominently displays Burger King cups and wrappers in one scene.

Mattel chipped in where they could, with advertising the film through a contest on action figure packaging, and with coverage in the monthly *He-Man and the Masters of the Universe Magazine*. The *Masters of the Universe* comic book rights had since changed from DC to Marvel's Star Comics line. The new series would be ending with issue 13 in 1987, they would also release a one-shot comic book adaptation of the movie.

The sixth wave of action figures would tie-in as well, offering plastic versions of Gwildor, Saurod, and Blade. The latter made a curious addition to the previous figures, as instead of brightly colored and animal themed, he was covered in chain mail and knives. The toys took longer to make than movie did, leading to some interesting discrepancies. Saurod, in particular, translated poorly from Stout's detailed costume in the bright, blocky plastic. That figure came with an action feature, the ability for sparks to be formed from its mouth to simulate firing lasers, which was likely an aspect of the character featured in much earlier drafts. The prototype of the Blade figure shown in advertisements had a muzzle-like grill over his mouth, also from an earlier design sketch, but this was corrected by the time the figure was released. Although it would not be made to resemble actor Anthony De Longis, it would at least look like the correct costume.

Packaged with the figures was a minicomic called "The Cosmic Key,"

The action figure of Gwildor from the *Masters of the Universe* film was one of the last in the original run. (Photograph by Rachael Layne.)

which introduced variations of the movie-originated characters who had been turned into toys. While it featured the Key, those characters, and Skeletor becoming more powerful thanks to supernatural forces, the plot had almost nothing to do with that of the film. As one of the last mini-comics produced, a mere six pages in length. This was less than half as long as the usual. The storytelling was muddled as a result.

To coincide with the film's release, Mattel also released a game titled *Masters of the Universe: The Movie* for 8-bit systems like Amstrad CPC and Commodore 64. The same year, two other He-Man games came out, though they had no connection to the live-action film. *Masters of the Universe: The Arcade Game* and *Masters of the Universe: The Super Adventure* were styled after the toy line and animated series, but they still boosted the brand name's signal as it struggled to expand into the new medium.

In theaters, the first teaser trailer proclaimed, "There is a place where legends are born, where the light confronts the dark ... a world of incredible mystery, magic, and adventure ... a world where colossal powers will collide in a battle to control the universe!" The words were matching by images of Lundgren as He-Man, well-oiled in a dark and misty room, swinging the massive Power Sword. This was intercut with a rapidly advancing camera movement toward the planet Earth, which then exploded.

The full promotional trailer emphasized the film's cosmic adventure and invasion of Earth, with red screaming laser bolts, explosions, or a sword clash in nearly every shot. As with the teaser trailer, the identities of the characters almost seem obscured. Due to the costume revisions and other design liberties taken by Stout and his crew, there is nothing to signify the people on the screen as representing the cartoons on the TV, or the toys on the shelves. It appears to be just another space opera / action flick until at the end, when the narrator booms, "Dolph Lundgren is He-Man! Frank Langella is Skeletor! Only they have the powers to be ... Masters of the Universe!"

The film was released on August 7, 1987, but it lacked the grand premiere its animated forefather managed. There were no He-Man hot air balloons this time around. Those involved in the *Masters* production were left to buy their own theater ticket. "I expected a cast and crew screening, but Cannon didn't give us one," Stout recalled. "I thought they were punishing us, but then later I'd found out, no, they were just bankrupt."[28]

Cannon Film's financial difficulties hampered advertising, and the toy line's drastically declining sales didn't guarantee the audience numbers Mattel had been counting on. As the companies looked on hopefully, both needing a hit, many in the cast and crew didn't have their hopes up. Teela actress Chelsea Field remembered going to the theater opening night and being excited to see her face on the big screen. She said, "of course we all hoped it was going to be a big hit, but I think by then we all had a feeling that it wasn't gonna do very well."[29]

Masters of the Universe grossed a lackluster $4,883,168 its opening weekend, a weekend noted for less than impressive ticket sales all around. It came in third, behind the crime comedy *Stakeout* and the James Bond film, *The Living Daylights*.

While audiences were largely disinterested, critics were mostly unimpressed. Though praising the makeup and costumes, *Variety* dismissed *Masters* as a "*Conan—Star Wars*" hybrid ripoff." The review stated, "The Epitome of Good takes on the Epitome of Evil for nothing less than the future of the Universe, and the result is a colossal bore."[30] The closest the *New York Times* came to a compliment was "If you liked the toy, you'll love the movie."[31]

Perhaps none were harsher than the *Washington Post*'s Rita Kempley. In her write-up, she also referenced the similarities to *Star Wars* and other successful franchises. "Unlike the characters in the *Superman* movies," she wrote, "[He-Man and Skeletor] lack humor and motivation.... Little kids at play have come up with craftier plots, better characterization and conceivably more spectacular effects—provided their mothers let them play with matches."[32]

Not all reviews were negative, though. The *Chicago Tribune* complimented *Masters'* "visual wit" and singled out Goddard as "effective at getting these quirkier bits on film."[33] The costumes and designs, along with Goddard's directing, garnered recognition in the scattered positive articles. Generally received as a special effects movie, most weren't blown away by the special effects. The film was lambasted by many for a perceived lack of originality in the story, along with Lundgren's thick accent.

Goddard expressed disappointment in the quick rejections from some reviewers, though said he wasn't too surprised: "I knew going in that this was based on a toy. When something is based on a toy, critics have a built in resistance to it and you're going to get those comparisons."[34]

Still, *Masters* also received some recognition from more genre-specific organizations. The film received a nomination for Best Film from Portugal's Fantasporto festival, and won its International Fantasy Film Award for Best Special Effects. It was nominated for Saturn Awards for Best Science Fiction Film, Best Costumes, and Best Special Effects from the Academy of Science Fiction, Fantasy, and Horror Films. While it lost in these categories, direct Gary Goddard was awarded the group's Silver Scroll Award for Outstanding Achievement. Billy Barty was nominated for Worst Supporting Actor at that year's Golden Raspberry Awards, but lost to David Mendenhall, the child actor featured in Cannon's Stallone film *Over the Top.*

The first-live action movie based on an action figure was largely greeted with confusion and derision, most based mainly on the fact of its adaptation. Movies based on books or TV shows was one thing, but a toy line was seen as too simplistic to support a real film. It was a concept that would become the norm in another two decades, with the debut of Michael Bay's *Transformers*, but it was too bizarre for the critics at the time. As for consumers, the iron had cooled too much before the film could strike it. Audiences showed up weakly at first, and their numbers dwindled. Certified as a box office bomb, *Masters of the Universe* was pulled from theaters after three weeks. It had managed to gross just over $17 million dollars, failing to recoup its adjusted budget of $22 million.

7

"I'll Be Back!"

The post-credit scene of *Masters of the Universe* is not well known. The brief clip was included at the very end of the film before such a thing became common: instead of a gag joke or a funny outtake, the film's villain pops his out of the water at the bottom of the pits of Castle Grayskull and tells the viewers to expect a sequel. That sort of snippet would become very common in decades to come, in the era of "shared cinematic universes," but not in 1987. At that point, most viewers didn't know better than to walk out of the theater during the credits, or to press "stop" on their VHS player's remote.

"I'll be back!" Skeletor promises. Such a boast is certainly something his character would say; Skeletor had already cheated death on plenty of occasions on television and in children's imaginations, always returning with a bigger scheme and more outlandish henchmen. You just can't keep a good villain down.

However, a sequel was far from an inevitability. Much depended on the film's reception from fans, critics, and the theatergoers-at-large, along with the grosses from the international territories and video rental stores Cannon Films had already pre-sold. Still, without contracts in place and before the numbers on any possible profit could be crunched, Golan and Globus were already talking up the next installment. Advertisements for *Masters of the Universe Part II* were posted in various newspapers and trade magazines. This came as a surprise to everyone involved in the making of *Masters of the Universe Part I*.

During the production of the film, Goddard had flirted with the ideal of a sequel story. If the first was received well enough, he figured, perhaps they'd be allowed to set the follow-up entirely on Eternia and eschew any human point-of-view characters. The director envisioned Skeletor escaping from the pit at the bottom of Grayskull and encountering either the evil Horde, or the Snake Men characters Goddard had been forced to discard in the first movie. "Armies would have been raised," he speculated, "and I had hoped to create something that fused Eternia into a kind of 'Middle Earth' world—with He-Man going on a journey into Skeletor's dark empire."[1]

His ideas were not fully formed, and no scripts or treatments were written. No actual plans were made. After *Masters* wrapped, Goddard had quickly moved on to create and produce the toy line and TV series *Captain Power and the Soldiers of the Future*. It was another endeavor with Mattel, and this time he was allowed to create the characters from whole cloth instead of working to adapt a zealously guarded brand name.

Despite his difficulties with Cannon and the out-of-pocket expense the first film required, Goddard still considered returning. "I would have welcomed working on the sequel," he said, "but another director had convinced them HE could make a He-Man movie for $6,000,000 or less."[2] This price tag, instead of the $22 million the first film had cost, was much more in the wheelhouse of Cannon Films. After *Masters of the Universe*, it seemed, the company had given up on big budget blockbusters. But not on He-Man.

Golan and Globus' plans to make another, cheaper He-Man movie involved one of their go-to directors, Albert Pyun.

Pyun had made a name for himself in low budget B-movies throughout the 1980s, and he'd made a few for Cannon by the time the studio started to get the ball rolling on *Masters II*. He'd been the director of Cannon's *Down Twisted* (1987), which also featured Courtney Cox, along with 1988's *Alien from L.A.*, which gained notoriety for starring model Kathy Ireland. He'd become so trusted by this point that the producers put him in charge of salvaging their over-budget, half-completed mess of a *Journey to the Center of the Earth* remake.

The proposed sequel was in progress by the end of 1987, as *Masters* was still opening across parts Europe. While the Cannon producers worried over the paltry domestic box office receipts, they could still convince themselves the money from the foreign territories would make up for it. As always, the company forged ahead to make their next movie. It was, however, in trouble almost immediately.

At their appearance at Cannes that year, Golan and Globus had talked up their *Masters* plans to anyone who'd listen. Not only would there be two more He-Man films, the cousins said, but they would both star Dolph Lundgren. This was news to Lundgren, who was in South-West Africa at the time, filming *Red Scorpion* (1988). The star publicly corrected the

Israeli moguls in interviews, stating he had not signed a contract, and had no interest in reprising his role.

So Pyun's production replaced Lundgren with big-wave surfer Laird Hamilton. The professional athlete had the prerequisite tan skin, fit physique, and bright blonde hair to play He-Man. Hamilton looked the part as good as, if not even better than, Lundgren did, and he had no pesky foreign accent to throw off filmgoers. He was also no stranger to cameras as a fashion model, and he'd just made his film debut that year in *North Shore*, a movie about surfers, starring surfers.

By the beginning of 1988, talk of the sequel was making its way into the trade papers. The *Los Angeles Times* reported: "Laird Hamilton takes over Dolph Lundgren's He-Man role in Cannon's 'Masters of the Universe II.' Albert Pyun directs the sequel, which takes the superhero to Earth disguised as a football quarterback."[3]

And so, heading in the opposite direction of Goddard's story ideas, *Masters II* would take the Eternians back to Earth. Nearly the entire film would take place there.

Working from the director's treatment, Stephen Tolkin, who did uncredited work on the first *Masters* script, fleshed out the full screenplay. Both Tolkin and Pyun have since confirmed the basics: After surviving his fall into the pits beneath Castle Grayskull, Skeletor was somehow able to return to Earth to be either disguised as, or reincarnated in the form of, billionaire industrialist Aaron Dark. Learning of this, He-Man has Gwildor teleport him back to Earth to thwart his nemesis. To do so, he embraces the Flash Gordon elements of his archetype and takes the form of / is disguised as a football star. As far as is known, neither character would appear in their traditional, recognizable forms for at least most of the movie.

Many He-Man fans had been disappointed with *Masters of the Universe Part I* for how much time the story spent on Earth. *Masters II* all but guaranteed those fans still would not have been happy.

With a set budget of $4.5 million, Pyun began preproduction. The costumes were being sewn and the sets were under construction in North Carolina. But as Cannon Films struggled to find the resources to keep afloat amid a collapsing junk bond market, the fate of *Masters of the Universe II* would be tied very closely to another tie-in film: the first big screen adaptation of the Marvel Comics character Spider-Man.

Much can, and has, been written about Cannon's aborted Spidey flick. The company had leased the rights from Marvel for a good time as their script went through various changes. The producers were not familiar

According to Cannon Film's advertisements, *Masters of the Universe Part 2* was an inevitability. Likely for the best, this never came to be.

with the character, and at first commissioned scripts that depicted him as a literal spider-man, a monstrous and murderous mutant with eight legs who yearned for his own death. Marvel executive and Spider-Man co-creator Stan Lee reportedly balked at the early drafts.

According to the project's assigned director, Joseph Zito, "Golan and Globus didn't really know what Spider-Man was.... They thought it was like the Wolfman."[4] While Zito and the various hired gun screenwriters tried to steer the project back toward a more comics faithful storyline, Cannon began to undergo their now formalized SEC investigation and other sorted money issues. The budget was asked to be scaled back, and then scaled back again. Way back.

Zito left the project, and was also replaced by Pyun. He agreed to direct *Spider-Man* and *Masters II* simultaneously, staggering the productions to his advantage. "The concept was to shoot 2 weeks of *Spider-Man* first," the director explained. "The section of Peter Parker's story before he was bitten. Then we would shoot 6 weeks of *Masters 2*."[5] While filming Hamilton as He-Man, the actor portraying Peter Parker would undergo a very intense muscle-building workout routine until Pyun's cameras could return to him, making him appear to have gained superhuman strength overnight from that radioactive spider's bite.

However, this was just as Cannon's money problems finally caught up with them. A check they'd sent to Marvel bounced, and the rights to their world-famous wall-crawler were rescinded. The deal with Mattel fell through at the same time, but the reasons for it vary depending on who you ask. According to Albert Pyun, Cannon owed money for the rights to He-Man but simply couldn't afford to pay it. Others insist that check bounced as well. Gary Goddard claims the sequel's vast departure from the source material was enough to scare away the toy company. "Mattel saw the script, or perhaps the storyboards, and pulled the license," he has said.[6]

Masters of the Universe Part II was no more, and yet according to Pyun, cash-strapped Cannon Films had already sunk $2 million into the sets and costumes.[7] The director also stated that both productions were mere days away from filming when the two deals fell through. However, there had been no one formally cast to play Peter Parker in *Spider-Man*, or Skeletor/Aaron Dark in *Masters II*. It's not believed that scripts were finished, though shooting without an actual script was not beyond the norm for the studio. Whatever phase of production the two films were actually in, and however much had been spent, it had all progressed too far for Golan and Globus to not get a movie out of it.

In what has become an infamous story in B-movie history, Albert Pyun and fledgling screenwriter Don Michael Paul took a mere weekend to draft an all new, original screenplay to incorporate the completed sets and costumes. Pyun had promised Cannon he'd keep the rest of the budget as low as conceivably possible. What resulted from this frenzied, penny-pinching scramble was *Cyborg* (1989), the post-apocalyptic karate picture starring a young Jean Claude Van Damme. It was shot in 24 days and, with a minuscule budget of $500,000, it even managed to turn a nice profit for the troubled studio.

The origin of *Cyborg* was a poorly guarded secret. Since it debuted, it's been connected to He-Man both in fan speculation and release titles; due to its unique production, certain wires were crossed and newspaper listings of *Cyborg* would occasionally be labeled *Masters of the Universe II: Cyborg*.

He-Man fans have long wondered how much of Pyun's intended *Masters II* script ended up in the Van Damme vehicle. There's been talk of the titular cyborg being the evil He-Man clone Faker, or the young woman Van Damme's character protects turning out to be an amnesiac She-Ra, in a spin on the *Secret of the Sword* story. As the actual film takes place in a violent, grim post-apocalyptic world, there has also been discussion if that was present in Pyun's original vision. If He-Man was sent to Earth to stop an evil industrialist, what if he arrived too late? As a director, Albert Pyun is noted for being drawn to post-apocalyptic and dystopian projects, so it would not be out of character.

The finished *Cyborg* film itself bears no ostensible resemblance to our Eternian heroes and villains. The characters and motivations are clearly distinct, and the tone is much too bleak and hard-edged to be mistaken for Masters of the Universe. It does, however, make for a fun footnote in He-Man's history. The two films are occasionally shown together as a double-feature.

Despite all the ups and downs of Cannon's sequel attempts, it's unknown if Mattel was even interested in taking He-Man back to the big screen. The hero had fallen on hard times back home. Although the franchise had made an estimated $2 billion on the sales of all the toys, playsets, and other collectables, they weren't flying off the shelves like they'd used to. The fad was dying.

The sixth wave of Masters of the Universe figures were released in 1987, in conjunction with the live-action film. This wave included movie characters Blade, Saurod, and Gwildor, along with Filmation characters like King Randor, and Snake Men like Sssqueeze, who hadn't appeared anywhere but the minicomics. Mattel, like Cannon, were disappointed in the box office grosses. The toymakers also did not see a bump in sales from the movie. For all the advertising Goddard's film had done for the characters, it hadn't sold more figures. The toy line managed to lose nearly $400 million that year, and the decision was made to bring the franchise to an end.

The '87 wave of figures would be the last Masters of the Universe toys officially released for a long time. There were a few stragglers from the next wave whose prototypes had been completed before the line folded. These figures, like Laser Power He-Man and Laser Light Skeletor, were released in non-domestic markets where the line was still in demand.

Other figures had been in the works when Mattel brought the axe down on the brand. Sensing the public's waning interest, the company was all set to shift the line in a different direction. Masters of the Universe would become The Powers of Grayskull, and it would focus on Eternia's distant past, called Preternia. The origins of many characters and concepts, such as the formation of Castle Grayskull and the rise of King Hiss and the villainous Snake Men, were due to be explored. Along with the new, imaginative characters would be a series of cyborg dinosaurs and giants.

The Powers of Grayskull would be headlined by He-Man's ancestor, He-Ro of Grayskull, the Most Powerful Wizard in the Universe. The new line had been set up in an issue of the minicomics titled "The Powers of Grayskull: The Legend Begins." Its story saw He-Man venturing back in time to visit Preternia, and He-Ro made a cameo, though veiled completely in shadow. The audience's interest was stoked, but nothing more would come of it. When Mattel canceled Masters of the Universe, the production on The Powers of Grayskull was also shut down.

A few figures did manage to escape, though. The line's three dinosaur figures, Tyrantisaurus Rex, Bionatops, and Turbodactyl, were sold domestically, but its two 12" giant figures, the heroic Tytus and villainous Megator, were only released in Italy. There was a prototype of He-Ro completed, and its image was included on various packaging, but it was never released.

It was all a bit sudden, but He-Man was no more.

With the public exhausted and retailers still frustrated, many at Mattel felt it best to let the franchise lay dormant for a few years. John Amerman, the company's new chairman and CEO, felt differently. The Marketing and Design departments were ordered to begin work on He-Man's rebranding immediately after the collapse of the Masters of the Universe line. The new figures would need to be released as soon as possible, and it would need to start making those massive profits all over again.[8]

New designs and illustrations were presented to retailers to gauge their interest, but none seemed to go over well. Many toy stores continued to suffer from Mattel's volume-driven strategy; they still had unsold product they were continually lowering the price on, taking a loss just to clear the space for toys that would be bought. No matter the quality of the pitch or the prospective new He-Man, they wanted nothing to do with it. Designers like Roger Sweet and Mark Taylor worked for a year, finding approaches that skewed more toward sci-fi and enhanced military themes. It took about a year for the retailers to agree to look into another Masters of the Universe line.

A space-fantasy theme was decided upon, and the usual process of focus testing and numbers crunching began. The name "Masters of the Universe" was dropped from marketing. The toys' packaging was all simply branded as "He-Man." It hit the shelves in 1989, only two years after the last line had bottomed out.

This new He-Man line would prove to be quite different in many ways. Physically, the musculature of every character was toned down to something more realistic, and they were made to stand up straight, instead of crouching. They all stood a uniform 5" tall. Sweet expressed his intense displeasure with the changes, but he also understood the rationale: "The result required less plastic, which meant it could be produced more cheaply."[9] On Eternia or even in deep space, the economics had to be considered.

Mattel also strove to distance the New He-Man from the old one. In addition to slimming down, the hero was given a haircut and had taken to wearing pants. The Power Sword went through a redesign to include a green laser blade.

Skeletor was the only other character who made the jump into the new line. His redesign was less drastic than the hero's, so while he became more slender, he maintained his blue skin, skull head, and the armor-and-briefs look. He was also given a new helmet and a cloak.

Orko, Man-At-Arms, and the other regular supporting Heroic Warriors disappeared, replaced with "Galactic Guardians," more sci-fi inspired and superheroic characters like Hydron and Tuskador. The Evil Mutants, like Slush Head and Staghorn, took the place of Skeletor's bumbling henchmen. As gimmicky as the new characters all turned out to be, they would've fit right in on Eternia.

The figures were again packaged with minicomics. The first of the four produced worked to bridge the continuities between the familiar Masters of the Universe line and this new space-faring one.

Titled "New Adventure," it introduces Galactic Warriors Flipshot and Hydron as their ship travels to the past, and to the planet Eternia. They are looking to recruit the legendary He-Man to resolve their long-standing war with the Mutants, but they've also been tricked by Skeletor into stealing the powers of Castle Grayskull. Their spaceship hovers over the castle and begins to funnel up the structure's magic.

Alerted by the Sorceress, Prince Adam attempts to transform into He-Man, but the weakening power of Grayskull fails him. Stuck in his normal, mortal form, he still rushes after Skeletor, who is about to be beamed up to the empowered spaceship. Through his usual treachery, he is finally about to take possession of the Castle's power.

Both are beamed onto the futuristic ship, and Adam convinces the new characters they've been tricked. He draws his sword and says, "By the power of Grayskull!" It works this time, and in the dramatic lightning crash and explosion of his transformation, Skeletor is badly injured. Scarring and mutilation from this are the stated excuse for the variation in his appearance. He-Man's new duds, however, are a gift from the Sorceress. She sends him into the future alongside the Galactic Guardians to defeat the Evil Mutants.

This New He-Man and his new allies watch as Skeletor flees in the ships' escape pod, screaming, "Evil's face is mine!"

As had become the trend with *He-Man and the Masters of the Universe* years earlier, no new toy line could be complete without its matching animated series. At first, Mattel turned back to Lou Scheimer and the Filmation company.

The writers and animators were brought on board fairly early, to attempt to build a cohesive story-world around the concepts before the toys were finished. This way, they could be much more involved with the new *He-Man* stories, the way they had been with the *She-Ra* spin-off.

In 1988, Filmation had their first ideas for a more space-oriented Masters of the Universe cartoon. It would be called *He-Ro, Son of He-Man*. Their proposal set the story as a direct sequel to the original series, with He-Man ruling Eternia in place of his father, with Teela by his side as his queen. After the birth of their son, the planet faces a catastrophe similar to Superman's homeworld of Krypton, and the young parents decide to send their son away in a rocket ship. Before it takes off, though, Skeletor sneaks his own infant son, born of the *She-Ra* character Shadow Weaver, onto the ship as well.

The ship reaches the Tri-Solar system, where the babies are taken in by the new good and evil characters, respectively. He-Man's son is named He-Ro, and Skeletor's is Skeleteen, as both characters would be teenagers in the show. Both young adults would be able to call to their parents for guidance, in segments which are rumored to have been shot in live-action.

Mattel did not sign off on the Son of He-Man pitch, as they were not likely interested in tossing out He-Man and Skeletor, the only previously existing characters their new He-Man line contained. Filmation went back to the drawing board.

The next pitch came in very early 1989 and was titled *He-Man and the Masters of Space*. He-Man, and his persona of Adam, would still be the star in this iteration, and he would also bring along Orko as he battled Skeletor across the stars. Much more is known about Filmation's *Masters of Space* proposal, including the great deal of thought the company put into fleshing out the various planets in the Tri-Solar system and new, original characters. This included Ephon Deveraux, a space-pirate queen who occupied a more morally gray area than the black-and-white He-Man and Skeletor, and new comedic villains like Skeletor's sister Skeletrix, his pet dog-alien Barque, and twin nephew and niece Funnybone and Hunnybone.

This show was also not meant to be. Less than a month after it was proposed to Mattel, Filmation went out of business.

The animation house had gone through some rough times at the end of the 1980s. The airwaves were flooded with toy-based cartoons in the years following *He-Man*'s release, each one mimicking the straight-to-syndication strategy Lou Scheimer's company had pioneered. Also, these competitors were made by animation studios who did not share Filmation's dedication to employing American animators. Most rival series, like *Transformers*, were imported and utilized cheaper Japanese animation. Economic realities caught up with them, and they were called upon to make fewer shows each year.

Looking for a way to avoid layoffs, Scheimer agreed to sell Filmation to the Paravision International, a company owned by L'Oreal cosmetics. Only after the ink was dry did he realize the French conglomerate had no interest in producing new cartoons, or even keeping the company intact. L'Oreal only wanted their back catalogue of completed films and television series. Scheimer's company was dismantled by 1989 and all its employees were let go.

Without Filmation, whom Mattel had worked with on other toy-based series like *Bravestarr*, the toymakers had to look elsewhere. For a new series, Mattel signed a deal with the young American-Japanese studio Jet-lag Productions, which had partnered with the established international DIC Entertainment company. A new 65-episode season was commissioned for syndication and set to air in fall 1990.

Titled *The New Adventures of He-Man*, the new series took advantage of how much animation had evolved since the first He-Man cartoon aired. *New He-Man*'s animation was smoother and less reliant on the versatile, yet repetitive, stock footage Filmation had leaned upon. This allowed the character to have more varied interactions and fights, and for the action to take place in more exotic locales, planets, moons, and spaceships. The regular cast was larger, with more varied heights and body shapes as well.

The animation style and character designs were influenced by the Japanese anime style that was popular in other cartoons of the time. This gave the characters larger eyes and made the violence more stylized. This approach also impacted the storytelling, infusing the show with a manic sense of humor. The Evil Mutants were impossibly doltish and inept, even compared to Skeletor's old minions on Eternia. The heroic Galactic Guardians weren't much better most of the time, with major characters like Flipshot depicted as panicky and easily frightened. The great scientists of the planet Primus, presented as the four greatest minds on the planet, were played for laughs as stupid, childish old men.

The jumps in both style and tone were jarring to seasoned He-Man fans. This was only intensified by the Jetlag/DIC series insisting on its connection to the old Filmation one. The hero's old friend Man-At-Arms had a brief cameo, as the Mutant Flogg shapeshifted to resemble the hero, and Teela appeared in the mid-season episode "Once Upon a Time." These two characters, along with He-Man's secret identity of Prince Adam, had been drastically redesigned.

Another change that had occurred in the realm of animation was the possibility of long-form storytelling instead of one-offs like *He-Man and the Masters of the Universe* had been. While each episode of the original cartoon could function as an introduction to He-Man, Skeletor, Orko and all the rest, *The New Adventures* allowed the stories to build and characters to develop to a greater extent while largely remaining generally episodic.

This meant the first episode of the series, "A New Beginning," could be a proper first chapter and actually set the new show in motion. It provided an explanation for He-Man to move from his home on Eternia into the future, and introduced his new allies and enemies. Like the original cartoon, the story would contradict the minicomic that had been packaged with the toy some months before. It both was, and was not, a reboot.

In the show's continuity, the planet Primus is protected by an energy shield which protects it from the Mutants' attacks. As the shield is slowly weakening, the planet's ruler, Master Sebrian, sends Flipshot and Hydron off in a time machine to find a mythic hero from the past who possesses "the power of the good and the way of the magic."

When the two arrive on Eternia, they are taken captive by a tribe of giants loyal to Skeletor and marched to Snake Mountain. Recognizing the duo's superior technology and utter naiveté, he tells them he's the hero they are searching for and happily agrees to accompany them back to the future.

The Sorceress of Grayskull alerts He-Man who, like Skeletor, is already in his revised *New Adventures* appearance. The hero is told he is needed in the future and must leave Eternia behind. Saddened, he changes back into the form of Prince Adam to say goodbye to his parents, King Randor and Queen Marlena, who have similarly been redesigned. As Skeletor is on his way back to the time machine with the two Galactic Guardians, the Sorceress telepathically contacts Adam to say he must leave now. Adam raises his sword and says the magic words, transforming into He-Man in front of his amazed parents. After they say how proud they are of him, he departs.

The transformation sequence is a holdover from Filmation; though Mattel's first minicomics alluded to the fact the hero would stay as He-Man full-time, but the new animators recognized the popularity of this aspect of the old show. The *New Adventures* transformation is less dramatic than the original, though. Now, Adam just raises his sword and says, "By the power of Eternia," and changes in a flash of light over a backdrop of flames. There's no Castle Grayskull in words or image, and no Cringer to change into Battle Cat. Prince Adam is, however, much more visually distinct from He-Man in this version.

He-Man catches up with Skeletor just before he boards the time machine, and the two begin to fight. Flipshot and Hydron are unsure which of the two has "the power of the good and the way of the magic," or think that maybe He-Man is good but Skeletor is magic. With their window to the future closing, they duo simply push them both inside their machine and take them both to Primus.

In the future, the adversaries tumble out of the machine and continue their fight. He-Man's heroics and feats of power convince the onlooking Sebrian he is the one they were searching for. Just then, the planet's safety shield cracks and a small group of Mutants invade. He-Man easily defeats them, and Skeletor hitches a ride with the retreating villains.

The first five episodes work as a long, loose story, but by this episode's end, the new status quo has been established: Skeletor is among the Mutants, claiming allegiance to Flogg but scheming and pulling the strings the same way he'd been manipulated by Evil-Lyn; He-Man is accepted as the protector of Primus and the leader of the Galactic Guardians; and his dual identity of Adam is taken in by Master Sebrian, who knows his secret, to pose as his nephew.

The *New Adventures of He-Man* aired its one 65-episode season in 1990–1991, and it was not picked up for a second. The He-Man toy line lasted significantly longer, from the first wave in 1989 to the fourth in 1992. But instead of aggressively expanding the way Masters of the Universe had, even after its cartoon ended, the New He-Man's releases became more and more conservative.

The first wave had three heroes and three villains, with each side getting their separate accessories and two sets of vehicles. The one big playset was the Starship Eternia, the heroes' main vehicle and base of operations. The next wave included four heroes, including a variant of He-Man, and five villains, including another Skeletor. There were no vehicles or accessories, just the playset the Evil Mutant's hideout, the skull-shaped Denebrian moon Nordor. Wave number three had four Galactic Guardians and three Mutants, with no He-Man or Skeletor in sight. The heroes had one vehicle and the villains had two. The final wave in '92 contained no vehicles or playsets, and all the figures were gimmicky variants of characters who had other figures earlier in the line.

The revamped He-Man made some money for Mattel, but was nowhere near the success its predecessor was. The new cartoon, and the new toys, were too drastic a change to be accepted by the more hardcore original fans. The casual fans were already outgrowing their interest in the franchise, and the new, younger crowds had so many more options for their TV adventure and action figure needs. He-Man couldn't grab them the way he had their older brothers. By 1990, the animation airwaves were dominated by *Teenage Mutant Ninja Turtles* and *GI Joe: A Real American Hero*, along with comedic, non-toy based Fox Kids shows like *Bobby's World* and *Tiny Toon Adventures*.

Despite the fresh air *New Adventures* breathed into the character, the new incarnation lacked the same power and novelty of the original. The line died quietly and the characters were finally laid to rest by the toy company.

For the next decade or so, He-Man was gone but not forgotten. The Filmation series and action figures crystalized in the minds of fans as they grew up. A whole generation looked back fondly on He-Man, Skeletor, She-Ra and the rest. As they grew up and gained disposable income, the books, games, comics, and toys became sought-after collectibles. All the hallmarks of the franchise, from the characters to the catchphrase "By the power of Grayskull," remained in the cultural lexicon. Even those who didn't grow up with He-Man knew who he was.

But there was no new Masters of the Universe material. There were clamorings from the more intense fan base, and also from another unexpected source.

After the dissolution of Filmation, Lou Scheimer had formed his own animation company to try to get back into the cartoon business. Lou Scheimer Productions did some minor work throughout the '90s and its founder was constantly pitching new projects. In 1996 he took one such series proposal to DIC, who had worked on the *New Adventures* cartoon.

It was called *He-Ro, Son of He-Man, and the Masters of the Universe*, and it was intended to be a direct sequel to his original Filmation series.

In *He-Ro*, Prince Adam has grown up to become king, and he's made Teela his queen. At least ten years have passed, and Skeletor has long been magically imprisoned in the Frozen Lands by He-Man and the Sorceress. Peace has finally come to Eternia. Meanwhile, in a forest outside of the kingdom, an abandoned child is found by a "she-bearcat" creature and raised as her own. He grows up to commune with the animals, unaware of his true family and unsuspecting of his destiny. His only other friend is a talking black crow, Craven.

King Adam is contacted by the Sorceress, who says, "It is time now for you to share the Power of the Sword."[10] She tells him to quest for the nameless boy in the dark valley across the Mountains of Fire, so that he may inherit the Power Sword. As Adam sets off with Man-At-Arms, Orko, and Cringer, Skeletor and his minions break free of their enchantments. The villains learn of this nameless boy as well, and they rush off to the dark valley to turn him evil before he can take hold of the magic sword.

Beast Man uses his control of animals to track down the boy, and the she-bearcat is killed trying to protect her adopted cub. Skeletor convinces the boy it was all Adam's fault, and he swears vengeance. The heroes arrive, and Adam transforms into He-Man, handily defeating the henchmen. Skeletor has escaped with the boy into the Mountains of Fire, laying traps behind him. He-Man catches up with them and tries to convince the boy of his error in judgment. As he waffles, uncertain, Skeletor runs out of patience and blasts Craven. With it gravely wounded, the boy makes his choice and sides with He-Man.

Adam and Teela adopt the boy, naming him Dare, and the king gives up the Power Sword. Dare raises it over his head and says, "I am He-Ro, son of He-Man.... I have the Power!" He transforms into a muscular, heroic identity, and changes the recovered Craven into Battle-Bird.

Scheimer's *He-Ro* pitch enthusiastically embraced the history of the Filmation series and strove to appeal to the original fans. He promised King Adam could still transform into He-Man on occasion, and that it would feature most of the reoccurring characters from *He-Man* in a more mature form. While moving the franchise forward, with a new generation of Heroic Warriors, the show would keep one foot very firmly planted in the past.

His pitch also showed a weakness concerning the elements of Masters of the Universe lore that didn't immediately impact his previous TV show. In 1996, many fervent fans would've recognized the name He-Ro as He-Man's powerful wizard ancestor from the aborted The Powers of Grayskull toy line, though this new He-Ro would bear no relation and the series made no mention of him. Other "new" characters for the series, like Tongue-Lasher and Odar bore a great deal of resemblance to Mattel characters Tung Lashor and Stinkor.

It was envisioned as a way to reinvigorate the franchise, but also to tell stories about growing up. The proposal and story bible Scheimer presented included breakdowns of characters and sketches of their updated appearances, and even a handful of episode storylines. As he remembered his meetings about the sequel series, Scheimer said, "I don't know why *He-Ro* never went anywhere, but DIC eventually let the project go."[11]

And just like that, He-Man was put back to sleep for a few more years.

Within a few more years, '80s nostalgia was in full bloom. As Mattel watched the prices climb for the original Masters of the Universe figures, an idea was hatched. Now that a collector's market existed for these weathered, 15 year old toys, there might be enough interest to sell some new ones.

In 2000, the company released a special commemorative edition of the classic action figures. They utilized the original molds and painted them just the way they'd looked before. Even the packaging was the perfect reproduction. The first wave contained ten figures, all of characters who had appeared in the first year or two of the classic toy line. It consisted of He-Man, Skeletor, Man-At-Arms, Teela, Evil-Lyn, Beast Man, Mer-Man, Faker, Tri-Klops, and Trap Jaw. There were two-packs of He-Man with Battle Cat and Skeletor with Panthor, and the collected set of ten in the impressive "Legends of Eternia" pack.

Mattel did a second wave of commemorative figures, but they were more limited in number and print run. Re-released in 2001 were Buzz-Off, Clawful, Stratos, Zodac, and the Battle Armor versions of both He-Man and Skeletor.

To say the re-release "did well" would be a massive understatement. Fans and collectors gobbled these new old toys up. As they were produced in very limited numbers, they quickly became hard to come by. In many cases, the brand new figures were more expensive than the toys they'd been molded after.

Even more rare and expensive were the five-packs sold. There was one for each wave, including four regular figures and another one only available in that pack. The first contained He-Man, Skeletor, Man-At-Arms, Beast Man, and the special figure of Prince Adam. The second packaged Battle Armor He-Man and Battle Armor Skeletor, Zodac, and Clawful with the fuzzy green Moss Man figure.

The re-release was cut short as Mattel began to rethink their strategy. With so many excited fans eager to spend their money, maybe the time was finally right. Maybe the world was ready for more He-Man.

In 2002, Mattel partnered with a toy design studio called Four Horsemen to make a new series of Masters of the Universe figures. The founders of Four Horsemen had all cut their teeth at the well-regarded McFarlane Toys, and their independent company became known for producing hyper-stylized figures with loads of minute details. They brought this same approach to their He-Man figures. Mattel was no longer interested in simply reproducing the past; they wanted something bold and modern.

While a new toy line promised a new vision of the beloved characters, this would not be a drastic redesign the way the *New Adventures* figures had been. All of the familiar heroes and villains from the '80s toy line and Filmation cartoon were made available. Even more, they were all recognizably the same characters, just tweaked and exaggerated to fit into the early 2000s toy market.

One thing missing from the newest toy line was the in-pack mini-comics. After sorting through some rights issues regarding the comic book license to the characters, there was not enough time to commission the comics, let alone investigate how it may have effected each figure's price point. One full-sized comic was created and packaged with a two-pack of He-Man and Skeletor exclusively released at Target stores. It featured artwork inspired by the new character designs, and the cover was provided by comic book legend Neal Adams.

A second issue was in the works, set to be packaged with a proposed Smash Blade He-Man and Spin Blade Skeletor two-pack. The script was provided by Robert Kirkman, creator of popular zombie comic *The Walking Dead*. Despite some tight deadlines, the comic was finished and submitted, but this was just as the two-pack was canceled. The second comic was not released with the action figures. It wouldn't see print until years later.

With a new toy line in the works, there needed to be a new cartoon. Mattel turned to Mike Young Productions to bring the new designs to the small screen. This new series, also called *He-Man and the Masters of the Universe*, remained as faithful to the '80s property as the Four Horseman designs did. The show brought back several key writers from the Filmation series, such as Larry DiTillio, to maintain the same spirit as the original.

This time around, characters were allowed to develop more over the course of a season, and there was a great deal of time spent on the backstory of each character, and of Eternia itself. The mythology of a world full of monsters, magic, and sci-fi technology was taken very seriously, though episodes still allowed for the moments of lightness from Orko, Cringer, and the other more comedic characters.

While the new *He-Man* series had plenty of old fashioned things to make the original fans happy, it had also been updated in many ways. The quality of animation was a big leap forward, but the biggest change came in the storytelling. This new show had a focus on tighter continuity from episode to episode, allowing for cliffhangers and multi-part story arcs. The show would also give the fans something the Filmation series never had: a definitive origin story for He-Man.

The three-episode arc titled "The Beginning" kicked off the first season in August of 2002. It opens with an extended flashback of soon-to-be king Randor warning Eternia's ruling Council of Elders that a warlord named Keldor will be coming to attack them and conquer the planet. But the council is not concerned. They say a great hero will be rising to defend Eternia.

Randor leads a group called The Defenders, comprised of Man-At-Arms, Stratos, Mekaneck, and Ram Man, as they defend the Elders from attack by Keldor, a blue-skinned man wearing familiar purple armor. As the Defenders battle with Keldor's forces, which includes recognizable faces like Beast Man, Randor duels with the warlord. Bested, Keldor attempts to throw a vial of acid. Randor blocks it with his shield, and it splashes back into Keldor's face. Screaming in pain, he and his forces retreat.

Years later, Keldor's forces have been sealed behind a mystic wall on the planet's dark hemisphere, separating them from the rest of Eternia. Randor has become king and his son, Prince Adam, is a fun-loving teenager. Man-At-Arm's daughter Teela, is shown to be about the same age as Adam but much more serious in her combat training.

One of the biggest design changes in the new *He-Man* series was the visual of these two characters. Adam and Teela were always intended to be younger, but they were typically drawn to look like adults. They were now very much young people in look and action, which made Adam's transformation into his heroic persona so much more convincing. He-Man may look the way Adam would as an adult, but it's not a very overwhelming similarity. As Scheimer's company had originally based the change on the young Billy Batson's transformation into the adult Captain Marvel, this would be a much better representation.

Keldor, now shown wearing a hood to hide his face, has discovered a way to break through the mystic wall. As he and his henchmen work on this, Man-At-Arms is telepathically contacted by The Sorceress. He escorts Prince Adam away from a party at the palace to Castle Grayskull, where he is told the power of Eternia's Elders are contained. The Sorceress tells him he must become the protector of the planet, and of the secrets of Grayskull. Adam declines.

On his way back to the palace, Adam is stunned to see plumes of smoke and signs of destruction. The origin story embraces the elements of Joseph Campbell's Monomyth to a T, leading to sequences like this which may appear familiar. Young, uncertain Adam turning down an exciting future to return home echoes Luke Skywalker's leaving Obi-Wan Kenobi behind to discover his murdered aunt and uncle in *Star Wars*.

The body count is lower in "The Beginning," however. Adam finds his mother alive in the palace, and she tells him Keldor's forces have attacked. His father and the rest of the Defenders are battling with them in the nearby Evergreen Forest. Adam rushes off to join them. His friends, the court magician Orko and his pet Cringer, who cannot speak this time, watch with concern. They sneak after him, wanting to help.

In the forest, Teela has joined the other heroes as they defend the palace from the villains. What follows is a fairly self-indulgent fight scene, introducing each redesigned character and what sorts of violence they are capable of. Once-bumbling henchmen like Whiplash and Clawful are now seen to be fearsome opponents, and the teenaged Teela holds her own alongside very capable warriors like Man-E-Faces. The battle is pitched, and the two sides are evenly matched.

All the while, the hooded Keldor duels King Randor once again. This time Keldor gets the upper hand, and then pulls back his hood to reveal what the acid has done to his face: all that now remains is a skull. His name, he says, is now Skeletor. "Not a pretty sight, is it?" he sneers at the King. "You did this." The villain now looks the way he had in the '80s cartoon, and the voice work by Brian Dobson resembles that of the first voice of Skeletor, as done by Alan Oppenheimer.

Prince Adam arrives and doesn't fare too well against the assembled villains. He watches Skeletor take Randor away for interrogation about where the Elders' power has gone, and recognizes just how powerless he is. He runs away in the midst of the fight, which astonishes Teela. What she thinks is cowardice is something else entirely: he is returning to Castle Grayskull to become the hero The Sorceress told him about.

He is taken into the depth of the castle and presented with a massive, magical sword. By raising it over his head and saying the right words, he is transformed into He-Man for the first time. The Sorceress uncovers Orko and Cringer, who have seen the whole thing. When he's told he needs a warrior-creature as a loyal companion, He-Man transforms Cringer into Battle Cat, and the two take off. Amazed and confused, Orko sees himself out.

On the battlefield, Skeletor's henchmen have taken the high ground. Evil-Lyn uses her considerable magical powers to call down a meteor storm, bombarding the heroes with chunks of flaming rocks from space. The biggest one is headed right for Teela, but He-Man arrives and steps in front of her. With one super-powered punch, he destroys the meteor and saves the group by lifting a gigantic rock to block the rest. He then throws the rock, scattering Evil-Lyn and the other villains.

He-Man rushes off after Skeletor, leaving his new allies to mop up the henchmen. Man-At-Arms is swallowed by one of Mer-Man's gigantic, flying fish, and Teela works to free him. Elsewhere, Skeletor realizes King Randor doesn't know the secret location of the Elders' powers, but he still continues to torture him for the sake of revenge. This is interrupted by He-Man. The two battle, and Skeletor proves himself as a more-than-capable swordsman, but even with his magical attacks, it's not enough to stop Grayskull's champion.

Sensing a weakness in He-Man's desire to save the king, Skeletor says he will push him down a nearby bottomless chasm unless He-Man allows him to leave unmolested. The hero obliges, and Skeletor sends the king falling to his death anyways.

He-Man dives after his father, and the two manage to stop their decent by jamming the Power Sword into the rock wall. They are then fished out by Stratos and the rest of the Defenders. Back topside, He-Man declares them all "masters of the universe," and tells the king he will be available to save Eternia again whenever he is needed.

The third episode ends with the newly established status quo: Prince Adam is back at the palace, unable to share his secret with Teela or his parents; the uptight Man-At-Arms quarrels with the playful Orko; and Skeletor is back at Snake Mountain, scheming new ways to eliminate He-Man while his underlings, namely Evil-Lyn, look for ways to replace him at the top of the villain's chain of command.

As the new cartoon aired, Mattel cast a wide net to recapture the expansive range of cross-media saturation they'd enjoyed some 15 years earlier. Video games were released, along with all the t-shirts and other goodies fans expected. Comic books were created by MVCreations to tie into the new continuity. They were released by Image Comics, and then by CrossGen.

The new figures were released in waves, as before, but the waves would come much more frequently this time. Instead of one new group of toys, vehicles, and plays sets every year, these were released seasonally, with four new waves every year. This new toy line also leaned more heavily on variants and different versions of the same characters. Every wave included a new outfit for the hero and villain, such as Jungle Attack He-Man or Fire Armor Skeletor.

There were several issues with the toys' release and distribution. Shipments of the new Masters of the Universe figures were subject to "short-packing," an error where certain toys are not made in the same numbers as others. Boxes sent to retailers contained an uneven number of figures of each character. Shelves ended up full of Samurai He-Mans, but collectors were unable to track down Teela or Ram Man.

The new *He-Man and the Masters of the Universe* aired for 26 episodes on Cartoon Network, which had become the new industry standard for a season of an animated series. In fall of 2003, the show returned in a slightly rebranded form. It was now called *Masters of the Universe vs. The Snake Men.* This second season would shift the focus away from Skeletor as the main villain, and introduce King Hiss and the Snake Men as an ancient, evil army that had plagued Eternia in the Preternia days. They had been imprisoned in a parallel universe by the planet's Council of Elders, but in the modern day, they escape to do battle with He-Man, Skeletor, and anyone else who stands in their way.

This second season was cut short in January of 2004 with its 12th episode, the 39th overall, titled "Awaken the Serpent." Canceled due to its underperforming toy line, the cartoon was unable to resolve its numerous plot threads. The second season had also been laying the groundwork for Hordak and the evil Horde, intending them to be the villains of season three. These plans too, never came to fruition. The completed script for episode 40, "Captured," was adapted into a comic book and released with the series' last DVD set in 2008.

The last toy wave was released in winter 2004. Unlike the others, it did not contain any vehicles or play sets. The figures were primarily new versions or repaints of previously released characters.

Though the latest incarnation of He-Man and his friends did not prove capable of succeeding in the modern toy market, there were still as many hardcore Masters of the Universe fans as there had ever been.

To fill this need, the National Entertainment Collectibles Association, or NECA, stepped in. The figurines they released were not articulated like standard action figures, but made to the same scale as the 2002 relaunch figures, and in the same Mike Young Productions/Four Horsemen style. The new "staction figures" were made for characters who had not yet had new toys made in the relaunch, such as Clamp Champ and Hordak. They were released for a collector's market, in much smaller print runs and often as exclusives at conventions like the San Diego Comic Con between 2005 and 2007.

After the collapse of the 2002 relaunch, Masters of the Universe returned to its previous spot in pop culture, as a once-ubiquitous property that was now known to all and loved by many. Its followers were not as many as some other cross-media brands, but just as dedicated and passionate.

Since 1987, He-Man had remained in the periphery of the public consciousness as Mattel staged various comebacks. As more time passed and there were more varied interpretations of the character, fans were able to look back at the different incarnations to decide which one they liked best. The general public, too, could look back on the things they saw as children and reevaluate their merit with a more adult mindset.

And just like that, people began to talk about the Lundgren / Langella *Masters of the Universe* film again.

8

He-Man Meets Cult Status

When *Masters of the Universe* broke new ground in 1987, the ground did not give away easily. There was resistance to it, an immediate and outraged dismissal by most in the world of entertainment. Audiences, even those who were still fans of the He-Man franchise, were not sure what to make of it. This has never been more apparent than in one article from the Chicago Tribune. Though noteworthy for being one of the most positive immediate reviews of the film, it's still titled "Surprise! 'Masters' Isn't Bad."

"'Masters of the Universe' claims the distinction of being 'the first live-action film created from a toy line,'" the first sentence reads. In the second, this distinction is called a "dubious pedigree."[1] Although the rest of the article is practically glowing compared to the other reviews, the newspaper's point was made clear right away: toys were considered beneath the esteemed world of cinema. Even the rest of Cannon Films' B-movie output was given the chance to fail before it was judged so thoroughly.

Mattel had faced an uphill battle adapting the action figures into animation years before, but that had turned the franchise into one of the company's biggest successes. Things did not work out so well in the live-action medium.

After *Masters* disappeared from cinemas, it moved into the second-run realm where Cannon made most of its money. Its VHS tapes were rented in much better numbers than theater tickets were bought. This was due either to casual filmgoers who were curious but not sold on the film's trailers, or who were possibly scared away by Cannon's name or the negative press. Many of rentals also came from repeat viewings, by action movie fans or the devoted He-Man crowd. Cannon had always enjoyed a stronger presence in the United Kingdom given their ownership of theater chains, and this dominance extended to video rental shops. *Masters* even became the most rented VHS in Britain for a time.[2]

When the film debuted, it was greeted as an oddity, but as more time passed it began to evolve into something else entirely: a cult classic.

Cult classics have a ubiquitous yet difficult to define part of popular culture. While they were born of the truly transgressive and stigma-shattering films of the 1950s, the term has since evolved into a catch-all for any movie that finds its audience well outside of the mainstream. Most journalists, specialists, and aficionados often refuse to lay out any kind of formula for what makes a cult movie, as they tend to consist of contradictions like "retro-futurism" (as seen in *Brazil* [1985] or *Dark City* [1998]) or "so bad it's good" (like Tommy Wiseau's *The Room* [2003] or *Troll 2* [1990]). Much of the definition also depends on the eye of the beholder; what is called cult is determined by taste and expectation, which are subjective, to say the least.

Still, several of the same elements tend to occur in most cult classic films: well-publicized difficulties with the film's production and/or famously disappointing box office return; a sense of nostalgia expressed or encouraged; a tongue-in-cheek tone, or it is so genuinely bad that it becomes fun to enjoy ironically; challenging the audience's cultural norms and/or genre expectations, or even their ideas of competent filmmaking; and no doubt, the biggest is the role of the audience. Cult film fans are famously passionate about these movies, organizing midnight showings, sing-alongs, costume parties, and all sorts of other ways to encourage the viewing and enjoyment of a movie which may not have been accepted by many others before.

This fan appreciation aspect of cult movies was best expressed by the late Umberto Eco in his classic essay "*Casablanca*: Cult Movies and Intertextual Collage." That fans love the movie, he says, is not enough. "It must provide a completely furnished world so that its fans can quote characters and episodes as if they were aspects of the fan's private sectarian world, a world about which one can make up quizzes and play trivia games so that the adepts of the sect recognize through each other a shared expertise."[3]

Masters of the Universe does not fit neatly inside the hazy definition of a cult classic but, then again, many don't. Firstly, it straddles the line in terms of quality. There's some camp humor inherent in the naiveté of the teenage couple and the bumbling Detective Lubic. The film's editing and special effects do not always come off smoothly, and neither does the dialogue from Dolph Lundgren. In their rooftop interaction, Langella's

Skeletor says, "Well said, He-Man," with sarcasm practically dripping from his words. Goddard seems to encourage a chuckle or two at the actor's expense.

Despite the unintentional humor, *Masters* looks objectively fantastic. The design is flawless and unique, bringing lizard-men and magical throne rooms, not to mention a toy franchise, to life. If it had been made with an even smaller budget, or without the talents of people like William Stout or Richard Edlund, the movie might move into the "so bad it's good" territory altogether. As it stands, though, it just dips in its toes.

It also benefits from the script's inclusion of Eternian expressions and terminology. Such minutia fill out the world of the movie and provide quotables for fans. There are no songs to sing along with, as such, but it's easy to picture a theater calling out "I have the power!" as Lundgren raises the Power Sword near the end.

Masters doesn't challenge an audience's views on sexuality or gender norms the way midnight movies like *Priscilla, Queen of the Desert* or *The Rocky Horror Picture Show* do, and it doesn't shock the viewer with gore or nudity. As much as the toys and cartoons blurred the world of science-fiction and sword-and-sorcery fantasy, the movie erred on the side of sci-fi. There's no surprising or innovative take on the genre expectations. While it may not have delivered exactly what He-Man fans were looking for, it's still recognizably He-Man.

As for the audience, they are not necessarily fans of Gary Goddard's movie alone. He-Man, as a household name, brought his audience with him to the cinema and no doubt asked their parents to bring home the video tape from rental shops.

Cannon Films brought its own fans, as well. By 1987, the studio had solidified its reputation as a producer and distributor of pure schlock. Their logo marked theatrical posters and cardboard VHS sleeves as bloody escapist action, comically inept low-budget spectacles, and more than often, both. In the U.S. and UK, their films were sought out by those looking for a brainless ninja flick or something to laugh at with friends. This status, along with the name recognition of He-Man and *Rocky IV* star Dolph Lundgren, was enough to rent some tapes and sell some tickets.

Masters would make appearances in revival movie houses and in other special showings alongside other cult classics, but the preexisting audience from the toys and cartoons set the live-action movie apart.

He-Man fans have had a difficult relationship with the film since day one, and the filmmakers have heard all about it. "The biggest complaint I always got at the time was 'why didn't you have ORKO in the film, and what happened to Battle Cat?'" Goddard would recall years later.[4]

The limitations of the technology and budgetary restrictions were not good enough answers for many young Masters of the Universe fans. While it was generally agreed that Lundgren at least looked the part of He-Man, and most praised the way Langella and Foster brought Skeletor and Evil-Lyn to life, the film's other elements and innovations were not embraced as well. Fans complained about the time spent on Earth instead of exploring Eternia. Many were torn on the number of new characters, as well. While the look of Saurod and fight scenes with Blade were cheered, Gwildor was not embraced as a worthy substitute for Orko. The series regular Beast Man was included, but he was downgraded to a savage, unspeaking brute. All of his lines in the original script, fans would later learn, were given to another new character, Karg.

If the movie had played things closer to the established tone and look of the cartoon series, many fans grumbled, maybe it would have gone over better. The fans weren't the only ones to feel this way. Filmation's Lou Scheimer said he'd met with the film's producer, Ed Pressman, early in preproduction to ask about the newest adaptation. He didn't like what he heard.

"As is Hollywood's style," Scheimer wrote, "they ignored completely the show that made the franchise so popular with the kids.... I said, 'You're f---ing the audience! This is not what they grew up on; it's not what they want to see. You're really hurting yourself.'"[5]

But not every He-Man fan was disappointed with *Masters*. One boy sitting in the theater was Tim Seeley, who would grow up to become a famed comic book writer and artist. "I'll always remember going to see that movie with my family in the theater," he said. "I had just gotten out of the hospital that very day after an appendectomy. I was sitting next to my dad, and the credits rolled up. My dad took one look at 'Produced by Golan & Globus' and he said, 'Oooooh, boy.' Like, out loud."

While the producers' reputation was known to his family, Seeley's impression wasn't tainted: "Despite that, I LOVED that movie. Yeah, sure, it's low budget, and occasionally stiltedly acted, but it's full of heart and imagination. And the bad guys looks cool as hell. Saurod is one of the coolest things I've ever seen."[6]

Future filmmaker Corey Landis didn't catch *Masters of the Universe* in the theaters, but rented a VHS copy as soon as it came to video stores. "With respect to Gary, whom I am a big fan of, I was not a fan of the movie," he remembered. "I've seen it several times in the last few years, and I can appreciate certain aspects more with the critical eye of an adult in the industry. I think Langella is incredible in it, and I think a lot of Stout's design elements are great. But it is NOT the [Masters of the Universe] movie I wanted or want."[7]

After the months of costume tests, rewriting dialogue, and traveling back and forth from California during filming, Frank Langella was excited to show his children *Masters*, the movie he made just for them. "In the end, they couldn't care less," he said. "I had a screening for them, and they both fell asleep!"[8]

Twenty years after *Masters of the Universe* was released, things began to look very different, yet very familiar at the multiplex. The year 2007 saw the release of *Transformers*, the first in a series of live-action films based on the toy line that had followed He-Man onto television. Optimus Prime, Megatron, and the rest had made their leap into live-action now as well, but they'd taken their time doing so.

Hasbro's *Transformers* animated series ended about the time Mattel's *Masters* movie was leaving theaters in 1987, but its toy lines and comic books continued on for years. New cartoons like 1993's *Transformers: Generation 2* and 1996's *Beast Wars* achieved varying levels of success, but they kept the brand going strong. The most dedicated fans were kept involved, and the new incarnations even recruited more. Unlike Masters of the Universe, the toy-buying public was never completely burned out on Autobots and Decepticons.

Despite the new toys, new comics, new cartoons and video games, Transformers always belonged to the past. While the brand could keep up with the modern expectations of a cross-media franchise, it always remaining a remnant of the 1980s. So when the nostalgia wave crested higher than ever before in the mid–2000s, Hasbro found itself with a very mutable property, a time-tested product already on shelves, a dedicated existing fan base, and a brand name that would be recognized by those seeking to relive their childhood, no matter if they were a child of the '80s, '90s, or '00s. All of the right pieces were in the right places for Transformers to go to the big screen.

From the get-go, the *Transformers* film had more in its favor than *Masters* did a generation before. While Goddard and his crew were given a substantial amount to make their film by Cannon's standards, $22 million in 1987 was generally not considered to be enough money to bring a movie full of monster costumes, lasers, alien planets, explosions and invading armies to life. The fact that Edlund's company was not paid for every SFX shot they completed, or that Goddard had to pay out of pocket to complete the last sequence, couldn't have been a surprise to Hollywood insiders in the late '80s.

Even adjusting for inflation, the budget for *Transformers* was astronomical compared to what Goddard was given to work with. The stated amount spent was $150 million, before marketing and other costs, but it was still considered lower than it could've been. By the mid–2000s, it wasn't uncommon for blockbuster action films like this adaptation to be upward of $200 million. Producers called the smaller budget a "bargain" and watched the money roll in from box office receipts.[9]

Like *Masters* before it, the first *Transformers'* star power was visible but still minimal. Former Disney child star Shia LaBeouf was cast as he was beginning to emerge into more prominent, less child-like roles. The film would be his breakout performance in the second phase of his acting career, allowing the producers to sign him to a multi-film contract for less money than an already established leading man. The love interest would be played by Megan Fox, who was best known for appearing on an ABC sitcom called *Hope & Faith*. She was signed for cheap before the movie would rocket her to stardom as well.

The other faces of *Transformers*, like former R&B singer Tyrese Gibson and seasoned character actor John Turturro, were recognizable to audiences without being an actual draw. Academy Award winner Jon Voight showed up to sleepwalk through a minor role as the Secretary of Defense.

The most high profile names attached were behind the camera. Director Michael Bay had already become well known for his shallow, flashy style where image tended to trump the story. His films were often lambasted by critics. Still, he could speak to the mainstream audiences like few others, already having massive box offices successes with films like *Armageddon* (1998) and *Pearl Harbor* (2001). The adaptation would also be executive produced by Steven Spielberg, whose input was minimal but involvement was heavily touted.

With actors cast to appeal to the youthful demographic, a director who practically guaranteed a big opening weekend, and the name of one of Hollywood's modern legends, the only thing Hasbro had left to do was secure the hardcore Transformers fan base with the new renditions of the old characters.

Technology had finally reached the point where a live-action movie starring cars that turned into robots was a possibility. George Lucas's Industrial Light and Magic, the most sought-after special effects company in Hollywood was hired to bring the robots of life. They were instructed to make the Autobots and Decepticons appear realistic, though recognizable to fans, and to be sure their personalities shone through.

Putting the project over the top in the eyes of Transformers fans was the inclusion of voice actor Peter Cullen, who had voiced the heroic Optimus Prime in the '80s. Though Bay cast Hugo Weaving to portray Megatron and replaced the other robot's voices, Cullen was brought back to add some legitimacy in the eyes of the nostalgic. Fans responded very positively to this bit of pandering. Though not all were happy with the alternations Bay's film made to the tone or characters, the inclusion of the "real" voice of the lead Autobot was enough to make fans give the film their seal of approval.

Transformers was a perfect pop cultural storm. It hit all the right notes and appealed to all the right markets, so nobody was surprised when it grossed well over $700 million. Paired with the special new movie-specific toy line, tie-in comic books and paperback novels, a new video game, and a relaunched cartoon series, not to mention the prerequisite t-shirts and fast food promotions, the movie all but reinvented the media franchise wheel.

That first *Transformers* movie in 2007 also showed the world that a movie based on an action figure was nothing to scoff at. It was one of the biggest releases in years, and its impact on the way movies are created and marketed in the modern area deserve recognition. The media franchise formula gelled in a way it never had before, but that was quick to be emulated.

Hasbro followed the film up two years later with their other popular, nostalgia-laden '80s property, GI Joe. Like the Transformer franchise, the Joe figures had remained a constant, more or less, on toy store shelves. They'd had several cartoons since the original in 1985 as well, keeping the new versions of the brand name in the public eye while similarly marketing to the nostalgia audiences with special retro-styled anniversary toy lines. It too was primed for a jump to the big screen. After the success of *Transformers*, Hasbro hurried along the production on *GI Joe: The Rise of Cobra*.

The high hopes of the toy company, and Hollywood in general, were visible in the title alone. Unlike the first Transformers film, the Joe's one featured a colon and a subtitle, warning viewers in advance this would be the first of an ongoing series of films. Perhaps producers had *Masters of the Universe* in mind when creating *Transformers* with no such subtitle; the movie could've been a flop, so the studio stayed a little cautious. This time, though, the budget was cranked up to $175 million and there was no doubt *GI Joe* would get a sequel.

By 2009, audiences didn't blink at the idea of a major motion picture based off of a toy property. They did not, however, embrace cartoonish military action-adventure flick the way they'd fallen for a tale of a boy and his car.

GI Joe: The Rise of Cobra offered little of the fan service *Transformers* had, leaving the lovers of the toys and animated series cold with the new interpretations. Much of the characters and mythos were altered for director Stephen Sommers' vision. As the fans grumbled, critics rolled their eyes at the plot holes and lackluster special effects. Hasbro's second attempt failed to capture the same lightning in a bottle. Though it turned a profit, it was nowhere near as successful as the first attempt, and the inevitable sequel was trapped in Development Hell for several years.

The Transformers film's own sequel, this one subtitled *Revenge of the Fallen*, had come out just weeks earlier. It boasted a higher budget, at $200 million, but it lacked the carefully crafted rollout of its predecessor. The film was sloppily constructed, full of pacing issues and plot holes, unintelligible special effects, and as was immediately pointed out by filmgoers, many of the robot's personalities had been condensed into offensively racist caricatures. While it was torn apart by critics and not-quite embraced by fans, it still pulled in more money than the first one.

The franchise turned out another two sequels by 2016, of varying degrees of quality but both cracking the $1 billion mark in terms of international box office grosses. As Hollywood fell under more pressure to create these massive cross-media branded movies, and multiple sequels and spin-offs and cinematic universes became the norm, Transformers was still setting the standard.

And so, 20 years after it was first attempted, live-action films based on toy brands became culturally acceptable, if not insisted upon. But this book was not written to suggest that *Masters of the Universe* was more deserving of the success that *Transformers* achieved. The latter achieved things the former never could, due to advances in computer generated effects and more importantly, timing. While Mattel attempted to strike while the iron was hot, it hadn't foreseen the immanent downfall of the toy line. *Masters* was a swing and a miss. Its successor was much more sure in its execution, waiting to accumulate a full generation's worth of good will and fond memories before taking the leap.

Transformers also had more support from Hasbro, as the company was willing to invest more money to attract the top talent and best special effects to bring the franchise to life. It was also more willing to step back and allow the folks it had hired make the adaptations needed for the live-action medium. In 2007, every move the toymakers made felt confident and surefooted as they expanded the brand across various media to capitalize, and it all came together perfectly. Mattel on the other hand, had been fumbling in the dark throughout every stage of the Masters of the Universe, from toy to cartoon to film. When it succeeded, it was masterful and revolutionary. When it failed, it was an absolute train wreck. Hasbro's success all came from the benefit of not being the first ones to attempt something risky.

What this book was written to support is the pivotal role *Masters of the Universe* played in the genesis of the *Transformers* film franchise, board game-based films like *Battleship* (2012), and the current Marvel Studios cross-media strategy that has become the norm for speculative fiction franchises. Successful films are not pulled from the ether, whole and uninfluenced. This goes double for an expansive cross-media brand whose spearhead is a live-action movie.

It is noteworthy that the Transformers brand was influenced by He-Man: the toys and cartoons debuted in America after He-Man first braved those waters, and animated series like *Transformers* fell into the tested mold of *He-Man and the Masters of the Universe* for the sake of survival. Hasbro merely had to look at what Mattel was doing right, namely a children's cartoon acting as marketing and produced for five-episodes-per-week syndication, and then try to improve the process to maximize their profits. They did the same with their GI Joe brand, as Playmate Toys would do with *Teenage Mutant Ninja Turtles* in 1988, and Saban Entertainment would do with *Mighty Morphin Power Rangers* in '93.

Masters of the Universe started that trend, just as they attempted to start the trend of the toy-based live-action movie. If Goddard's film in 1987 had been successful, it is very likely that it would've quickly been followed by imitators the same way. Instead, it became a cautionary tale for overzealous toy companies. Along with the collapse of the toy line, Mattel was offered up as an example of how not to market your product, alongside its example of how to market it correctly. While the cartoon was mimicked, the movie was avoided.

This does not mean it was not influential in that way. Development is impacted by failures as well as successes, and more so, a first attempt that failed due to marketing issues rather than quality can teach quite a bit. If Mattel had not flooded the market with He-Man figures and playsets, not utilized frustrating sales gimmicks for expensive toy accessories, and perhaps selected a less shady film studio, the audiences may have shown up. The movie might have grown the brand as it was intended to.

It could have been as pivotal to He-Man as the Filmation cartoon had been. There could've been a sequel, maybe Cannon's strange, earthbound one or Goddard's dream of an epic, Tolkienesque fantasy. The completed movie was more than competent enough to serve its purpose if it had not been undermined from the start.

However disappointing the actual results were, *Masters of the Universe* occupies an important place in the history of media franchises. The film was the cornerstone in the foundation laid by Mattel, Filmation, and He-Man himself. It may have taken 20 years for the set-up to pay off, and it may have paid off for another company and franchise, but it finally happened. When the second blockbuster film based on a toy franchise hit, it hit big and changed the media landscape forever.

And it couldn't have happened without He-Man.

9

"Good Journey"

After the cancellation of *Masters of the Universe vs. The Snake Men* cartoon and the discontinuation of the rebooted action figure line, it didn't take long for He-Man get back up on his feet.

The final wave of "station figure" statuettes from NECA came out in 2007, just as Mattel was making its next announcement about the franchise. The Four Horsemen studio would be designing another line of figures, these ones modeled after the '80s toys and the iconic Filmation cartoon. Though made to resemble the designs of the originals, the figures would come from all aspects of the varied He-Man franchise. The company promised toys from the comic books and minicomics, both *He-Man* and *She-Ra* cartoons from the '80s, the less fondly remembered '90s incarnation, and characters introduced in the different animated series who had never been turned into toys before. They would be made for the collectors' market directly, no longer worrying about finding space on toy store shelves or winning over a new, jaded generation; they were selling directly to the pre-existing, hardcore fans. Fittingly, it was titled Masters of the Universe Classics.

The new line debuted at the San Diego Comic Convention in 2008, and the first offerings were old favorites He-Man and Beast Man, plus a figure of King Grayskull, a character only briefly seen in the 2002 cartoon. The new toys were better constructed and more minutely detailed, and had more points of articulation than the originals had. They were thoroughly modern while still appearing retro.

The Classics line was very successful in its more modest marketplace, and began releasing more figures each successive year. Mattel also followed through on its promise to release an eclectic group of characters. In 2009 they released the long-delayed toy of He-Ro, the Most Powerful Wizard in the Universe, from the aborted The Powers of Grayskull line. In 2015, there came another figure called He-Ro II, designed off of the sketches in the Lou Scheimer sequel series pitch, *He-Ro, Son of He-Man, and the Masters of the Universe*. Between those two were new editions of previously released characters like She-Ra and the Evil Mutant Slush Head, along with characters only seen in the minicomics, like Procrustus, the four-armed god who lives at Eternia's planetary core, and Evilseed, who had been created for the Filmation cartoon.

Three of the previously released characters who received a new figure were from the *Masters of the Universe* film: Gwildor, Saurod, and Blade. The new editions more closely resembled the makeup and costumes featured in the film instead of the preproduction design sketches. The Classics figure of Blade, while still as absurdly muscular most of the He-Man characters, now had multiple movie accurate sword accessories and a laser whip. No matter how controversial the film remained in certain fan circles, it still had its place alongside the other incarnations.

The new Classics figures were also packaged with minicomics. The latest series was produced by Dark Horse Comics, a Portland-based publisher best known for comic books like Mike Allred's *Madman*, Mike Mignola's *Hellboy*, and Frank Miller's *Sin City* stories. The writer hired was Tim Seeley, the He-Man fan who'd been fascinated by watching the *Masters* film on the big screen.

After growing up reading the minicomics packaged with his He-Man figures, Seeley had been inspired and grew up to be a comics writer and artist. While making the horror comic *Hack/Slash* for Image Comics, he became friendly with editor Scott Allie. "He and I discovered mutual interests in all kinds of horror and crime stuff," Seeley said, "with the one thing that we totally didn't share being [Masters of the Universe]. It was kind of a joke even. When Dark Horse got hired to do the pack in minicomics for the new [Masters of the Universe] Classics figures, Scott called me right away, and my career came full circle!"[1]

Keeping with the throwback flavor of the new toy line, Seeley's minicomics picked right up where the last ones had left off. They began with a retelling of "The Powers of Grayskull: The Legend Begins," the final minicomic story of the original line. That original comic was labeled as the first of a three-part story, but the toys were canceled before the second or third could come out. In the new story, we again see He-Man traveling to Preternia to encounter the various Snake Men and cybernetic dinosaurs that would have been featured in the aborted toy line. The following stories would finally introduce He-Ro, He-Man's wizard ancestor, and the other characters who would be featured in the Classics line.

These new Classics minicomics were as targeted at an older, collecting fan base as the toys were. The artwork and stories had become more sophisticated, and each minicomic was now intended to do more than showcase a new figure or advertise their special action feature. Seeley and the other creators used the pages to tie together the various continuities of Masters of the Universe, fill in plot holes or explain away long-dangling story threads or other unanswered questions. The franchise had evolved in a fascinating way, with the toys and minicomics being created for fans, by fans.

Mid-2016, Mattel announced the Masters of the Universe brand would be handed off to Super7, a company well known for retro kitsch like their vintage-style ReAction figures. To celebrate this massive change for the franchise, Super7 debuted "The Curse of the Three Terrors" at the San Diego Comic Con. It was a short cartoon, touted as the first new animation in the classic Filmation style since 1985.

"The Curse of the Three Terrors" was a quick, fun romp through Eternia's Dark Hemisphere as Skeletor searched for yet another ultimate weapon to use against He-Man. It was made to look as much like the old cartoons as possible, utilizing the same music and iconic opening credits. As the ultimate tip of the hat to fans, original Skeletor voice actor Alan Oppenheimer returned to the role at 86 years of age.

In 2012, the rights for He-Man comic books returned to DC Comics. The company replaced Dark Horse as the producer of the minicomics and began telling new stories delving into the lore, namely the newest version of the origin of Skeletor. They also told the final battle of He-Man and Skeletor after their space-bound *New Adventures* arc, as the '90s cartoon series ended without a climactic confrontation between the two. As with the Dark Horse material, the Classic minicomics filled in the holes in continuities to tie the canon together for the keen-eyed He-Man fans.

At the same time, DC brought Masters of the Universe back to full-sized comics as well. The company began cautiously: after a brief, weekly comic first released online to introduce readers to the revamped Eternia, a six-issue *He-Man and the Masters of the Universe* series followed. Once it concluded, the ongoing *Masters of the Universe* title lasted for 19 issues. The comic retold some of the more well-known stories, such as the discovery of She-Ra and the Horde, in greater depth and for a more mature palate. In the meanwhile, a separate miniseries brought the characters to the Earth of the mainstream DC Comics universe, allowing He-Man to once again battle Superman. There were also a series of one-shot comics exploring the origins of characters like He-Man and Hordak.

In 2014, this was followed by a new comic series called *He-Man: The Eternity War*, another ongoing series set in a grim, battle-sieged Eternia after the Horde capture Castle Grayskull and He-Man must lead a resistance.

Though typically thought of as a children's property, many modern Masters stories have been keyed for an adult audience of former child-fans. There is also the '80s kitsch nostalgia in play, as well, as t-shirts and other memorabilia are still made with their character's Filmation look. He-Man based fan groups, websites, and conventions like Los Angeles' Power-Con have all sprung up over the past few decades and continue to go strong.

In 2015, Dark Horse Books, an off-shoot of Dark Horse Comics, began releasing thick, hardcover tomes about the Masters of the Universe franchise. First came *The Art of He-Man and the Masters of the Universe*, full of illustrations and historical footnotes. It was compiled by Tim Seeley and his brother, Steve. A few months later saw the release of the first volume of the *He-Man and the Masters of the Universe Minicomic Collection*. At well over one thousand pages, it contained all of the original mini-comics from the Masters of the Universe line, the She-Ra line, the four made for the *New Adventures* figures, and the two for the 2002 reboot. Both books also contained interviews with creators. In 2016, they followed up with *He-Man and the Masters of the Universe: A Complete Guide to the Classic Animated Adventures*, which covered every episode of the Filmation *He-Man* and *She-Ra* series. A collection of the newspaper comic strips and a character guidebook were both announced for release in 2017.

With the years of fond memories built up in the fans, and all the recognition from a new generation thanks to jokes on shows like *Robot Chicken* and *Family Guy*, there has also been plenty of official talk and fan speculation about a new live-action film. The project has been kicked around Hollywood since the 2000s, trapped in a circle of so-called "Development Hell." Mattel took the property to Sony to produce, and then moved it to Columbia Pictures. Directors like Jon M. Chu (*GI Joe: Retaliation*) have been attached and removed, and many talented writers, such as Chris Yost (*Thor: The Dark World*), have submitted screenplays which were ultimately discarded. Any advances on the project were tossed out when a new director came on board or a new creative approach was decided upon.

In early 2016, Columbia Pictures Senior Vice President DeVon Franklin announced the newest director attached was McG, the director responsible for the campy adaptations of the '70s TV series *Charlie's*

Angels. This meant the latest script would require another rewrite. Still, interest in the remake was high, both for fans and actors. Both former American Gladiator Mike O'Hearn and *The Legend of Hercules* (2014) star Kellan Lutz began personal casting campaigns to be hired on as the newest He-Man.

As the 30th anniversary of the original live-action *Masters of the Universe* approaches, more interest is building and more audiences are eager to see He-Man and Skeletor on the big screen once again.

When the first *Masters of the Universe* movie was released, director Gary Goddard had already moved on to new projects. After its rocky preproduction, stressful production, and personally expensive postproduction, he had moved onto another project with Mattel. *Captain Power and the Soldiers of the Future*, Goddard's brainchild with Landmark Entertainment Group co-founder Tony Christopher, sought to push the boundary between television and action figures, making each episode of the live-action and computer-animated show interact with the toys the viewers at home were playing with. The toy line's vehicles were equipped with sensors which reacted to the flashing laser blasts on the screen. *He-Man* and *She-Ra* alumni Larry DiTillio and J. Michael Straczynski wrote most of the series.

Goddard's goal was to create something truly innovative with *Captain Power*. He succeeded at this goal, but that did not mean the show was accepted warmly. The same parents groups who complained about *He-Man*'s double-duty as toy advertisement did not approve of any programming that required a separately bought action figure to complete the experience. The show also came under fire for adult themes and storytelling. Episodes were built for longer story arcs, which was uncommon for 1987, and they also featured fascistic and post-apocalyptic imagery, mild swearing such as "Go to hell," and implied sexual liaisons between characters. Such story elements were included to bridge a generational gap, for the parents of the target toy-buying audience to be entertained along with their children. Some parents, however, were horrified by the on-screen death of one of the Soldiers of the Future at the end of the 22-episode season.

After criticisms were leveled, many TV stations moved the show to a dumping ground timeslot, a block that was too early or too late to attract viewers, in order to burn through the remaining episodes. Without a highly visible show to promote them, the toy line tanked as well.

Captain Power maintained a small but loyal group of fans who appreciated the innovative approach and more mature stories. Goddard has remained a strong backer of the series, and after several years of working behind the scenes, in 2016 he announced the Captain Power concept would be returning in a new series called *Phoenix Rising.*

Still, Goddard never directed an episode of *Captain Power.* When asked if his experiences with Cannon during *Masters of the Universe* had put him off directing, he responded, "Not at all. I love directing. I love being in the thick of the battle and figuring out solutions. But I had a company then—and I left it for a year to make this film. When I came back, we had some major new projects in Japan and elsewhere, and for Universal Studios, too."[2]

Business was picking up for the Landmark Group, and the company found itself designing attractions for theme parks and high-end resorts across the globe. This kept him moving within Hollywood circles, as he worked with Steven Spielberg to make the Jurassic Park River Adventure ride, among other partnerships. He directed many of the short films which were including in the roller coaster or theme park experiences, which led to him experimenting with the 3D format. He was involved in the making of *T2 3-D: Battle Across Time*, a well-received Universal Studios show. "I introduced [director James Cameron] to 3D film making during that project," Goddard has said.[3]

Additionally, he has provided memorable design work for Caesar's Palaces' Forum Shops, and Star Trek: The Experience, both in Las Vegas. In 2002, Goddard split from Landmark Entertainment to form The Goddard Group. He has since designed more theme parks and resorts internationally, with a focus on the expanding markets of East Asia, such as the Macau region of China.

Goddard has returned to TV, creating the short-lived series *Skeleton Warriors* in 1994 and *Mega Babies* in 1999, and he has also made a splash on Broadway. He produced a one-night special *Jesus Christ Superstar* revival, featuring the stars of its movie adaptation, and earned a Tony Award for the 2009 revival of *Hair.* He got another nomination the same year for *Reasons to be Pretty.* He is keeping busy with the various projects in various media, he said, "But I would actually love to direct another film."[4]

The *Masters* director has remained a proud supporter of his film, giving enthusiastic yet candid interviews about his experience with the project. He's appeared for big screen presentations of the movie on many occasions to give an introduction and do question and answer sessions.

By 2012, the rights to the film belonged to Warner Brothers. Talk began about a special 25th anniversary edition Blu-Ray to replace the very early, minimalist DVD release from years before. Brand new special features were assembled, including a "Making of *Masters of the Universe*" video with on-screen interviews with Goddard, William Stout, and others. Goddard's friend, *X-Men* director Bryan Singer, had agreed to moderate a new commentary track with Goddard and Frank Langella. However, after much of the new retrospective material had been finished, the Warner executives changed their minds. Perhaps uncertain such a release could recoup the costs of the new materials, a more bare-bones Blu-Ray was released. It featured the same extras that had been on the DVD, and the picture had not been much improved for the new format. Goddard, and many He-Man fans, expressed disappointment.

The company that made *Masters of the Universe*, Cannon Films, didn't survive its release.

The failure of the He-Man film and *Superman IV: The Quest for Peace* are generally regarded as the one-two punch that finally brought the studio down. Neither brought in the kind of money Golan and Globus needed, especially the "*Star Wars* of the '80s" level money *Masters* was optimistically predicted to generate. They'd made too many box office bombs, especially with too high of budgets, to get away with hiding the failure anymore. Bankruptcy was right around the corner, but they limped onward.

In 1987, Cannon began selling off the film library they'd amassed to pay off some of their debt. Their films continued to be produced and released, but the scrappy company had become desperate, hurrying out their *Cannon Movie Tales* fairy stories and violent Chuck Norris vehicles, all with lower production values than before. Here and there, Golan and Globus would turn a small profit, namely with cheaply made Jean Claude Van Damme actioners like *Bloodsport* and *Kickboxer*, but it was nothing to turn back the company's downward slide.

Cannon was eventually taken over by wealthy Italian financier Giancarlo Parretti for the sum of $200 million. This was all part of a scheme by Parretti to appear savvy enough in the ways of filmmaking to buy the famed French studio Pathé. So confident was Parretti that he changed the name of Cannon Film Group, Inc. to Pathé Communications in anticipation of the larger purchase. But this scheme fell apart when the French government reportedly found some unsavory details in his murky past; like Golan and Globus, the origins of much of Parretti's money was difficult to trace.

He was hounded by rumors of Mafia ties in Europe, and these soon followed him to America as well. According to an article in the *Los Angeles Times* from 1990, "Parretti issued a statement to denounce a story in

Business Week magazine that said he had indirect ties to at least one Mafia family and that accused him and Pathé Chairman Florio Fiorini of money laundering through a network of private foreign holding companies."[5]

Blocked from acquiring the actual, historically prestigious Pathé studio, Parretti instead borrowed well over $1 billion from international banks to purchase MGM, one of the largest American studios at the time. They were then merged with his own Pathé, Pathé Communications. He kept the Cannon group together to utilize their distribution network and churn out some more quick, cheap films.

Menahem Golan had met his match in the shady profiteer. Parretti pushed down hard on the company, forcing painful spending cuts and restructuring the company to begin paying off Cannon's various debts. Under the strain of money troubles, Golan quarreled with Parretti and even his cousin, Yoram Globus. He would leave the company in 1989 to form his own studio, the 21st Century Film Corporation, and continue making his own brand of low-budget thrillers, like *Death Wish V: The Face of Death* and Albert Pyun's Marvel Comics adaptation *Captain America*. Globus's newly formed Cannon Pictures countered this with films like *American Ninja 4: The Annihilation* and *Delta Force 3: The Killing Game*.

Perhaps the strangest thing to come out of the Golan-Globus split was their dueling dance movies. Both cousins wanted to make a quick flick to cash in on the Lambada dance craze, and knowing how briefly such fads would last, the producers put their own projects together almost overnight. Globus's movie was titled *Lambada*, so the copyright on the word was snatched up. Golan was forced to call his *The Forbidden Dance*. They were released the same day in 1990, cannibalizing each other's ticket sales. Neither film was well received, nor made any real profit.[6]

Parretti, meanwhile, was overseeing his MGM-Pathé Communications empire and doing little else. Under his management, MGM released almost no films and money problems began to mount. Checks were bouncing. Others, from staffers to film laboratories and even Sean Connery, were not being paid at all. The conglomerate's loans were beginning to default.

Within a year of Parretti's power-play, MGM-Pathé was in U.S. bankruptcy court. As the company circled bankruptcy, Parretti's own banking contacts refused to loan more money until he was removed from power. Shortly thereafter, he was facing fraud charges from the U.S. Securities and Exchange Commission, and the French government charged him with defrauding Credit Lyonnais, the national bank. "Parretti also was indicted by a Delaware grand jury in 1992 on perjury and evidence tampering charges related to the Credit Lyonnais dispute."[7] He fled the United States before he could be charged, or extradited to France to face other charges.

MGM retained control of Globus's Cannon Pictures, which went out of business in 1994. The 21st Century Film Corporation went bankrupt the same year. The cousins would later reunite and bury the hatchet over, what else, making more movies together.

The impact of Cannon Films was not forgotten in Hollywood, or in the minds of filmgoers. The company served as a cautionary tale for other studios, warning of the dangers of over-expanding and over-leveraging, and also provided dozens of new favorite movies for a generation of cult movie watchers. In 2014, Australian director Mark Hartley began putting together a documentary called *Electric Boogaloo: The Wild, Untold Story of Cannon Films*. Golan and Globus refused to participate, reportedly telling Hartley they were making their own documentary. In true Cannon fashion, *The Go-Go Boys: The Inside Story of Cannon Films* was released the same year. It debuted at the Cannes Film Festival, of course.

After *Masters of the Universe*, production designer William Stout stayed busy in Hollywood and beyond. The same year the film was released, he was hired on by Walt Disney Imagineering to design Disney-land attractions at different locations across the globe. Other theme parks he contributed to include Universal Studio's Islands of Adventure and Michael Jackson's Neverland Ranch.

With a growing reputation in the worlds of design and cartooning, Stout was also able to begin focusing on projects that personally interested him more.

One such interest was dinosaurs and paleontological art. His artwork was included in a traveling exhibition of paleoart, and was displayed in locations such as the Smithsonian and the British Museum. He served as designer for the animated *Dino-Riders* series, based on the toy line, and for Hanna-Barbera's short-lived *Dink, the Little Dinosaur* show. In 1993, he was hired by Universal Cartoon Studios to design an animated series spinning off of the popular *Jurassic Park* film. After extensive preproduction and a finished trailer showcasing what the series would be like, producer Steven Spielberg canceled the project before he could even watch it.

"I'm also very, very proud of my mural work that accurately depicts the pantheon of early prehistoric life," Stout said. "I've created nineteen public murals of this type so far. You can see them at the San Diego Natural History Museum, the San Diego Zoo, the Houston Museum of Natural Science and at Walt Disney's Animal Kingdom."[8]

Stout has illustrated children's books, including several Oz titles and his award-winning work on Richard Matheson's *Abu & The 7 Marvels*. Back on the big screen, he did design work for animated movies like *Dinosaur* (2000) and *The Ant Bully* (2006), and live-action and CGI creatures in Guillermo del Toro's *Pan's Labyrinth* (2006) and director Frank Darabont's adaptation of Stephen King's novella *The Mist* (2007).

He has also received recognition, and a grant, from the National Science Foundation for his paintings made after traveling to Antarctica. In 1992, Stout spent the summer in the Antarctic Artists and Writers Program observing nature and wildlife for a new series of paintings. He has spoken proudly of his work concerning the Antarctic, stating he is "adding to the movement to make Antarctica the first World Park and protect it forever."[9]

Stout has received numerous awards for his work in cartooning and design throughout the '70s and '80s, and up to the mid–2000s. He remained close friends with Jean "Moebius" Giraud until the French artist's death in 2012.

Initially, Dolph Lundgren did not speak fondly of his experiences making *Masters of the Universe*. In the next few years after its release, he would complain to interviewers about the long night shoots in Whittier, California, and the disorganization of Cannon Films. "Playing He-Man was pretty much my lowest point as an actor," he said in 1989, when he'd gotten a few more films under his belt.[10]

The burgeoning action star followed up *Masters* with another troubled production, *Red Scorpion*, the next year. Next he portrayed the title character in an adaptation of Marvel Comics' *The Punisher* (1989) Throughout the '90s, he played the lead in lower budget action and sci-fi movies, along with memorable turns in ensemble films like *Universal Soldier* (1992) and *Johnny Mnemonic* (1995).

Still, to most audiences he would always be Ivan Drago, the nearly unstoppable Russian boxer from *Rocky IV*. This role, more than *Masters* or anything else, welcomed him into an upper echelon of '80s and '90s action stars. His name would come up in conversations alongside actors like Arnold Schwarzenegger, Sylvester Stallone, and Jean-Claude Van Damme. Work was constant, but as the years progressed, his films were given much smaller theatrical releases, then sent directly to video. In the mid–2000s, Lundgren began directing. He worked behind the camera as well as in front for films like *The Defender* (2004) and *Icarus* (2010), and even provided the scripts for other actor/director projects like *Missionary Man* (2007) and *Command Performance* (2009). Although these films were released direct-to-video and not particularly celebrated, they allowed Lundgren to branch out creatively.

With '80s nostalgia picking up steam in the latter half of the 2000s, the actor returned to the *Universal Soldier* franchise alongside Jean-Claude Van Damme. 2010 held a turning point, as Lundgren played Gunner Jensen in *The Expendables*. The film was a tribute to '80s and '90s action movies, directed by and starring Sylvester Stallone, and featured other action stars like Bruce Willis and Arnold Schwarzenegger. Lundgren was given one of the meatier roles in the project: the character of Jensen is an aging mercenary with a drug addiction. He betrays the Expendables team and fights with the characters played by Stallone and martial artist Jet Li. After appearing to die, Jensen then reappears at the end of the film, recovering, sober, and back on the side of the good guys. In an ensemble film with such a large cast, he was given more to do than most.

The Expendables received mixed reviews but killed at the box office. It was Lundgren's first widely released theatrical film in 15 years, and one of the biggest successes of his career. He returned for the film's two sequels in 2012 and 2014, both of which grossed even more money.

Though hailed as the beginning of a career renaissance, Lundgren seemed content to return to the world of smaller budget movies where he could have more creative control. He has continued to direct and write his films occasionally, and moved into the world of producing as well.

Time has changed the way the star viewed his time making *Masters of the Universe*. As there were more rumors about the next He-Man film, interviewers would ask Lundgren again about his experiences, or if he'd been approached to reprise the role. On the circuit promising *The Expendables 2* in 2012, he admitted he'd had fun the first time around. He was still not a fan of the exposing outfit He-Man would require, but expressed an openness to taking another role. "I think He-Man is a cool character, and I had fun doing [the movie]," he told one interviewer. "I'd rather play the king. But yeah, good idea. All of these old superheroes are coming back, and I'm sure that's one that people could enjoy."[11]

Boosted by his appearance in *The Expendables* series, he has become more of a public figure and fitness celebrity, releasing an autobiography / fitness book called *Train Like an Action Hero: Be Fit Forever*, and giving interviews to explain his dietary and exercise practices.

Even when not on the big screen like other name brand action heroes, Lundgren has remained well within the public consciousness. This is no more apparent than in a frightening scenario from 2009: British tabloid *The Daily Mail* reported on an attempted home invasion in Lundgren's family's home in Marbella, Spain. While the actor was away filming, three masked men snuck in and tied up his wife, jewelry designer Anette Qviberg. While threatening her at knifepoint, the men spotted a family photo including the actor who still very much possessed a He-Manly set of muscles. They immediately fled the scene.[12]

After his turn as Skeletor, Frank Langella's career became even more varied than before. In addition to his work both on and off-Broadway, he played in highbrow comedies like *Dave*, lowbrow adventure like *Cutthroat Island*, and even in alien makeup for a multi-episode arc on *Star Trek: Deep Space Nine*. He did small parts in TV movies on children's networks, and appeared in short-lived sitcoms. While not every project he was involved with was well received by audiences or critics, Langella was always seen as a reliable, hard-working, and talented character actor who added a bit of class to anything he touched.

He won his second Tony Award in 2002 for the play *Fortune's Fool*, and was nominated again two years later for *Match*. In 2005, he was cast in George Clooney's *Good Night, and Good Luck*. The serious period piece was nominated for several awards, including a Screen Actors Guild Award for Outstanding Performance by a Cast in a Motion Picture.

Starting Out in the Evening, a quiet, somber adaptation of Brian Morton's novel, won Langella more acclaim in 2007. It earned him a Best Actor Award from the Boston Society of Film Critics, along with nominations from the Independent Spirit Awards and several others. That same year he won his third Tony for his role former president Richard Nixon in the play *Frost/Nixon*. He and costar Michael Sheen reprised the roles the next year in Ron Howard's film adaptation of the play. The big screen version of *Frost/Nixon* brought him a flurry of new award nominations, including one for Best Actor from the Academy Awards.

With the recognition and stature his career had been steadily gaining, Langella was occasionally asked about his role in *Masters of the Universe*. Interviewers phrased their questions to demean the film as pure camp or cheese, but the actor would have none of it. In 2008, while being interviewed by *USA Today* about *Frost/Nixon*, Langella proudly said: "I loved playing Skeletor, and people sometimes say, 'Aren't you embarrassed?' Not in the least! I loved my performance in that. I worked very hard to make him as exciting as I could. It was a great paycheck. But it was also delicious."[13]

Though he did not win the coveted Oscar, Langella's success continued in his various roles. He received another Saturn Award nomination for Best Supporting Actor for 2009's *The Box*, and another Tony nomination for Actor in a Leading Role in a Play for *Man and Boy* in 2012. In the 2010s he was involved in projects as diverse as *Muppet's Most Wanted* (2014) and the gritty FX drama series *The Americans*. While promoting the independent sci-fi movie *Robot & Frank* in 2012, he was asked again his role in *Masters of the Universe*.

After acknowledging that playing Skeletor introduced him to a whole generation of filmgoers, he smiled. "It's one of my very favorite parts."[14]

Evil-Lyn was the first of many memorable sci-fi/fantasy roles for Meg Foster. After *Masters*, she would appear would appear prominently in genre films like *Leviathan* (1989) and *Blind Fury* (1989), and into the '90s in Full Moon Entertainment pictures like *Shrunken Heads* (1994), the space-western *Oblivion* (1994) and its 1996 sequel. Though the films were often mere B-movies, Foster's icy on-screen demeanor and icier blue eyes constantly made her stand out. Her unique look, along with a turn in John Carpenter's outrageous 1988 film *They Live*, ensured her status as a cult movie icon. Though her career began to dry up at the turn of the century, things picked up again in the 2010s. She was cast in two musician-turned-director Rob Zombie films, *The Lords of Salem* (2012) and *31* (2015).

After portraying Blade and acting as the film's fight coordinator, Anthony De Longis has enjoyed a long and varied career in front of and behind the camera. He played more evil henchman, such as opposite Patrick Swayze in *Road House* (1989), and displayed his expertise with a sword in appearances on the TV series *Highlander*. He was often called upon to lend realism to cinema, such as choreographing bare knuckle boxing matches for Tom Cruise in *Far and Away* (1992), in which he was also featured as one of the fighters. Despite the SFX added for *Masters*, his skill with a whip gained even more renown in the industry. He was called in to teach Michelle Pfeiffer how to handle a bullwhip for her role as Catwoman in *Batman Returns* (1992), and to freshen up Harrison Ford's abilities before he filmed *Indiana Jones and the Kingdom of the Crystal Skull* (2008). Toward the mid–2000s, De Longis moved away from acting and choreographing to focus on voice acting. His voice work appeared in video games like *Red Dead Redemption* and *Bulletstorm*. He also became a go-to expert for historically accurate weapons and fighting techniques: De Longis appeared on shows like *Mythbusters* and *Deadliest Warrior*, and demonstrated how comic book superhero Green Arrow's signature boxing glove arrow might work on *DC Nation*. He kept both prop swords from his time as Blade, and donated one to a charity auction in the late 2000s.

The same year as he was Gwildor, Billy Barty appeared in two Cannon

Movie Tales, *Rumpelstiltskin* and *Snow White*. He had a special appearance in Ron Howard and George Lucas's fantasy epic *Willow* the next year, and then carried on making guest appearances on TV shows or taking bit parts in movies. Barty appeared more sporadically as the '90s progressed and his health declined. He passed away from heart failure in 2000.

The last episode of *Hill Street Blues* aired some months before *Masters of the Universe* debuted. With his longest-lasting and most recognizable role behind him, and no sign of a sequel for Man-At-Arms, Jon Cypher began popping up in TV movies and guest spots on various shows. His next most prominent and career-defining part came in the form of General Marcus Craig on the family comedy series *Major Dad*. Cypher appeared in a majority of the show's episodes. After a brief foray into voice acting for the *Batman Beyond* cartoon, the hard-working character actor finally allowed himself to retire.

The role of Teela was Chelsea Field's big break into acting, and though *Masters* didn't exactly take off at the box office, it gave her plenty of momentum for her new career. She was cast in prominent roles for horror movies like *Prison* (1988) and *Dust Devil* (1993), along with high profile turns in *Harley Davidson and the Marlboro Man* (1991) and *The Last Boy Scout* (1991). In the mid–'90s, Field began to transition into more mature, motherly roles in family-friendly movies; she appeared in the films *Andre* (1994) and *Flipper* (1996), which were both about a child's adventures with an aquatic mammal. She has acted less since 1996, when she married former *Quantum Leap* star Scott Bakula. They have two children together.

As for our Earthlings, James Tolkan returned to his most famous role as Principal Strickland in *Back to the Future Part II* in 1989, and as that character's ancestor in *Part III* the next year. He continued to play to his strengths as a hardnosed, authoritarian figure throughout the late '80s and '90s in appearances on TV shows like *The Fresh Prince of Bel-Air* and *The Wonder Years*. In 2001, he appeared as a regular cast member on the award-winning *A Nero Wolfe Mystery* series on A&E. He also directed two episodes. Tolkan has popped up in films periodically since the '90s, including 2015's indie western *Bone Tomahawk*.

After his time on the big screen as Kevin Corrigan in *Masters of the Universe*, Robert Duncan McNeill found better luck on television. He made some guest appearances on shows like *Quantum Leap* and *Murder, She Wrote*, and multi-episode arcs on *Homefront* and *Second Chances*, before becoming a regular on the medical drama *Going to Extremes*. It lasted less than one season. In 1992, McNeill was cast as a young cadet on an episode of *Star Trek: The Next Generation*. Having suitably impressed producers, he would return to the franchise in 1995 when he was cast as a different character, Tom Paris, on *Star Trek: Voyager*. He was a regular cast member for the show's full seven seasons, becoming well known and respected by the Trekkie community. He also shared the screen for several episodes with his *Masters* costar, Anthony De Longis. McNeill used his lengthy run on the sci-fi series to expand his talents behind the camera: he began directing, writing, and producing. He has become a prolific and sought after TV director, helming episodes of series like *Dawson's Creek*, *Supernatural*, and *Chuck*.

Courtney Cox's star was on the rise, and the initial box office disappointment of *Masters of the Universe* did nothing to slow it. After her role as "American Everygirl" Julie Winston, she was hired a recurring character on *Family Ties*, appearing opposite Michael J. Fox for over 20 episodes in the show's sixth and seventh seasons. Along with guest spots on TV shows and appearing in TV movies, she returned to the big screen for films like *Cocoon: The Return* (1988). 1994 proved to be a big year for the actress, as she played the love interest in the breakout Jim Carrey vehicle *Ace Ventura: Pet Detective*, while on the small screen she was a girlfriend-of-the-week on *Seinfeld*, and debuted in her best-known role as Monica Geller on *Friends*. Throughout that hit sitcom's 10-year run, she would also host *Saturday Night Live*, and star in the horror-satire *Scream* (1996) and its two sequels. Once *Friends* ended, Cox became a regular in the short-lived tabloid drama *Dirt*, and produced and starred in the cult favorite sitcom *Cougar Town*. Since the mid–'90s, she's been nominated for dozens of awards, including People's Choice, Teen Choice, and the Golden Globes.

Christina Pickles, the live-action Sorceress of Grayskull, finished out her run on the celebrated TV drama *St. Elsewhere*. The year *Masters* was released, she was nominated for her fourth Outstanding Supporting Actress Emmy for the series. The next year, the show's last, she'd get her fifth. Pickles continued to bring her calm, quiet dignity to appearances on TV shows like *Matlock* and *Roseanne*, and in films like *Legends of the Fall* (1994) and Baz Luhrmann's *Romeo + Juliet* (1996). She was reunited with Courtney Cox on *Friends*, playing her former costar's mother. She appeared as Judy Geller in 19 episodes over the ten-year span, earning another Emmy nomination for the episode "The One Where Nana Dies Twice." After popping up in sporadic TV roles throughout the 2000s, Pickles has moved into voice acting, frequently on the Public Radio International program *Selected Shorts*.

Lou Scheimer Productions never managed to take off the way Filmation had. The aging cartoonist put together short features and pitched many ideas to other companies, but almost nothing was released. Into the late '90s, his health became more of a concern. After undergoing heart surgery, he was diagnosed with Parkinson's disease. He passed away in 2013, just days before his 85th birthday.

Scheimer was mourned throughout the world of animation. While best known for the *He-Man* and *She-Ra* cartoons which impacted the childhoods of so many, he was still remembered for his work on *Star Trek: The Animated Series*, *The Archie Show*, and for the boundaries broken by an all African American cast of characters on *Fat Albert and the Cosby Kids*. He was also noted as the last great holdout against outsourcing American animation jobs to cheaper countries. Although the quality of Filmation's products is not remembered fondly, the man and the characters he brought to life are.

Roger Sweet left the Masters of the Universe design group but stayed on at Mattel for some time. He received his severance and left in 1991. Feeling burnt out from the industry, he moved to the Pacific Northwest and never returned to work in the world of action figures.

In the early 2010s, Sweet was approached by filmmakers Roger Lay, Jr., and Corey Landis for their documentary, *Toy Masters*. He agreed to tell his side of the story and explain what he had been positing for years: that he was the sole creator of the Masters of the Universe concept. After speaking with Lay and Landis, Sweet reportedly became difficult to work with. He stopped returning their calls and emails.

The former toymaker's argument is explained in *Mastering the Universe: He-Man and the Rise and Fall of a Billion-Dollar Idea*. Sweet co-wrote the book, which operated as an autobiography, a tell-all, and platform for his claim. The book brings across Sweet's unique voice and the intercompany politics quite well, but it had no silver bullet to settle the dispute of He-Man's origin. Though some common inspirations can be inferred for both Sweet and Mark Taylor, much of the beginnings of Masters of the Universe still falls to a word-versus-word argument.

He-Man, like his fellow Masters of the Universe and their shared world of Eternia, is a concept that struck hard, capturing the dreams and imaginations of a generation and never letting them go. It has reverberated outward, through the decades and across different forms of entertainment. It connected the way few toys, TV shows, and movies do. But even those involved with its creation have a hard time placing their finger on what made it the success it is. Many of them have gone as far as to call it luck.

After interviewing former Mattel executives along with Sweet and

Taylor, *Toy Masters*'s Corey Landis said, "It's like taking a number one song and asking why it was such a hit. The melody was just so, the chord structure was just so, etc. It just hit the right notes, at the right time."[15] He-Man happened because the world was ready for He-Man. If the toy had debuted a few months earlier, or a few months later, it may not have worked. The same could be said of the Filmation series. If another media franchise had beaten *He-Man and the Masters of the Universe* to the air, the series may not have commanded the same sense of originality or novelty. If it had debuted any sooner, it would have likely been slapped down by the FCC.

The sense of design in the characters and their world are also cited for that certain special something. The mixture of science-fiction and fantasy elements opened the franchise up wider than most concepts, making a universe of play where anything in a child's imagination was possible. Another thing that set the figures apart from their competition was the overly muscled sculpts, grimacing facial expressions, and squat, battle-ready positions. This brought the proportions of Frank Frazetta warriors and comic book superheroes to 3D, letting children act out their power fantasies.

The characters themselves were also crafted in broad enough strokes that, while the minicomics, storybooks, and cartoons were a fun extension, the explanation they provided were hardly necessary. Tim Seeley remembered getting his first Masters of the Universe figures, saying, "I instantly understood, in my 5-year-old mind, who was who, and what they did, and whether they were good or bad."[16]

Playing off such archetypes connected He-Man, Skeletor, and the secrets of Castle Grayskull to the larger, timeless world of mythology. "People from all walks of life and cultures have responded favorably to heroes," William Stout explained. "They've loved tales of good vs. evil ever since storytelling began."[17] Mattel's concern for keeping things "generic" in the line's early days bestowed, perhaps inadvertently, a mythic element to the toys. Combined with the story elements developed by the Filmation cartoon, namely the secret identity of young and uncertain Prince Adam, pushed the franchise even deeper into the time-tested tropes of the Campbellian "Hero with a Thousand Faces" story structure.

The loose, yet inherently recognizable design and characterizations also gave the franchise an elasticity. The toys could be shifted from medium to medium across a variety of styles. They could be updated to remain contemporary and still maintain the same sense of the characters. Stories from the minicomics could be retold as cartoon episodes. Small details or entire backstories and motivations could be altered, even the visuals tweaked as needed, and it would make no real difference overall. The Skeletor of the toys was the same as the Skeletor of the minicomics, the cartoon, the live-action film, and the imagination of the audience.

And He-Man? Everybody knows He-Man.

The brawny, blond barbarian of the magical, sci-fi world came pre-packaged as the perfect hero. He was born standing on the shoulders of the greats that came before him, from John Carter of Mars and Flash Gordon, to Conan the Barbarian and Tarzan of the Apes, to Superman and Captain Marvel. He condensed what worked before him into something timeless and instantly recognizable. He was as simple as his name, He-Man, a symbol of power and masculinity and the boundless imaginations of children across the world. That classic sense of his character, the simplicity of his mission, and the nobility of his cause have all kept him in the public's periphery even during the wilderness years between TV series or their next reboot.

His timeless nature is what has aided in the varied adaptations and translations, from toys to comics to cartoons and live-action. Big audiences will always want a super-strong hero with a pure heart. They will always respond to magic swords and spaceships and Battle Cats and skull-faced despots who are bested each and every time. He-Man will always be looked to because nobody else has ever done what he does quite as well. Even those who have never seen the Filmation cartoon or played with the original toys know who he is, so the building clamor to bring him back to the big screen hasn't surprised anyone.

As much as the Masters of the Universe franchise is looking forward now, it's important to not forget the past. That brand name has earned its rightful spot in history, even if that spot is not always recognized; it is fondly remembered as the first to leap the chasm between the toy store aisles and the television screens, but Goddard's 1987 film is often overlooked. Time has been good to the film, and many are viewing it more favorably after the distance of 30 years and the comparisons of less faithful Transformers and GI Joe adaptations, but it is still left out of the chain of events.

Regardless of quality or reception or casting or anything else, *Masters of the Universe* is important to the evolution of cross-media franchises. It is a cornerstone to the foundations of what audiences have grown to expect. It showed the entertainment industry how things could work, even if the lesson didn't sink in for 20 more years. The film is an important, even pivotal, link in the chain.

After all this time, it still has the power.

Filmography

Masters of the Universe (1987). 106 minutes. Produced by Yoram Globus and Menahem Golan. Executive Producer Edward R. Pressman. Co-Producer Elliot Schick. Associate Producers Michael Flynn and Evzen Kolar. Based on the toy line developed by, and copyrights and trademarks owned by Mattel, Inc., used under license. Written by David Odell, with uncredited rewrites by Stephen Tolkin and Gary Goddard. Directed by Gary Goddard.

CAST: He-Man: Dolph Lundgren; Skeletor: Frank Langella; Evil-Lyn: Meg Foster; Gwildor: Billy Barty; Julie Winston: Courtney Cox; Kevin: Robert Duncan McNeill; Man-At-Arms: Jon Cypher; Teela: Chelsea Field; Lubic: James Tolkan; Sorceress: Christina Pickles; Beastman: Tony Caroll; Saurod: Pons Marr; Blade: Anthony DeLongis; Karg: Robert Towers; Charlie: Barry Livingston; Monica: Jessica Nelson; Mrs. Winston: Gwynne Gilford; Mr. Winston: Walter Scott; Carl the Janitor: Walt P. Robles; Gloria: Cindi Eyman; Narrator: Peter Brooks; Pigboy: Richard Szponder.

CREW: Music: Bill Conti; Cinematography: Hanania Baer; Film Editing; Anne V. Coates; Casting: Vicki Thomas; Production Design: William Stout; Art Direction: Robert Howland; Set Decoration: Daniel Gluck, Mike Johnson, Kathe Klopp; Costume Design: Julie Weiss; Makeup Article: Robin Beauchesne; Hair Stylist: Lori Benson; Hair Stylist for Mr. Lundgren: Angelo Di Biase; Body Makeup: Lauren Hartigan; Makeup Lab Sculptor: James Kagel; Makeup Department Head: Todd McIntosh; Hair Stylist: Zandra Platzek; Makeup Lab Foreman: Gerald Quist; Makeup Artist: June Haymore-Pipkin; Makeup Designer: Michael Westmore; Post-Production Supervisor: Michael Alden; Production Manager: Alan Gershenfeld; Post-Production Supervisor: Alain Jakubowicz; Production Supervisors for Mattel, Inc.: Joe Morrison, John Weems, and Leslie Levine; Production Manager: Elliot Schick; Executive in Charge of Production: Rony Yacov; First Assistant Director: Frederic B. Blankfein; Second Assistant Director: John Eyler; Second Second Assistant Director: Barbara Bruno and Gere LaDue; Set Dresser: Nancy Booth; Assistant Art Director: Lynn Christopher; Lead Scenic Painter: Sharlene Ciraolo; Concept Designer: Edward C. Eyth; Property Manager: Ellen Freund; Special Designer: Jean 'Moebius' Giraud; Concept Designer: Joe Griffith; Carpenter:

Allan Johnson Set Dresser: Andrew Kennedy; Prop Maker: Frederick Lietzman; Lead Man: Douglas E. Maxwell; Set Dresser: John Hammer Maxwell; Concept Designer: Claudio Mazzoli; Carpenter: David McKlveen; Set Dresser: Jimy Murphy; Storyboard Illustrator: David Negron; Art Department Production Assistant: Josh Olson; Art Department Coordinator: Mary K. Perko; Construction Foreman: Michael Reinhart; Lead Sculptor: Leo Rijn; Production Design Coordinator: Rachel Rosenthal; Carpenter: Benjamin Thompson; Property Assistant: David Touster; Armor Construction Coordinator: Douglas Turner; Assistant Property Master: Ron Woods; Carpenter: Curtis Yackel; ADR Mixer: Bob Baron; Sound Recordist: Anna Behlmer; ADR Supervisor: George Berndt; Assistant Sound Editor: Steve Borne; Sound Re-Recording Mixer: Gary C. Bourgeois; Sound Editor: Ed Callahan; Sound Re-Recording Mixer: Chris Carpenter; Assistant Sound Editor: Mick D'Andrea; Boom Operator: Mary Jo Devenney; Special Sound Effects: John P. Fasal; Sound Recordist: Stanley B. Gill; Boom Operator: Mark Goodermote; ADR Mixer / Foley Mixer: Tommy Goodwin; Assistant Sound Editor: Douglas Kent; Sound Editor: Elliott Koretz; Supervising Sound Editor: John A. Larsen; Foley Editor: Robert Martel; ADR Editor: Marilyn McCoppen; Sound Editor: Harry B. Miller III; Sound Designer: Ed Novick; Sound Re-Recording Mixer: Dean Okrand; Sound Editor: David Pettijohn; Supervising Foley Editor: Barry Rubinow; Supervising Sound Editor: Robert R. Rutledge; ADR Assistant: Peter Michael Sullivan; ADR Editor: Jenny Weyman-Cockle; Sound Editor: John S. Wilkinson Jr.; Special Effects Lead: Arthur Brewer; Special Effects Technician: R.J. Hohman; Assistant Special Effects Foreman: Daniel Hutten; Special Effects Supervisor: Ellen Kitz; Special Effects Crew: Robert Hohmen, Karl G. Miller, Malton Right, and Larry Roberts; Special Effects Supervisor: Paulette Smook Marshall; Special Effects Assistant: Leo Leoncio Solis; Assistant Production Coordinator: Gretchen Van Zeebroeck; Pyro Technician: Joseph Viskocil; Model Shop Coordinator: Susan Alpert; Visual Effects Animation Production Assistant: Maura Alvarez; Visual Effects Project Leader, Swords: Larz Anderson; Visual Effects Editor: Michael Backauskas; Visual Effects Camera: Don Baker and Mat Beck; Visual Effects Art Director: Brent Boates; Visual Effects Special Consultant: Laura Buff; Visual Effects Grip: Mark Cane; Visual Effects Animator: Glenn Chaika; Model Shop Production Assistant: Dave Chamberlain; Visual Effects Optical Camera: Charles Cowles; Visual Effects, Technical Supervisor: Philip Crescenzo; Visual Effects Optical Line-Up: Mark Dornfeld; Executive Visual Effects Supervisor, Boss Film Studios: Richard Edlund; Model Maker / Visual Effects Project Leader, Flying Discs: Leslie Ekker; Visual Effects Chief Lighting Technician: Robert Eyslee; Visual Effects Production Advisor: James Nelson; Visual Effects Chief Financial Officer: Donald Fly; Visual Effects Animation Production Assistant: Meg Freeman; Visual Effects Animator: Deborah Gaydos; Visual Effects Optical Camera: Alan Harding; Visual Effects Optical Coordinator: Leslie Falkinburg; Moldmaker / Caster / Fabricator / Body Impressions, Weapons, Stunt Suit, Boss Films: Adam Hill; Visual Effects Production Supervisor: Robert Hippard; Visual Effects Illustrator: George Jenson; Visual Effects Animation Production Assistant: Lisa Krepela; Visual Effects Matte Department Supervisor: Neil Krepela; Visual Effects Animator: Mauro

Maressa; Visual Effects Production Coordinator: Mary Mason; Visual Effects Project Leader, Weapons: Pat McClung; Visual Effects Director of Photography, Second Unit: Rexford L. Metz; Visual Effects Editor: Dennis Michelson; Visual Effects Still Photographer: Virgil Mirano; Visual Effects Matte Artist: Michele Moen; Visual Effects Foreman: Thaine Morris; Visual Effects Director of Photography: William Neil; Visual Effects Animation Coordinator: Lisa Neil; Visual Effects First Assistant Photographer: Eric Peterson; Visual Effects Technical Animator: Samuel Recinos; Visual Effects Optical Supervisor: Chris Regan; Visual Effects Head Lab Technician: Patrick Repola; Visual Effects Project Leader, Battle Station: Eugene P. Rizzardi; Visual Effects Animation Production Assistant: Anjelica Casillas; Visual Effects Special Projects Assistant: Jon Schreiber; Visual Effects Project Leader, Puppets: Nick Seldon; Visual Effects Optical Camera: James Sleeper; Visual Effects Model Shop Supervisor: Mark Stetson; Visual Effects Optical Line-Up: Michael Sweeney; Visual Effects Animator: Eusebio Torres; Model Maker: George Trimmer; Visual Effects Grip: Patrick Van Auken; Software Programmer: Paul Van Camp; Visual Effects Coordinator: Michael Van Himbergen; Visual Effects Supervisor: Garry Waller; Visual Effects Chief Engineer: Gene Whiteman; Visual Effects Art Director: Terry Windell; Visual Effects First Assistant Photographer: Stefanie Wiseman; Visual Effects Editorial Production Assistant: Debra Wolff; Visual Effects Chief Matte Artist: Matthew Yuricich; Visual Effects Project Leader, Cosmic Key: Stuart Ziff; Stunt Double for Mr. Langella: Anthony De Longis; Stunt Choreographer: Loren Janes; Stunt Coordinator: Walter Scott; Stunts: Robert N. Bell, Bradley J. Bovee, Janet Brady, Tony Brubaker, Brian Burrows, Doc D. Charbonneau, Danny Costa, Charles Croughwell, Kent Jordan, Clint Lilley, Ben Scott, John-Clay Scott, Brian Smrz, and Gregg Smrz; Best Boy Electric: Mark Buckalew; Key Grip: Skip Cook and Brian H. Reynolds; Dolly Grip: Rick Davis; Camera Operator: Dan Elsasser; Electrician: Christopher Fenney, David M. Rakoczy, Don Tomich, and John E. Vohlers; Additional Cinematographer: Michael Hofstein; Best Boy: Warren Kroeger; Best Boy Grip: Richard Kuhn and Ric Urbauer; First Assistant Camera: Michael E. Little; Grip: Robert W. McCarty, Bob Myers, Vince Onken, Mark Roemmich, and Mark A. Shelton; Key Rigging Grip: Ron McCausland; Gaffer: James Rosenthal; Still Photographer: Ken Sax; Videographer: David Schmalz; Assistant Camera: Randy Shanofsky; Casting Assistant: Renee Milliken; Extras Casting: Sally Pearle; Co-Special Costume Supervisor: Allan A. Apone; Wardrobe Production Assistant: John Franzblau; Wardrobe Supervisor: Lawrence Richter; Assistant Wardrobe: Isabella B. Van Soest and Mira Zabadowski; Costumer: Carol Kunz, Lisa Lovaas, Marcie Olivi, Frank Palinski, Joseph A. Porro, and Sharon Swenson; Assistant Editor: Christopher Cibelli; Second Assistant Editor: Sam Citron; Negative Cutter: Helen Hahn; Apprentice Editor: James D.R. Hickox; Post-Production Coordinator: Omneya Mazen; Color Timer: Stephen R. Sheridan; Music Coordinator: Corrie Behrhorst; Orchestrator: Bill Conti; Music Supervisor: Paula Erickson; Orchestrator: Ralph Ferraro; Music Editor: Stephen A. Hope; Music Supervisor/Orchestrator: William Kidd; Music Coordinator: Stephanie Lee; Conductor/Music Arranger: Bruce Miller; Conductor: Harry Rabinowitz;

Orchestrator: Joel Rosenbaum; Score Mixer: Dan Wallin; Music Mixer Assistant: Rick Winquest; Transportation Co-Captain: John Conte and Edward Flotard; Transportation Manager: Jimmy Jones; Transportation Captain: H. William Miller; Transportation Coordinator: Joel Renfro; Location Manager: Steve Anderson; Title Designer: Wenden K. Baldwin; Assistant to Mr. Kolar: Denise Lanzetta; Development Assistant: Fern Baum; Production Assistant: Arthur Borman; Intern: Bea Ellen Cameron; Design Maquettes: Terri Cardinali; Creature Crew: Craig Caton; Set Medic: Bundy Chanock; Design Maquettes: Joe De Reis; Skeletor Armory Crew: Edward J. Franklin; Creative Advisor to Mr. Lundgren: David Gamberg; Production Assistant: Brian Gaughan; Dialogue Coach to Mr. Lundgren: Lillian Glass; Script Supervisor: Adrienne Hamalian-Mangine; Location Manager: Bart Heimburger; Design Maquettes: Michael Hood and Laine Liska; Lead Puppet Sculptor: Michael Hosch; Assistant Production Coordinator: Gretchen Iverson; Unit Publicist: Karine Jonet; Armor Supervisor: James D. McGeachy; Production Executive: Rick Nathanson; Unit Accountant: Robert Pederson; Trainer to Mr. Lundgren: Josef Poma; Specialty Prop Builder: Brent Scrivener; Title Designer: Kyle Seidenbaum; Armor Production Executive: Barbara Slifka; Production Assistant: Susan Lee Smith; Production Accountant: Joe Straw; Assistant to Mr. Goddard: Merie Weismiller Wallace; Assistant to Mr. Edlund: Claire Wilson; Location Manager: Cynthia R. Woodard.

Animated Series

He-Man and the Masters of the Universe. Executive Producer: Lou Scheimer; Executive Vice President, Creative Affairs: Arthur H. Nadel; Vice President in Charge of Production: Joe Mazzuca.

Referenced Episodes:

"The Shaping Staff" (October 20, 1983). Writer: Paul Dini; Director: Lou Kachivas.

CAST: He-Man/Prince Adam/Beast Man/Faker: John Erwin; Skeletor/Man-At-Arms/Cringer/Battle Cat: Alan Oppenheimer; Teela/Evil-Lyn/The Sorceress/Magestra: Linda Gray; Orko/King Randor: Erik Gunden (Lou Scheimer).

CREW: Production Director: Hal Sutherland; Associate Producer: Patricia Ryan; Music: Shuki Levy, Haim Sabin, and Erika Lane (Lou Scheimer); Cinematography: R.W. Pope; Film Editing: Bob Crawford, Joe Gail, and Sam Moore; Post-Production Supervisor: Joe Simon; Storyboard Supervisor: Bob Arkwright; Graphic Designer: Michael Randall; Supervising Editor: George Mahana; Music Editor: Sam Horta; Film Coordinator: June Gilham; Final Checker: Teri McDonald; Film Coordinator: Christie Meyer; Educational and Psychological Consultant: Donald F. Roberts; Assistant to Directors: Keith Sutherland; Production Coordinator: Carol A. Tracy; Production Controller: Robert W. Wilson.

"A Tale of Two Cities" (November 1, 1983). Writer: Richard Pardee; Director: Marsh Lamore.

CAST: He-Man / Prince Adam / Beast Man / Gargon Warrior: John Erwin; Cringer / Battle Cat / Draca: Alan Oppenheimer; Princess Rhea / Queen Balina: Linda Gray; Garn / Gargon Warrior / King Thales: Erik Gunden (Lou Scheimer).

CREW: Production Director: Hal Sutherland; Associate Producer: Patricia Ryan; Music: Shuki Levy, Haim Sabin, and Erika Lane (Lou Scheimer); Cinematography: R.W. Pope; Film Editing: Bob Crawford, Joe Gail, and Sam Moore; Post-Production Supervisor: Joe Simon; Storyboard Supervisor: Bob Arkwright; Graphic Designer: Michael Randall; Supervising Editor: George Mahana; Music Editor: Sam Horta; Film Coordinator: June Gilham; Final Checker: Teri McDonald; Film Coordinator: Christie Meyer; Educational and Psychological Consultant: Donald F. Roberts; Assistant to Directors: Keith Sutherland; Production Coordinator: Carol A. Tracy; Production Controller: Robert W. Wilson.

"Double Edged Sword" (October 25, 1983). Writer: Robert London; Director: Gwen Wetzler.

CAST: He-Man / Prince Adam / Elden: John Erwin; Cringer / Battle Cat / Man-At-Arms / Mer-Man: Alan Oppenheimer; Teela / The Sorceress: Linda Gray; Orko / King Randor / Trap Jaw: Erik Gunden (Lou Scheimer).

CREW: Production Director: Hal Sutherland; Associate Producer: Patricia Ryan; Music: Shuki Levy, Haim Sabin, and Erika Lane (Lou Scheimer); Cinematography: R.W. Pope; Film Editing: Bob Crawford, Joe Gail, and Sam Moore; Post-Production Supervisor: Joe Simon; Storyboard Supervisor: Bob Arkwright; Graphic Designer: Michael Randall; Supervising Editor: George Mahana; Music Editor: Sam Horta; Film Coordinator: June Gilham; Final Checker: Teri McDonald; Film Coordinator: Christie Meyer; Educational and Psychological Consultant: Donald F. Roberts; Assistant to Directors: Keith Sutherland; Production Coordinator: Carol A. Tracy; Production Controller: Robert W. Wilson.

"The Arena" (September 29, 1984). Writer: Warren Greenwood; Director: Ernie Schmidt.

CAST: He-Man / Prince Adam / Om: John Erwin; Skeletor / Man-At-Arms: Alan Oppenheimer; Teela / Queen Marlena: Linda Gray; Orko / King Randor / General Tataran / Guard / Eternians / Goblin warrior: Erik Gunden (Lou Scheimer).

CREW: Music: Shuki Levy, Haim Sabin, and Erika Lane (Lou Scheimer); Editing: Bob Crawford, Joe Gail, and Rick Gehr; Post-Production Supervisor: Joe Simon; Storyboard Supervisor: Bob Arkwright; Graphic Designer: Connie Schurr; Head of Visual Effects: Shurl Lupin; Supervising Editor: George Mahana; Music Editor: Sam Horta; Film Coordinator: June Gilham; Final Checker: Teri McDonald; Film Coordinator: Christie Meyer; Creative Technical Advisor: R.W. Pope; Educational and Psychological Consultant: Donald

F. Roberts; Assistant to Directors: Keith Sutherland; Production Coordinator: Carol A. Tracy; Production Associate: Pamela Vincent; Production Controller: Robert W. Wilson.

"Jacob and the Widgets" (October 19, 1984). Writer: Harvey Brenner; Director: Ed Friedman.

CAST: He-Man / Prince Adam / Squinch / Jacob: John Erwin; Cringer / Man-At-Arms / Mer-Man / Battle Cat: Alan Oppenheimer; Teela / Lara: Linda Gray; Orko / Trap Jaw / Kando / Biro: Erik Gunden (Lou Scheimer).

CREW: Music: Shuki Levy, Haim Sabin, and Erika Lane (Lou Scheimer); Editing: Bob Crawford, Joe Gail, and Rick Gehr; Post-Production Supervisor: Joe Simon; Storyboard Supervisor: Bob Arkwright; Graphic Designer: Connie Schurr; Head of Visual Effects: Shurl Lupin; Supervising Editor: George Mahana; Music Editor: Sam Horta; Film Coordinator: June Gilham; Final Checker: Teri McDonald; Film Coordinator: Christie Meyer; Creative Technical Advisor: R.W. Pope; Educational and Psychological Consultant: Donald F. Roberts; Assistant to Directors: Keith Sutherland; Production Coordinator: Carol A. Tracy; Production Associate: Pamela Vincent; Production Controller: Robert W. Wilson.

"The Problem with Power" (October 9, 1985). Writer: Bob Forward, Leslie Wilson; Idea: Tom Tataranowicz; Director: Gwen Wetzler.

CAST: He-Man / Prince Adam: John Erwin; Skeletor / Man-At-Arms: Alan Oppenheimer; Teela / Queen Marlena / The Sorceress: Linda Gray; Orko / King Randor / General Tataran / Trap Jaw / Goblins: Erik Gunden (Lou Scheimer).

CREW: Music: Shuki Levy, Haim Sabin, and Erika Lane (Lou Scheimer); Editing: Bob Crawford, Joe Gail, and Rick Gehr; Post-Production Supervisor: Joe Simon; Storyboard Supervisor: Bob Arkwright; Graphic Designer: Connie Schurr; Head of Visual Effects: Shurl Lupin; Animation Special Effects: Brett Hisey, Dardo Velez; Supervising Editor: George Mahana; Music Editor: Sam Horta, Mary R. Smith; Film Coordinator: June Gilham; Final Checker: Teri McDonald; Film Coordinator: Christie Meyer; Creative Technical Advisor: R.W. Pope; Educational and Psychological Consultant: Donald F. Roberts; Production Assistant: John J. Blough, Michael P. Sowa; Production Coordinator: Carol A. Tracy; Production Associate: Pamela Vincent; Production Controller: Robert W. Wilson.

Screenplays

Odell, David. *Masters of the Universe*, December 5, 1985.

Chapter Notes

Preface

1. Edmund L. Andrews, "Toy-Based TV Shows Win Ruling" (*New York Times*, November 9, 1990).

Introduction

1. Jay Lemke, *Critical Analysis Across Media: Games, Franchises, and the New Cultural Order* (First International Conference on CDA, 2004), p. 3.

2. *Fifty Shades of Grey* famously began its life as fan fiction, with author E.L. James writing about the steamy relationship of the characters Edward Cullen and Bella Swan from the young adult novel and film *Twilight*. Although fan fiction is a beloved and prolific aspect of media franchise fandom, it will not be touched upon in this book. There's just far too much of it.

3. Edward Jay Epstein, *The Midas Formula: How to Create a Billion-Dollar Movie Franchise* (Slate.com, 2005).

4. Joseph Campbell, *The Hero with a Thousand Faces*, 3d ed. (Novato, CA: New World Library, 2008), p. 23. Originally published 1949.

5. "This movie is a brain-bubble symptom, a 107-minute Technicolor aneurysm; it is an extended, incoherent Tourette's-style yelping of design-ideas, soundtrack-styles, FX flourishes, rewrites and mismatched performances." Peter Bradshaw, review of *Wild Wild West*, *The Guardian* (August 13, 1999).

6. "Tri-Star originally planned two sequels to *Godzilla* (1998), but decided against the idea when the film turned out to be a critical and commercial disaster." Robert Greenberger, *Meet Godzilla* (The Rossen Publishing Group, 2004), p. 36.

7. The Golden Raspberry Awards, or "Razzies," are a set of annual awards that works like the Bizarro Oscars: they give out awards for the year's Worst Movie, Worst Actress, and so on. They're by no means a definitive example of what's bad, but they're typically fairly on point. In a book talking about Cannon Films, the Razzies will come up a few times.

8. Jake Rossen, *Superman Vs. Hollywood: How Fiendish Producers, Devious Directors, and Warring Writers Grounded an American Icon* (Chicago: Chicago Review Press, 2008), p. 1.

9. Jake Rossen, *Superman Vs. Hollywood: How Fiendish Producers, Devious Directors, and Warring Writers Grounded an American Icon* (Chicago: Chicago Review Press, 2008), p. 3.

10. The history of Superman and the phone booth is best explained in an essay on the Superman Homepage. Steve Younis, *Superman and the Phone Booth* (http://www.supermanhomepage.com/other/other.php?topic=phonebooth).

11. Gregg Kilday, "Paramount, Hasbro Creating Movie Universe Around G.I. Joe, Four Other Brands (Exclusive)" (*Hollywood Reporter*, December 15, 2015).

12. Brett Lang, "How Universal Plans to Bring Its Monster Movies Back to Life (Exclusive)" (*Variety*, November 17, 2015).

13. Case in point is *Young Justice*, a well-loved animated series featuring teenage DC heroes like Robin, Superboy, and

Speedy. It aired on Cartoon Network between 2010 and 2013 before it was dropped after the conclusion of its second season, leaving dangling plot threads and many unhappy fans behind. When asked about the cancellation on Twitter in October of 2015, the show's producer, Greg Weisman (@Greg_Weisman), said it came about due to "lack of toy sales, which is where the money for our budget came from." Ratings were high and critical reception was all but glowing, but *Young Justice* died from a lack of tie-in success.

14. "Reason Interview with Mark S. Fowler," *Reason*, November 1, 1981.

Chapter 1

1. Roger Sweet and David Wecker, *Mastering the Universe: He-Man and the Rise and Fall of a Billion-Dollar Idea* (Cincinnati: Emmis Books, 2005), p. 77.

2. Tim and Steve Seeley, *The Art of He-Man and the Masters of the Universe* (Milwaukee, OR: Dark Horse Books, 2015), p. 9.

3. Roger Sweet and David Wecker, *Mastering the Universe: He-Man and the Rise and Fall of a Billion-Dollar Idea* (Cincinnati: Emmis Books, 2005), p. 80.

4. Roger Sweet and David Wecker, *Mastering the Universe: He-Man and the Rise and Fall of a Billion-Dollar Idea* (Cincinnati: Emmis Books, 2005), p. 86.

5. Interview with Corey Landis, February 4, 2016.

6. "In a fit of monumental stupidity, I threw away a manila envelope chock full of documents, illustrations, and other information regarding He-Man's creation." Roger Sweet and David Wecker, *Mastering the Universe: He-Man and the Rise and Fall of a Billion-Dollar Idea* (Cincinnati: Emmis Books, 2005), p. 201.

7. This information was obtained from the Battle Ram fansite. "Zodac—Cosmic Enforcer (1982)" (https://battleram.word press.com/2016/02/15/zodac-cosmic-enforcer-1982/, February 15, 2016).

8. Roger Sweet and David Wecker, *Mastering the Universe: He-Man and the Rise and Fall of a Billion-Dollar Idea* (Cincinnati: Emmis Books, 2005), p. 116.

9. Matthew Chernov, *10 Things We Learned from Mark Taylor, the Designer of He-Man* (http://www.therobotsvoice.com/ 2015/11/man-masters-universe-mark-taylor-mattel-toy-masters.php, November 5, 2015).

10. Interview with Gary Cohn, *He-Man and the Masters of the Universe Minicomic Collection* (Milwaukee, OR: Dark Horse Books, 2015), p. 175.

11. Interview with Mark Texeira, *He-Man and the Masters of the Universe Minicomic Collection* (Milwaukee, OR: Dark Horse Books, 2015), p. 108.

12. Interview with Gary Cohn, *He-Man and the Masters of the Universe Minicomic Collection* (Milwaukee, OR: Dark Horse Books, 2015), p. 177.

13. Interview with Michael Halperin, *He-Man and the Masters of the Universe Minicomic Collection* (Milwaukee, OR: Dark Horse Books, 2015), p. 269.

14. The court's specifics and quotes for this section were taken from an essay on a Robert E. Howard fan site. Paul Herman, "Copyrightable Conan?" (http://www. robert-e-howard.org/AnotherThought2. html, September 2001).

15. Paul Herman, "Copyrightable Conan?" (http://www.robert-e-howard.org/ AnotherThought2.html, September 2001).

16. Roger Sweet and David Wecker, *Mastering the Universe: He-Man and the Rise and Fall of a Billion-Dollar Idea* (Cincinnati: Emmis Books, 2005), p. 138.

Chapter 2

1. Lou Scheimer with Andy Mangels, *Lou Scheimer: Creating the Filmation Generation*, 2d ed. (Raleigh, NC: TwoMorrows Publishing, 2015), p. 45.

2. Lou Scheimer with Andy Mangels, *Lou Scheimer: Creating the Filmation Generation*, 2d ed. (Raleigh, NC: TwoMorrows Publishing, 2015), p. 62.

3. "The Man with the Golden Ear" was an industry nickname for Don Kirshner. It was also the title of a 2012 biography written by Rich Podolsky.

4. In 1969, a gold record indicated over one million units sold. The threshold was later halved.

5. Dick Kleiner, "'Trek' Tracks Adults" (*Sumter Daily Item*, July 21, 1973).

6. Lou Scheimer with Andy Mangels, *Lou Scheimer: Creating the Filmation Gen-*

eration, 2d ed. (Raleigh, NC: TwoMorrows Publishing, 2015), p. 199.

7. Roger Sweet and David Wecker, *Mastering the Universe: He-Man and the Rise and Fall of a Billion-Dollar Idea* (Cincinnati: Emmis Books, 2005), p. 123.

8. Tim and Steve Seeley, *The Art of He-Man and the Masters of the Universe* (Milwaukee, OR: Dark Horse Books, 2015), p. 120.

9. Charles Solomon, "Syndication Threat: Saturday Kidvid on the Way Out?" (*Los Angeles Times*, November 15, 1986).

10. Sydney Shaw, "A Children's Television Watchdog Group Filed a Complaint Tuesday..." (Archived on http://www.upi.com/Archives/1983/10/11/A-childrens-televison-watchdog-group-filed-a-complaint-Tuesday/9006434692800/, October 11, 1983).

11. The transcript from this episode has not been archived online. This quote from taken from Scheimer's book. Lou Scheimer with Andy Mangels, *Lou Scheimer: Creating the Filmation Generation*, 2d ed. (Raleigh, NC: TwoMorrows Publishing, 2015), p. 206.

12. Peter J. Boyer, "Toy-Based TV: Effects on Children Debated" (*New York Times*, February 3, 1986).

13. Peter J. Boyer, "Toy-Based TV: Effects on Children Debated" (*New York Times*, February 3, 1986).

14. Jane A. Welch, "'He-Man' is a Wimp Master" (*Washington Post*, April 21, 1985).

15. The quotes used for this section are logged on the He-Man.org website. "J. Michael Straczynski: Interview by Various Usenet Users—1995" (http://old.he-man.org/cartoon/cmotu-pop/interview-straczynski.shtml).

16. Lou Scheimer with Andy Mangels, *Lou Scheimer: Creating the Filmation Generation*, 2d ed. (Raleigh, NC: TwoMorrows Publishing, 2015), p. 230.

17. Lou Scheimer with Andy Mangels, *Lou Scheimer: Creating the Filmation Generation*, 2d ed. (Raleigh, NC: TwoMorrows Publishing, 2015), p. 204.

Chapter 3

1. Dolph Lundgren, *Train Like An Action Hero* (New York: Skyhorse Publishing, Inc., 2014), p. 12.

2. Dolph Lundgren, *Train Like An Action Hero* (New York: Skyhorse Publishing, Inc., 2014), p. 13.

3. Stallone has told this story a few times, including in a Q&A with the website Ain't It Cool News before the debut of *Rocky Balboa* (2006): "I saw Dolph Lundgren pick up Carl and heave him three feet into the corner when I was directing the scene between them; rather than retaliate, Carl got out of the ring and said something ferocious like, 'I'm calling my agent.... I quit!'" (http://www.aintitcool.com/node/30932, December 16, 2006).

4. "Stallone Answers December 9th & 10th Questions in a Double Round" (http://www.aintitcool.com/node/30932, December 16, 2006).

5. Blake Harris, "How Did This Get Made: Masters of the Universe (An Oral History)" (http://www.slashfilm.com/masters-of-the-universe-oral-history/, October 2, 2015).

6. This quote from Morrison is included in a "Making of" video prepared by the Toy Masters filmmakers. It has been loaded onto YouTube. As of this writing, it is set to be included as a special feature on the DVD release of *Toy Masters* (https://www.youtube.com/watch?v=p_u1nlmiGU8, April 16, 2012).

7. Mark Goodman, "Crime: Joe and Arville" (*Time*, December 7, 1970).

8. Andrew Yule, *Hollywood A Go-Go: The True Story of the Cannon Film Empire* (London: Sphere Books, Ltd., 1987), p. 14.

9. This was discussed in the Mark Hartley documentary, *Electric Boogaloo: The Wild, Untold Story of Cannon Films* (2014).

10. Paul Talbot, *Bronson's Loose! The Making of the* Death Wish *Films* (Lincoln: iUniverse, 2006), p. 33.

11. Paul Talbot, *Bronson's Loose!: The Making of the* Death Wish *Films* (Lincoln: iUniverse, 2006), p. 77.

12. The studio's accounting practices are explained in exhaustive depths in Yule's *Hollywood A Go-Go* book. I've summarized as best I can, but there were an awful lot of figures cited.

13. The makers of *Missing in Action* went as far as to cite Cameron for the inspiration for their story, thanks to his early draft of *First Blood Part II*.

14. Ebert's original review of *The Delta Force* is logged on his website (http://

www.rogerebert.com/reviews/the-delta-force-1986, February 14, 1986).

15. "Review: 'The Delta Force'" (*Variety*, December 31, 1985).

16. Nancy Rivera Brooks, "Cannon Group Will Buy Theater Chain" (*Los Angeles Times*, May 8, 1986).

17. Al Delugach, "Cannon Bid as Major Studio is Cliffhanger: Firm's Future at Risk in High-Stakes Gamble" (*Los Angeles Times*, August 24, 1986).

Chapter 4

1. Blake Harris, "How Did This Get Made: Masters of the Universe (An Oral History)" (http://www.slashfilm.com/masters-of-the-universe-oral-history/, October 2, 2015).

2. The earliest drafts of the script had Teela using a "somnotron," an Eternian blaster which put Earthlings, such as the over-eager young police officer, to sleep. She used it so much, the characters began to overhear panicked news reports about an outbreak of sleeping sickness across the Midwestern town. And the two biker's names were Greaser and Big Daddy. Let those examples show the tone Odell's early scripts were aiming for.

3. Interview with Gary Goddard, January 6, 2016.

4. Interview with Gary Goddard, January 6, 2016.

5. Blake Harris, "How Did This Get Made: Masters of the Universe (An Oral History)" (http://www.slashfilm.com/masters-of-the-universe-oral-history/, October 2, 2015).

6. Interview with William Stout, December 29, 2015.

7. Goddard's letter explained the Jack Kirby influence and his desire to make the film a "motion picture comic book." It begins: "As the director of *Masters of the Universe*, it was a pleasure to see someone got it. Your comparison of the film to Kirby's New Gods was not far off" (*John Byrne's Next Men* 26, Dark Horse Comics, 1994).

8. Interview with Gary Goddard, January 6, 2016.

9. A photo from this location scouting expedition was posted on MOTUmovie.com with the caption: "In the Cavern in Iceland that was to be part of the Eternia sequence (before the first budget cut)."

10. Goddard has told this story in several interviews over the years. This quote is from my interview with him via email in January of 2016.

11. Tim and Steve Seeley, *The Art of He-Man and the Masters of the Universe* (Milwaukee, OR: Dark Horse Books, 2015), p. 179.

12. This quote was taken from Goddard's answers to questions posed by fans on the MOTUmovie site and He-Man.org. James Sawyer, "Q&A with Director Gary Goddard" (http://www.motumovie.com/2010/02/q-with-director-gary-goddard.html, February 24, 2010).

13. James Sawyer, "Q&A with Director Gary Goddard" (http://www.motumovie.com/2010/02/q-with-director-gary-goddard.html, February 24, 2010).

14. Blake Harris, "How Did This Get Made: Masters of the Universe (An Oral History)" (http://www.slashfilm.com/masters-of-the-universe-oral-history/, October 2, 2015).

15. James Sawyer, "Q&A with Director Gary Goddard" (http://www.motumovie.com/2010/02/q-with-director-gary-goddard.html, February 24, 2010).

16. Interview with William Stout, December 29, 2015.

17. Interview with Gary Goddard, January 6, 2016.

18. James Sawyer, "Q&A with Production Designer William Stout" (http://www.motumovie.com/2010/06/q-with-production-designer-william.html, June 29, 2010).

19. Interview with Gary Goddard, January 6, 2016.

20. Interview with Gary Goddard, January 6, 2016.

21. Blake Harris, "How Did This Get Made: Masters of the Universe (An Oral History)" (http://www.slashfilm.com/masters-of-the-universe-oral-history/, October 2, 2015).

22. Rick Marshall, "Frank Langella Calls Skeletor 'One of My Very Favorite Parts'" (IFC, http://www.ifc.com/2012/08/frank-langella-skeletor-masters-of-the-universe, August 7, 2012).

23. Blake Harris, "How Did This Get Made: Masters of the Universe (An Oral History)" (http://www.slashfilm.com/

masters-of-the-universe-oral-history/, October 2, 2015).

24. John Atkin, "Q&A with Actor Jon Cypher (Man-At-Arms)" (http://www.motumovie.com/2013/10/q-with-actor-jon-cypher-man-at-arms.html, October 13, 2013).

25. Blake Harris, "How Did This Get Made: Masters of the Universe (An Oral History)" (http://www.slashfilm.com/masters-of-the-universe-oral-history/, October 2, 2015).

26. Blake Harris, "How Did This Get Made: Masters of the Universe (An Oral History)" (http://www.slashfilm.com/masters-of-the-universe-oral-history/, October 2, 2015).

27. Goddard has told this story a few times, namely on the DVD commentary and for his interview for Slash Film: "And that next day, she was fantastic. And afterwards I said to Vicky, 'You're right. That was her.' So Vicky gets the accolades for the smarts on that one." Blake Harris, "How Did This Get Made: Masters of the Universe (An Oral History)" (http://www.slashfilm.com/masters-of-the-universe-oral-history/, October 2, 2015).

28. John Atkins, "Q&A with Actor Robert Towers (Karg)" (http://www.motumovie.com/2013/10/q-with-actor-robert-towers-karg.html, October 12, 2013).

29. Blake Harris, "How Did This Get Made: Masters of the Universe (An Oral History)" (http://www.slashfilm.com/masters-of-the-universe-oral-history/, October 2, 2015).

30. John Atkin, "Q&A with Actor Anthony De Longis (Blade)" (http://www.motumovie.com/2010/11/q-with-actor-anthony-de-longis-blade.html, November 18, 2010).

31. John Atkin, "Q&A with Actor Anthony De Longis (Blade)" (http://www.motumovie.com/2010/11/q-with-actor-anthony-de-longis-blade.html, November 18, 2010).

32. James Sawyer, "Q&A with Production Designer William Stout" (http://www.motumovie.com/2010/06/q-with-production-designer-william.html, June 29, 2010).

33. James Sawyer, "Q&A with Production Designer William Stout" (http://www.motumovie.com/2010/06/q-with-production-designer-william.html, June 29, 2010).

34. Interview with William Stout, December 29, 2015.

35. Interview with Gary Goddard, January 6, 2016.

36. Andrew Yule, *Hollywood A Go-Go: The True Story of the Cannon Film Empire* (London: Sphere Books, Ltd., 1987), p. 212.

Chapter 5

1. This quote was pulled from the commentary track Goddard recorded for the original 2001 DVD release of *Masters*.

2. Goddard also called this out in the film's commentary. In my interview with him, he cited JRR Tolkien as one of his many influences from an early age: "I was also reading a lot of books—Doc Savage, Tarzan, Prydain Chronicles (The Book of Three), Over Sea Under Stone five book series, Frank Herbert, Tolkien. I was pretty much into sci-fi, and fantasy adventure books" (Interview with Gary Goddard, January 6, 2016).

3. In his Q&A session for the MOTU Movie site, Stout mentioned an odd bit of *Masters* trivia about this filming location: "The front parking lot of Robby's Ribs 'n' Chicken in reality is where Rodney King was beaten years later." (http://www.motumovie.com/2010/06/q-with-production-designer-william.html, June 29, 2010).

4. Metron is also the name of a character from Jack Kirby's *New Gods* comics. He is the inventor of "boom tube" technology, which allowed the characters to travel through teleportation. To some, Gwildor is a stand-in for Metron, just as Skeletor stands in for Darkseid. There are enough similarities between this film and the comic that a persistent theory was born: many believe *Masters of the Universe* began as a *New Gods* film. This has been roundly rejected by Goddard, Stout, and everyone else involved in its creation.

5. Any deliberate allusions have never been confirmed. Goddard is, however, a big *Star Wars* fan.

6. DVD commentary, 2001.

7. The first draft of the script called for unnamed town to be placed somewhere in the Midwest. This was amended

to match the shooting location in Whittier, California, as evidenced by Skeletor's crew zooming in on their enormous monitor a few scenes earlier. Though unnamed in the film, supplemental material such as Cannon's Media Press Kit identifies the town as Colby, California.

8. This quote came from a draft of the script attributed to David Odell, dated December 5, 1985, pp. 60–61.

9. DVD commentary, 2001.

10. The quotes from this section are all from the MOTU Movie site. John Atkin, "Q&A with Richard Szponder (Pigboy)" (http://www.motumovie.com/2010/06/q-with-richard-szponder-pigboy.html, June 21, 2010).

11. John Atkin, "Q&A with Actor Anthony De Longis (Blade)" (http://www.motumovie.com/2010/11/q-with-actor-anthony-de-longis-blade.html, November 18, 2010).

12. DVD commentary, 2001.

13. This also came from Odell's script from December 5, 1985, p. 75.

14. John Atkin, "Q&A with Actor Anthony De Longis (Blade)" (http://www.motumovie.com/2010/11/q-with-actor-anthony-de-longis-blade.html, November 18, 2010).

15. James Sawyer, "Q&A with Director Gary Goddard" (http://www.motumovie.com/2010/02/q-with-director-gary-goddard.html, February 24, 2010).

Chapter 6

1. James Sawyer, "Q&A with Director Gary Goddard" (http://www.motumovie.com/2010/02/q-with-director-gary-goddard.html, February 24, 2010).

2. James Sawyer, "Q&A with Production Designer William Stout" (http://www.motumovie.com/2010/06/q-with-production-designer-william.html, June 29, 2010).

3. Bruce Cook, "'Masters' A Lesson in More Thrills for Less" (*Los Angeles Daily News*, August 13, 1987).

4. Bruce Cook, "'Masters' A Lesson in More Thrills for Less" (*Los Angeles Daily News*, August 13, 1987).

5. "Juggling Mattel's desires and goals with the fact that Cannon Films was (unbeknown to us working on the movie) months away from going Chapter 11, created a very fluid environment during pre-production and then especially during production." James Sawyer, "Q&A with Director Gary Goddard" (http://www.motumovie.com/2010/02/q-with-director-gary-goddard.html, February 24, 2010).

6. Roger Sweet and David Wecker, *Mastering the Universe: He-Man and the Rise and Fall of a Billion-Dollar Idea* (Cincinnati: Emmis Books, 2005), p. 142.

7. S.J. Diamond, "Marketing to Children Raises Big Questions" (*Los Angeles Times*, June 30, 1986).

8. Tim and Steve Seeley, *The Art of He-Man and the Masters of the Universe* (Milwaukee, OR: Dark Horse Books, 2015), p. 61.

9. These figures, like all of the toy sales numbers, come from Roger Sweet's book.

10. Goddard has told this story in many interviews, but this exact quote came from the "Making Of" video set to be included on the *Toy Masters* DVD (https://www.youtube.com/watch?v=p_u1nlmiGU8, April 16, 2012).

11. Blake Harris, "How Did This Get Made: Masters of the Universe (An Oral History)" (http://www.slashfilm.com/masters-of-the-universe-oral-history/, October 2, 2015).

12. This also came from the *Toy Masters* clip (https://www.youtube.com/watch?v=p_u1nlmiGU8, April 16, 2012).

13. Blake Harris, "How Did This Get Made: Masters of the Universe (An Oral History)" (http://www.slashfilm.com/masters-of-the-universe-oral-history/, October 2, 2015).

14. James Sawyer, "Q&A with Director Gary Goddard" (http://www.motumovie.com/2010/02/q-with-director-gary-goddard.html, February 24, 2010).

15. Various anecdotes of this were shared in the *Electric Boogaloo* documentary.

16. Jake Rossen, *Superman Vs. Hollywood: How Fiendish Producers, Devious Directors, and Warring Writers Grounded an American Icon* (Chicago: Chicago Review Press), p. 159.

17. Jake Rossen, *Superman Vs. Hollywood: How Fiendish Producers, Devious Directors, and Warring Writers Grounded an American Icon* (Chicago: Chicago Review Press), p. 158.

18. The story in the comic adaptation was based on an earlier draft of Odell's script, and much of the character designs came from preliminary sketches from Stout and his crew. As such, Blade is much more alien, with yellow skin, and is not able to speak. The main established characters—He-Man, Teela, Man-At-Arms, Skeletor, the Sorceress, and Evil-Lyn—are drawn to look like their action figure or cartoon incarnations. Beastman, for whatever reason, appeared in his redesigned movie form.

19. *Toy Masters* (https://www.youtube.com/watch?v=p_u1nlmiGU8, April 16, 2012).

20. John Atkin, "Q&A with Actor Anthony De Longis (Blade)" (http://www.motumovie.com/2010/11/q-with-actor-anthony-de-longis-blade.html, November 18, 2010).

21. *Toy Masters* (https://www.youtube.com/watch?v=p_u1nlmiGU8, April 16, 2012).

22. Blake Harris, "How Did This Get Made: Masters of the Universe (An Oral History)" (http://www.slashfilm.com/masters-of-the-universe-oral-history/, October 2, 2015).

23. *Toy Masters* (https://www.youtube.com/watch?v=p_u1nlmiGU8, April 16, 2012).

24. Interview with Gary Goddard, January 6, 2016.

25. Interview with Gary Goddard, January 6, 2016.

26. Blake Harris, "How Did This Get Made: Masters of the Universe (An Oral History)" (http://www.slashfilm.com/masters-of-the-universe-oral-history/, October 2, 2015).

27. Golan and Globus's catchphrase was utilized by Jim Whaley, who hosted the *Cinema Showcase* program on WPBA-TV/ Atlanta, a public access station. It was then used on most of Cannon's marketing. Neither Whaley or Cannon Films mentioned the fact that two of the three original *Star Wars* films were released in the 1980s.

28. Blake Harris, "How Did This Get Made: Masters of the Universe (An Oral History)" (http://www.slashfilm.com/masters-of-the-universe-oral-history/, October 2, 2015).

29. Blake Harris, "How Did This Get Made: Masters of the Universe (An Oral History)" (http://www.slashfilm.com/masters-of-the-universe-oral-history/, October 2, 2015).

30. "Review: 'Masters of the Universe'" (*Variety*, December 31, 1986).

31. Walter Goodman, "Movie Review: 'Masters of the Universe'" (*New York Times*, August 8, 1987).

32. Rita Kempley, *Masters of the Universe* Review (*Washington Post*, August 10, 1987).

33. Johanna Steinmetz, "Surprise! 'Masters' Isn't Bad" (*Chicago Tribune*, August 12, 1987).

34. Blake Harris, "How Did This Get Made: Masters of the Universe (An Oral History)" (http://www.slashfilm.com/masters-of-the-universe-oral-history/, October 2, 2015).

Chapter 7

1. James Sawyer, "Q&A with Director Gary Goddard" (http://www.motumovie.com/2010/02/q-with-director-gary-goddard.html, February 24, 2010).

2. James Sawyer, "Q&A with Director Gary Goddard" (http://www.motumovie.com/2010/02/q-with-director-gary-goddard.html, February 24, 2010).

3. Leonard Klady, "Cinefile—Outtakes:The Sequel" (*Los Angeles Times*, January 24, 1988)

4. Michael A. Hiltzik, "Untangling the Web" (*Los Angeles Times*, March 24, 2002).

5. The origins of *Cyborg* have become legendary in the B-Movie and filmmaking communities. Pyun has told the story many times, but this quote comes from an interview to a Spanish language magazine, which was also logged on dolph-ultimate.com. Interviewer: Nicanor Loreti (*La Cosa Fantastico* 113, July 2005).

6. James Sawyer, "Q&A with Director Gary Goddard" (http://www.motumovie.com/2010/02/q-with-director-gary-goddard.html, February 24, 2010).

7. This number is dubious at best. In Cannon Film's heyday, they had been infamous for exaggerating their movie costs. A more expensive picture, they apparently thought, meant it would seem more credible to audiences and critics. By this point in Cannon's history, though, they had also

begun to tilt the other way. As the company's money problems became more public, they would deny spending so much money to make a movie that flopped. All the talk over the years about the build-up to the studio's *Masters 2* and *Spider-Man* movies always list this $2 million price tag, but it's best to take it with a grain of salt.

8. Mattel's quick turnaround on the He-Man property, along with the behind-the-scenes shuffling of executives, is chronicled in Roger Sweet's book.

9. Roger Sweet and David Wecker, *Mastering the Universe: He-Man and the Rise and Fall of a Billion-Dollar Idea* (Cincinnati: Emmis Books, 2005), p. 177.

10. This quote, and most of the information in this section, is from Scheimer's He-Ro series bible, which laid out the opening episode(s) and the characters. Years after the series failed to come together, the series bible was turned over to the He-Man.org website where it has been posted in its entirety (http://old.he-man. org/cartoon/exclusivefeatures/exclusive-heroseriesbible-intro.shtml).

11. Lou Scheimer with Andy Mangels, *Lou Scheimer: Creating the Filmation Generation*, 2d ed. (Raleigh, NC: TwoMorrows Publishing, 2015), p. 267.

Chapter 8

1. Johanna Steinmetz, "Surprise! 'Masters' Isn't Bad" (*Chicago Tribune*, August 12, 1987).

2. This information comes from an interview Lundgren gave to a French language magazine. The relevant section has been translated and logged on the dolph-ultimate.com fansite: "I'd like to forget. On the other hand, it helped me in my career and taught me a lot. *Masters of the Universe* was number one in rental videos in England but I didn't get much money in the story. Anyway, what counts it what we want to become" (*Impact*, issue 20, April 1989).

3. Umberto Eco, "Casablanca: Cult Movies and Intertextual Collage," *Travels in Hyperreality* (English translation copyright: Orlando: Harcourt, 1986), p. 198.

4. James Sawyer, "Q&A with Director Gary Goddard" (http://www.motumovie. com/2010/02/q-with-director-gary-goddard.html, February 24, 2010).

5. Lou Scheimer with Andy Mangels, *Lou Scheimer: Creating the Filmation Generation*, 2d ed. (Raleigh, NC: TwoMorrows Publishing, Second edition, 2015), p. 228.

6. Interview with Tim Seeley, January 25, 2016.

7. Interview with Corey Landis, February 4, 2016.

8. Anthony Breznican, "Langella is Perfectly Clear: Nixon Role Proves Haunting" (*USA Today*, December 3, 2008).

9. "But the producers of 'Transformers,' Lorenzo di Bonaventura and Ian Bryce, say they have spent only $150 million on 'Transformers,' and they reckon they got a bargain" (Bob Tourtellotte, "'Transformers' Films Yields Big Bang on Fewer Bucks" [http://www.reuters.com/article/us-transformers-idUSN2943327020070702, July 1, 2007]).

Chapter 9

1. Interview with Tim Seeley, January 25, 2016.

2. Interview with Gary Goddard, January 6, 2016.

3. Interview with Gary Goddard, January 6, 2016.

4. Interview with Gary Goddard, January 6, 2016.

5. Paul Richter, "The Mogul Behind Pathe's Bid" (*LA Times*, March 8, 1990).

6. This is considered one of the most defining stories of Golan and Globus as filmmakers. It is told wonderfully in the *Electric Boogalo* documentary.

7. Rob Wells, "Financier Settles Fraud Charges with SEC" (*Associated Press*, January 5, 1996).

8. Interview with William Stout, December 29, 2015.

9. Interview with William Stout, December 29, 2015.

10. This was another interview logged on dolph-ultimate.com (*Comics Scene 9*, Summer 1989).

11. "He-Man and the Masters of the Universe—Lundgren on He-Man Reboot" (IGN, http://www.ign.com/videos/2012/08/03/dolph-lundgren-on-he-man-reboot, August 3, 2012).

12. Gerald Couzens, "Burglars Tie Up Woman—But Flee the House When They

Realize She's Married to Action Hero Dolph Lundgren" (*Daily Mail*, May 5, 2009).

13. Anthony Breznican, "Langella is Perfectly Clear: Nixon Role Proves Haunting" (*USA Today*, December 3, 2008).

14. Rick Marshall, "Frank Langella Calls Skeletor 'One of My Very Favorite Parts'" (IFC, http://www.ifc.com/2012/08/frank-langella-skeletor-masters-of-the-universe, August 7, 2012).

15. Interview with Corey Landis, February 4, 2016.

16. Interview with Tim Seeley, January 25, 2016.

17. Interview with William Stout, December 29, 2015.

Bibliography

Books

Byrne, John. *John Byrne's Next Men* 26 (Dark Horse Comics, 1994).

Campbell, Joseph. *The Hero with a Thousand Faces*, 3d ed. (Novatno, CA: New World Library, 2008). Originally published 1949.

Greenberger, Robert. *He-Man and the Masters of the Universe Minicomic Collection* (Milwaukie, OR: Dark Horse Books, 2015).

_____. *Meet Godzilla* (The Rosen Publishing Group, 2004).

Lemke, Jay. *Critical Analysis across Media: Games, Franchises, and the New Cultural Order* (First International Conference on CDA, 2004).

Lundgren, Dolph. *Train Like an Action Hero* (New York: Skyhorse Publishing, 2014).

Rossen, Jake. *Superman Vs. Hollywood: How Fiendish Producers, Devious Directors, and Warring Writers Grounded an American Icon* (Chicago: Chicago Review Press, 2008).

Seeley, Tim, and Steve Seeley. *The Art of He-Man and the Masters of the Universe* (Milwaukie, OR: Dark Horse Books, 2015).

Schiemer, Lou, with Andy Mangels. *Lou Scheimer: Creating the Filmation Generation*, 2d ed. (Raleigh, NC: TwoMorrows Publishing, 2015).

Sweet, Roger, and David Wecker. *Mastering the Universe: He-Man and the Rise and Fall of a Billion-Dollar Idea* (Cincinnati: Emmis Books, 2005).

Talbot, Paul. *Bronson's Loose! The Making of the* Death Wish *Films* (Lincoln: iUniverse, 2006).

Yule, Andrew. *Hollywood A Go-Go: The True Story of the Cannon Film Empire* (London: Sphere Books, Ltd., 1987).

Articles and Essays

Andrews, Edmund L. "Toy-Based TV Shows Win Ruling" (*New York Times*, November 9, 1990).

Atkin, John. "Q&A with Actor Anthony De Longis (Blade)" (http://www.motumovie.com/2010/11/q-with-actor-anthony-de-longis-blade.html, November 18, 2010).

Atkin, John. "Q&A with Actor Jon Cypher (Man-At-Arms)" (http://www.motumovie.com/2013/10/q-with-actor-jon-cypher-man-at-arms.html, October 13, 2013).

Atkin, John. "Q&A with Richard Szponder (Pigboy)" (http://www.motumovie.com/2010/06/q-with-richard-szponder-pigboy.html, June 21, 2010).

Atkin, John. "Q&A with Actor Robert Towers (Karg)" (http://www.motumovie.com/ 2013/10/q-with-actor-robert-towers-karg.html, October 12, 2013).

Boyer, Peter J. "Toy-Based TV: Effects on Children Debated" (*New York Times*, February 3, 1986).

Breznican, Anthony. "Langella Is Perfectly Clear: Nixon Role Proves Haunting" (*USA Today*, December 3, 2008).

Brooks, Nancy Rivera. "Cannon Group Will Buy Theater Chain" (*Los Angeles Times*, May 8, 1986).

Chernov, Matthew. *Comics Scene* 9 (Summer 1989).

_____. *10 Things We Learned from Mark Taylor, the Designer of He-Man* (http:// www.therobotsvoice.com/2015/11/man-masters-universe-mark-taylor-mattel-toy-masters.php, November 5, 2015).

Cook, Bruce. "'Masters' A Lesson in More Thrills for Less" (*Los Angeles Daily News*, August 13, 1987).

Couzens, Gerald. "Burglars Tie Up Woman—But Flee the House When They Realize She's Married to Action Hero Dolph Lundgren" (*Daily Mail*, May 5, 2009).

Delugach, Al. "Cannon Bid as Major Studio is Cliffhanger: Firm's Future at Risk in High-Stakes Gamble" (*Los Angeles Times*, August 24, 1986).

Diamond, S.J. "Marketing to Children Raises Big Questions" (*Los Angeles Times*, June 30, 1986).

Ebert, Roger. "*The Delta Force* Movie Review" (http://www.rogerebert.com/reviews/ the-delta-force-1986, February 14, 1986) .

Eco, Umberto. "Casablanca: Cult Movies and Intertextual Collage," *Travels in Hyper-reality* (English translation copyright: Orlando: Harcourt, 1986).

Epstein, Edward Jay. *The Midas Formula: How to Create a Billion-Dollar Movie Franchise* (Slate.com, 2005).

Goodman, Mark. "Crime: Joe and Arville" (*Time*, December 7, 1970).

Goodman, Walter. "Movie Review: 'Masters of the Universe'" (*New York Times*, August 8, 1987).

Harris, Blake. "He-Man and the Masters of the Universe—Lundgren on He-Man Reboot" (IGN, http://www.ign.com/videos/2012/08/03/dolph-lundgren-on-he-man-reboot, August 3, 2012).

_____. "How Did This Get Made: Masters of the Universe (An Oral History)" (http:// www.slashfilm.com/masters-of-the-universe-oral-history/, October 2, 2015).

Herman, Paul. "Copyrightable Conan?" (http://www.robert-e-howard.org/Another Thought2.html, September 2001).

_____. "*He-Ro, Son of He-Man, and the Masters of the Universe* Series Bible" (http:// old.he-man.org/cartoon/exclusivefeatures/exclusive-heroseriesbible-intro. shtml).

Hiltzik, Michael A. "Untangling the Web" (*Los Angeles Times*, March 24, 2002).

_____ *Impact* 20 (April 1989).

Kempley, Rita. *Masters of the Universe* Review (*Washington Post*, August 10, 1987).

Kilday, Gregg. "Paramount, Hasbro Creating Movie Universe Around G.I. Joe, Four Other Brands (Exclusive)" (*Hollywood Reporter*, December 15, 2015).

Kleiner, Dick. "'Trek' Tracks Adults" (*Sumter Daily Item*, July 21, 1973).

Knowles, Harry. "Stallone Answers December 9th & 10th Questions in a Double Round" (http://www.aintitcool.com/node/30932, December 16, 2006).

Klady, Leonard. "Cinefile—Outtakes:The Sequel" (*Los Angeles Times,* January 24, 1988).

Lang, Brett. "How Universal Plans to Bring Its Monster Movies Back to Life (Exclusive)" (*Variety*, November 17, 2015).

Loreti, Nicanor. *La Cosa Fantastico* 113 (July 2005).

Marshall, Rick. "Frank Langella Calls Skeletor 'One of My Very Favorite Parts'" (IFC, http://www.ifc.com/2012/08/frank-langella-skeletor-masters-of-the-universe, August 7, 2012).

_____. "Reason Interview with Mark S. Fowler" (*Reason*, November 1, 1981).

_____. "Review: 'Masters of the Universe'" (*Variety*, December 31, 1986).

_____. "Review: 'The Delta Force'" (*Variety*, December 31, 1985).

Richter, Paul. "The Mogul Behind Pathe's Bid" (*LA Times*, March 8, 1990).

Sawyer, James. "Q&A with Director Gary Goddard" (http://www.motumovie.com/2010/02/q-with-director-gary-goddard.html, February 24, 2010).

Sawyer, James. "Q&A with Production Designer William Stout" (http://www.motumovie.com/2010/06/q-with-production-designer-william.html, June 29, 2010).

Shaw, Sydney. "A Children's Television Watchdog Group Filed a Complaint Tuesday..." (Archived on http://www.upi.com/Archives/1983/10/11/A-childrens-televison-watchdog-group-filed-a-complaint-Tuesday/9006434692800/, October 11, 1983).

Solomon, Charles. "Syndication Threat: Saturday Kidvid on the Way Out?" (*Los Angeles Times*, November 15, 1986).

Steimetz, Johanna. "Surprise! 'Masters' Isn't Bad" (*Chicago Tribune*, August 12, 1987).

Tourtellotte, Bob. "'Transformers' Films Yields Big Bang on Fewer Bucks" (http://www.reuters.com/article/us-transformers-idUSN2943327020070702, July 1, 2007).

Welch, Jane A. "'He-Man' is a Wimp Master" (*Washington Post*, April 21, 1985).

Wells, Rob. "Financier Settles Fraud Charges with SEC" (*Associated Press*, January 5, 1996).

Younis, Steve. *Superman and the Phone Booth* (http://www.supermanhomepage.com/other/other.php?topic=phonebooth).

_____. "Zodac—Cosmic Enforcer (1982)" (https://battleram.wordpress.com/2016/02/15/zodac-cosmic-enforcer-1982/, February 15, 2016).

Interviews

Interview with Gary Goddard, January 6, 2016.
Interview with Corey Landis, February 4, 2016.
Interview with Tim Seeley, January 25, 2016.
Interview with William Stout, December 29, 2015.

Index